Adult, Continuing and Extension Education: At a Glance

The Authors

Hema Sarat Chandra N completed his M.Sc. Agriculture in Extension Education from Banaras Hindu University, Varanasi. By securing UGC JRF he has done his Ph.D. in Agricultural Extension education from ICAR-National Dairy Research Institute (NDRI), Karnal, Haryana. Presently, he is working as teaching faculty for Agricultural Extension at College of Horticulture, Anantharajupeta, Dr.Y.S.R. Horticultural University, Andhra Pradesh. He has developed ATMA coordination index (ACI) and Group dynamics index (GDI) to measure the coordination of ATMA and group dynamics of farmer interest groups under ATMA. He has published research articles in national as well as international journals in agriculture and rural development sectors.

Gajanand Palve has graduated in B.Sc. Agriculture from Agricultural College- Jagtial of Acharya N. G. Ranga Agricultural University in 2014. Thereafter, he has attended to Bidhan Chandra Krishi Vishwavidyalaya (BCKV), Mohanpur, West-Bengal and completed his M.Sc. Agriculture in Agricultural Extension. He has secured ICAR SRF in Agricultural Extension and presently pursuing Ph.D. in Agricultural Extension education from ICAR-National Dairy Research Institute (NDRI), Karnal, Haryana. He has specialised in studying technology adoption behaviour of farmers.

Adult, Continuing and Extension Education: At a Glance

For UGC-NET, JRF, SRF, ARS, IARI, Ph.D.
SAU's, UPSC and Allied Agricultural Exams

Hema Sarat Chandra N
Gajanand Palve

Daya Publishing House®
A Division of
Astral International Pvt. Ltd.
New Delhi – 110 002

ISBN: 9789390384020 (PB)

Published by : **Daya Publishing House®**
A Division of
Astral International Pvt. Ltd.
– ISO 9001:2015 Certified Company –
4736/23, Ansari Road, Darya Ganj
New Delhi-110 002
Ph. 011-43549197, 23278134
E-mail: info@astralint.com
Website: www.astralint.com

Digitally Printed at : **Neelam Graphics, Delhi**

Preface

The concept of adult, continuing and extension has been manifested in different forms and as such today, it is conceived as a persuasive concept that touches all individuals, professionals and people of all walks of life. The report of UNESCO 1996 of international commission on education for 21st century also reiterated the importance and significance of life-long learning especially in the era of information and communication technology. Life-long learning is the continuous and self-motivated pursuit of knowledge and skills both for personal and professional development either through formal or informal learning. It enhances social inclusion and active citizenship. It shares mixed connotation with other educational concept like- adult education, literacy programmes, counseling and guidance, population and women education; health education, environmental education, vocational and extension education. The present book is a compilation of latest information which provides an overview of concise and point wise information on adult, continuing and Extension Education. It contains concepts and theories in adult education, trends of adult education and continuing education in India, history of modern Indian education, important in educational indicators, development efforts in a chronological order, important literacy programmes and schemes, important facts about teaching and research, important definitions and technologies. Assertion reason type, matching type and memory based questions embedded which will enable the readers to update their knowledge quickly and understanding of the subject in depth.

This book is designed to serve as a handy guide for students, teachers, researchers, special emphasis has been given to students appearing for various competitive examinations like post-graduate entrance examinations, SAUs Entrance, Ph.D., Junior Research Fellowship (JRF), Senior Research Fellowship (SRF), Agricultural Research Service (ARS), ICAR- Nation Eligibility Test (NET), SET, Civil Services, Agricultural Officers, Bank P.O. (Agriculture) and allied examinations.

All suggestions for the future improvement of book will be highly solicited. We are highly thankful to the publishers Astral International (Pvt) Ltd., New Delhi for arranging easily publication of this book.

Hema Sarat Chandra N.
Gajanand Palve

Contents

Chapter 1

Concepts and Theories in Adult Education

- Andragogy is the **Greek term**, literal meaning is **ADULT LEADING** it explains the theory and practice of how adults learn.
- Father of adult learning is **Malcolm Knowles**.
- **Malcolm Knowles** explained the process of adult learning by his publication **The Modern Practice of Adult Education: Andragogy vs. Pedagogy.**
- Theory and practice of teaching children is known as **PEDAGOGY.**
- Andragogy is the art and science of helping adults learn.
- Andragogy—initially a term coined by the German teacher Alexander Kapp.
- **Malcolm Shepherd Knowles** (August 24, 1913 – November 27, 1997) was an American Adult Educator, famous for the adoption of the theory of andragogy.
- **John Dewey :** philosophy of pragmatism, is considered one of the founders of functional psychology.
- Theory of instinct- M. C. Dougal
- Drive reduction theory – Hall
- Social urges theory – Adler

- ☆ Self actualization theory – Maslow
- ☆ In the conditioning approach to learning the unnatural stimulus follows the natural stimulus
- ☆ Ethno-methodology is a method of qualitative research
- ☆ J. B. Watson – "give me a dozen of healthy children i can make them doctor, judge, beggar, and even a thief "
- ☆ The view that "anything can be taught at any stage of development " was expressed by - Bruner.
- ☆ Sign theory of learning – Tolman
- ☆ Field theory of learning –kurt Lewin
- ☆ Trial and error theory of learning – Thorndike
- ☆ Lever Act: Extension
- ☆ 'extension term: Charles Mc Arthy
- ☆ Praxis term: Paulo Friere
- ☆ Learning : The Trearure (publication): UNESCO
- ☆ SatyenMaitra Award: NLMA
- ☆ Ontological View of Education: Paulo Friere
- ☆ Self Actualisation: Maslow
- ☆ Deschooling of Society 1871:Evan Ellich/Paulo Friere
- ☆ Lifelong Learning: Faure
- ☆ How adults learn: Robby Kidd
- ☆ Pragmatism: John dewey
- ☆ Conscientization: Paulo Friere
- ☆ Self Realization: Rabindranath Tagore
- ☆ Folk high school: grundtwig
- ☆ Cultural action for freedom: Evan Ellich/Paulo Friere
- ☆ term information and communication technology first used by: Stevenson
- ☆ Learning through connection: Thorndike
- ☆ Discriminated operant: Skinner
- ☆ Instrumental Response: Kimble

- ☆ Conditional Learning: Pavlov
- ☆ Folk School :Finland/Denmark
- ☆ Paulo Freire's Radical Approach to Literacy (1970s)
- ☆ Broadening the Concept of Literacy (1980s-1990s)
- ☆ USA: Slogan foundation
- ☆ Britain: Extra mural dept
- ☆ Canada: Frontire college
- ☆ Denmark: Folk High School (1844)
- ☆ Vietnam: fight famine, illiteracy, external attack
- ☆ Philippines: Adult education throuh radio
- ☆ Adult education, Worker,s Education association: Britain
- ☆ Social education: Maulana Abul kalam Azad
- ☆ Mass education: James Ven, China
- ☆ Community education: Southern countries of America
- ☆ Public education: Lenin, Russia
- ☆ Basic education : M.K. Gandhi
- ☆ Learning by Doing (Trial and Error): Thorndike

Chapter 2

Trends of Adult Education and Continuing Education in India

- **Farmer's Functional Literacy Programme** (Kisan Saksharta Yojana): started in **1967-68** in 3 districts.
- **Gram Shikshan Mohim** (Gram Shikshan Mohim):The Village Literacy Movement that started in Satara District in Maharashtra in **1959.**
- **NAEP** (national adult education programme)**:** Started in **1978** which was intended to be a mass program remained traditional centre based program.
- The target of NAEP IS **100 Million** a total of 44.22 million learners were enrolled in Adult education centers.
- **NLM (1988)** aimed at making non literate persons in 15-35 age group literates.
- NLM launched 2 year PLC for neo literates.
- The NLM scheme covered 148 million non literates in the age group 9-35 years has achieved 199 million enrolments by 2001.
- **TLC (1990)** 1st campaign in Kerala came into the picture. The campaigns are Area specific, time bound, volunteer based, cost effective and outcome oriented.
- TLCs include two year follow up programs of PLCs in the district which have completed successfully both TLC and PLC phases.

- ☆ The main objectives of the continuing education scheme is to institutionalizing the continuing education for neo-literates and provide considerable flexibility in designing and implementing a diverse kind of CE programs suited to the neo-literates.
- ☆ The continuing education scheme divided the continuing programs mainly into four categories.
  - i. **Equivalency programs:** designed alternative educational programs to the existing formal, general or vocational education.
  - ii. **Income generating programs:** upgrade vocational skills enable them to take up income generating activities.
  - iii. **Quality of life improving programs:** equip the members and the community with the essential knowledge, attitude, skills both as individual and the members of the community.
  - iv. **Individuals interest promotion programs:** learners can learn about their chosen social, cultural, spiritual, health, physical and artistic interests.
- ☆ CE Programmes has been executed through **Zilla Saksharata Samiti (ZSS)** which were expected to establish durable infrastructure for continuing education.
- ☆ **ZSS** were given the freedom and flexibility in developing the need based, location based and resources availability etc.
- ☆ **Continuing education centers (CECs):** are prime mode of implementing the CE programs and these are established one in each village to serve the population about 1500 including about 500 neo-literates, dropouts and pass outs from primary schools and non formal education centers.
- ☆ **One CEC** work as a nodal CEC meant for a **8-10 CECs** and main function of the center is to provide following facilities: Library, reading room, learning centre, training centre, information centre, charcha mandals, sports centre and cultural centre.
- ☆ NLM collaboration with the **National Open schools (NOS)** has developed a program of open basic education for the neo-literates to help them in pursuing the beyond the basic literacy in a non formal mode.
- ☆ **ZSS** remains in charge of implementing the scheme under the guidance and supervision of the state resource centers (SRCs) and state open schools.
- ☆ "NLM **(1988)** the scheme of continuing education for neo-literates is an attempt to provide the systematic, organized and well coordinated to mobilize the resources in support of literacy, post literacy and continuing education in the perspective of lifelong education."

- **CECs** are function as non formal education forums to provide holistic lifelong education. These are localized community based learning centers, usually organized and managed by the people themselves.
- These NFE centers are also called **multipurpose learning institutions** providing a systematic infrastructure for continuing education.
- The concept of the CE aims at establishing *"learning society" and "Lifelong education"* which imply the growing demand of CE.
- **Population education** emerged as an educational innovation in 1970, many of countries introduces this population in their educational system.
- World Population Plan of Action in 1974 encouraged population education in formal and non formal education.
- "Population Education is an educational process which develops among learners an understanding of interrelationship between population and development, causes and consequences of population change and criticality of conditions of population stabilization.
- "Population Education" includes in them the rationale attitude and responsibility to population and development."
- In India based on the National Seminar in 1969 NCERT made a population education syllabus in **1971**.
- **Population education clubs** were started in **1983-84**.
- **UGC-UNFPA** joint project on population education launched in 1986, for this technical assistance given by UNESCO and funded by United Nations Fund For Population Activities (UNFPA).
- UGC introduced UG and PG courses, Population and development in higher education system was commenced in **1997**.
- **Population Education Resource Centers (PERC)** established in Adult, continuing Education and Extension department.
- Finally 17 PERCs, 100 Adult education departments and 1400 population education clubs were set up in colleges and Universities.
- National Population Policy in 2000 aimed the stabilization of the population by 2045.
- **National Policy on women (2001):** aimed the women empowerment so they still strengthen the efforts which targeted the women gradually efforts mooted up for the accessibility of the education especially to women since education is the first rung of the development.

- ☆ Kasturba Gandhi Balika Vidyalaya **(KGBV):** started in **2004.**
- ☆ Sakshara Bharat Mission on **Sept 8, in 2009** started to raise the female literacy and to give skill training etc besides that special emphasis given to the women empowerment.
- ☆ **States reported with literacy rate greater than 90 per cent :** Kerala (94 per cent), Lakshadweep (91.85 per cent) and Mizoram (91.33).
- ☆ In 1999 UNESCO conferred upon it their Noma Literacy Prize.

Chapter 3

History of Modern Indian Education

- ☆ Hunter Commission, officially known as Indian Education Commission (1882)
- ☆ Indian Universities Commission (1902)
- ☆ Government Resolution on Educational Policy (1913)
- ☆ Calcutta University Commission (1917) also called Sadler Commission
- ☆ Hartog Committee (1929)
- ☆ Sapru Committee (1934)
- ☆ Abbot-Wood Report (1936-37)
- ☆ Zakir Hussain Committee (1937)
- ☆ Wardha Education Committee of the Central Advisory Board of Education (1939) also called B. G. Kher Committee
- ☆ Central Advisory Board of Education Report (1944) or Post-War Educational Development Report, popularly called the Sargent Report (1944).
- ☆ Secondary Education Commission (1952-53) popularly called Dr. Mudaliar Commission
- ☆ Committee on Higher Education for Rural Areas, Rural Institutions (1954) — Shri K. L. Shrimali Committee

- National Committee on Women's Education (1958) — Shrimati Durgabai Deshmukh Committee
- University Grants Commission's Review Committee on Education (1960) — Prof. K.G. Saiyidain Committee
- U. N. Dhebar Commission (1960)
- Committee on Emotional Integration (1961) — Dr. Sampurnanand Committee
- Committee on Plan Projects: Study Team for Selected Educational Schemes (1961) – Shri B. N. Jha Committee
- National Policy on Education: Programme of Action (1986)
- National Curriculum for Elementary and Secondary Education – A Framework (1988)
- National Curriculum for Teacher Education: A Framework (1988)
- Committee for Review of NPE 1986: Towards an Enlightened and Humane Society (1990) — Acharya Ramamurhty Committee
- University Grants Commission's Report of the Curriculum Development Centre in Education (1990)
- NCTE Committee for Teacher Education Programme Through Distance Education Mode (1990)
- Central Advisory Board of Education Committee on Distance Education (1992)
- CABE Committee on Policy, 1992
- National Policy on Education 1986: Programme of Action 1992
- National Advisory Committee: Learning Without Burden (1992)
- The National Council for Teacher Education Act, 1993
- Group to Examine the Feasibility of Implementation of the Recommendations of the National Advisory Committee (1993) — Prof. Yashpal Committee
- Committee on B.Ed. Correspondence (1993) — Prof. Ramlal Parikh Committee
- Study Group on the Training of Elementary Teachers in India (1961)
- Kothari Committee on Model Act for Universities (1961)
- University Grants Commission's Committee on Education as an Elective Subject at the Undergraduate Stage (1963) — Mr. A. R. Wadia Committee

- ☆ Study Group on the Study of English in India (1964) – Prof. Gokak Committee
- ☆ Education Commission (1964-66), popularly called Dr. D. S. Kothari Commission
- ☆ Committee of Members of Parliament on Education (1967)
- ☆ Three Delegations by University Grants Commission (1967-1971)
- ☆ Steering Committee of Planning Group on Education (1968)
- ☆ National Policy on Education (1968)
- ☆ Review Committee on the Working of National Council of Educational Research and Training (1968) — Dr. Nag Chaudhuri Committee
- ☆ Study Group on the Development of Pre-school Child (1970) – Shrimati Mina Swaminathan Committee
- ☆ Gajendragadkar Committee on Governance of Universities and Colleges (1971)
- ☆ National Committee on 10+2+3 Educational Structure (1972) — Dr. Shukla Committee
- ☆ Committee on Secondary Teacher Education of NCTE (1973-77) — Dr. Jha Committee
- ☆ Committee on Elementary Teacher Education of NCTE (1975) — Dr. Malcolm S. Adiseshaiah Committee
- ☆ University Grants Commission's Panel on Teacher Education During Fifth Plan Period (1974)
- ☆ The Curriculum for Ten-Year School: A Framework (1975)
- ☆ Standing Committee of National Council for Teacher Education (1975-76)
- ☆ Review Committee on the Curriculum for Ten-Year School (1977) — Shri Ishwarbhai Patel Committee
- ☆ Working Group on Vocationalisation of Education (1977-78) — Dr. Malcolm S. Adiseshaiah Committee
- ☆ Draft National Policy on Education (1979)
- ☆ Study Group on INSAT Television Utilisation for Education and Development (1980) — Shri S. Sathyam Committee
- ☆ National Commissions on Teachers – I and II: The Teacher and Society (1983-85) – Prof. Chattopadhyaya Commission

- ☆ Working Group to Review Teachers' Training Programme (In the Light of the Need for Value-Orientation) (1983)
- ☆ Challenge of Education: A Policy Perspective (1985)
- ☆ National Curriculum for Primary and Secondary Education: A Framework (1985)
- ☆ National Policy on Education (1986)
- ☆ National Knowledge Commission (NKC) 2006-09, which is popularly called Sir Sam Pitroda Commission.
- ☆ National Knowledge Commission (NKC) a high-level advisory body to the Prime Minister of India, was set up with the objective of transforming India into a knowledge society.
- ☆ University Grants Commission's Committee on B.Ed. Correspondence, Distance Education Programme (1994)
- ☆ Special Orientation Programme for School Teachers (SOPT) (1994-97)
- ☆ Committee of National Council for Teacher Education on Different Modes of Education Used for Teacher Preparation in India (1995)
- ☆ University Grants Commission's Committee on B.Ed. Through Correspondence for In-service Teachers (1995) — Prof. Takwale Committee
- ☆ Planning Commission's Report on Teacher Education in Five Year Plans (1951-97)
- ☆ NCTE Curriculum Framework for Quality Teacher Education (1998)
- ☆ National Curriculum Framework for School Education (2000)
- ☆ National Curriculum Framework (2005)
- ☆ Curriculum Framework for Teacher Education (2006)
- ☆ National Curriculum Framework for Teacher Education (2009)
- ☆ Panel to Review the functioning of the University Grants Commission (UGC) and the All-India Council for Technical Education (AICTE) (2008), later rechristened as The Committee to Advise on Renovation and Rejuvenation of Higher Education (2009) — Prof. Yashpal Committee
- ☆ The Right of Children to Free and Compulsory Education Act, 2009.

Chapter 4

Improvement in Educational Indicators

- ☆ The census 2011 estimated 20.78 crore children in the 6-13 age group.
- ☆ As per UDISE 2015-16, enrolment in elementary schools was 19.67 crore children in 14.49 lakh elementary schools.
- ☆ There has been a significant reduction in the number of out of school children in the 614 years age group, from 134.6 lakh in 2005 to 81 lakh in 2009 and further to 61 lakh in 2014.
- ☆ The annual average dropout rate at primary level has come down from 9.11 per cent in 2009-10 to 4.13 per cent in 2015-16.
- ☆ The transition rate from primary to upper primary has gone up from 83.53 per cent in 2009-10 to 90.14 per cent in 2015-16.
- ☆ The Pupil Teacher Ratio (PTR) has improved from 32 in 2009-10 to 24 in 2015-16.
- ☆ Department of School Education and Niti Aayog are jointly developing a School Education Quality Index (SEQI) in consultation with all States and UTs. This index aims to institutionalize a focus on improving education outcomes (learning, access, equity) as the principle aim of school education policy in India. This is expected to launch by January 2017.
- ☆ Shagun portal – an Initiative to monitor the implementation of SSA.
- ☆ ShaGun a web portal (from the words Shaala and Gunvatta) is being developed by Ministry of HRD. It has two components *i.e.* one is a

Repository of best practices, photographs, videos, studies, newspaper articles etc on elementary education.

- The 'Padhe Bharat Badhe Bharat' (PBBB) a subprogramme of the SSA, in classes I and II focusing on foundational learning in early grades with an emphasis on reading, writing and comprehension and Mathematics.
- The Rashtriya Avishkar Abhiyan (RAA) It is also under the SSA, was launched by Late Dr. A.P.J. Abdul Kalam. This aims to motivate and engage children of the age group 618 years, in Science, Mathematics and Technology by observation, experimentation, inference drawing and model building, through both inside and outside classroom activities.
- Vidyanjali This is subprogramme under SSA launched to enhance community and private sector involvement in Government run elementary schools across the country under the overall aegis of the SSA.
- Accreditation for Teacher Education Institutions (TEIs) by National Council for Teacher Education for better management and improved quality of teacher education.
- Mid Day Meal is a centrally sponsored programme designed with a view to enhancing enrollment, retention and attendance and simultaneously improving nutritional levels among children.
- Mid Day Meal Rules, 2015 notified on 30th September 2015 to ensure quality nutrition and effective monitoring.
- Rashtriya Madhyamik Shiksha Abhiyan (RMSA) is a Centrally Sponsored Scheme that envisages interalia provision of a secondary school within a reasonable distance of any habitation and to improve quality of education imparted at secondary level by making all secondary schools conform to prescribed norms, removing gender, socioeconomic and disability barriers etc.
- Shaala Siddhi: School Standards and Evaluation Framework and its web portal were launched on 7th November 2015. It is a comprehensive instrument for school evaluation leading to school improvement. Developed by the National University of Educational Planning and Administration (NUEPA), it aims to enable schools to evaluate their performance in a more focused and strategic manner and facilitate them to make professional judgments for improvement.
- The "Shaala Darpan Project" to cover all the 1099 Kendriya Vidyalayas was launched on 05.06.2015. The objective of this project is to provide services based on School Management Systems to Students, Parents and Communities.
- E-PATHSHALA: It is a single point repository of eresources containing, NCERT textbooks and various other learning resources. It is a joint

initiative of Ministry of Human Resource Development (MHRD), Govt. of India and National Council of Educational Research and Training (NCERT) developed for showcasing and disseminating all educational eresources including textbooks, audio, video, periodicals, and a variety of other print and nonprint materials.

- Kala Utsav is an initiative of MHRD to promote Arts (Music, Theatre, Dance, Visual Arts and Crafts) in education by nurturing and showcasing the artistic talent of school students at secondary stage in the country.
- Rashtriya Avishkar Abhiyan was launched on 9th July 2015 to focus on Science and Mathematics.
- GIAN is aimed at tapping the talent pool of scientists and entrepreneurs, internationally to encourage their engagement with the institutes of Higher Education in India so as to augment the country's existing academic resources, accelerate the pace of quality reform, and elevate India's scientific and technological capacity to global excellence.
- The Uchhatar Avishkar Yojana (UAY) was launched to promote industryspecific need based research so as to keep up the competitiveness of the Indian industry in the global market.
- Establishment of Higher Education Financing Agency (HEFA) for creating capital assets in Higher Educational Institutions in 12th September 2016.
- The SWAYAM PRABHA has been conceived as the project for telecasting high quality educational programmes through 32 DTH channels on 24X7 basis.
- UNESCO organized the 50th Anniversary of International Literacy Day at its Headquarters in Paris on 89th September, 2016 on the theme 'Reading the past, writing the future'.
- Ministry of Human Resource Development, Government of India, in collaboration with SAARC Secretariat, held SAARC Technical Meeting of Senior Officials on Education on 1516th September, 2016 in New Delhi.
- The 4th BRICS Education Ministers Meeting (EMM) took place in New Delhi on 30th September, 2016. It was preceded by a BRICS Senior Officials Meeting on Education on 29th September, 2016.
- New Delhi Declaration on Education was signed during the 4th BRICS Education Ministers Meeting.
- The 2nd meeting of the International Governing Board (IGB) of the BRICS Network University (NU) has taken place at IIT Bombay on 27th September, 2016.
- Indian Delegation visited Ekaterinburg, Russia for the 1st meeting of the International Governing Board (IGB) of the BRICS Network University

(NU) from 68 April, 2016, to draft regulations/statute for the functioning of the BRICS Network University.

- The National Policy on Early Childhood Care and Education (ECCE) adopted in 2013.
- The National Youth Policy (NYP), 2014.
- The National Policy for Skill Development and Entrepreneurship, 2015.
- The Constitution (Eighty-sixth Amendment) Act, 2002 that inserted Article 21-A in the Constitution of India envisages free and compulsory education for all children in the age group of six to fourteen years as a Fundamental Right.
- The Right of Children to Free and Compulsory Education (RTE) Act, 2009 which represents the consequential legislation envisaged under Article 21-A of the Indian constitution entitles every child of the age of six to fourteen year with the right to free and compulsory education in a neighbourhood school till completion of elementary education.
- Regional disparities in Gross Enrolment Ratio (GER) in higher education are large.
- The global Sustainable Development Goal 4 (SDG 4) within the Agenda 2030 seeks to 'Ensure inclusive and equitable quality education and promote lifelong learning opportunities for all'.
- Realizing the need to boost vocational education on a larger scale, the ugc propose to establish as many as 100 'deen dayal upadhyay centres for knowledge acquisition and upgradation of skilled human abilities and livelihood (kaushal) during the xii plan period.
- Incharge of implementation of open basic education programme is Zilla Saksharatha Samithi (ZSS).
- Continuing education centre are called as multipurpose learning institutions.
- Continuing education centre has the micro and macro level planning process.
- The continuing education centres are local specific and need based programme.
- The national resource centre for literacy at the lal bahadur shastri national academy of administration in mussoorie is a training cell setup on behalf of the national literacy mission for 5 years.
- The NLM has introduced the two kinds of evaluation concurrent and external in order to ensure greater authenticity and transparency in the system.

- Concurrent evaluation is a midterm appraisal that offers corrections in operation.
- External evaluation contains both the quantitative and qualitative aspects of the campaign.
- Illiteracy rate was highest in the 15-35 age groups.
- The national adult education programme intended to be a mass programme remained traditional centre based programme
- National adult education programme (NAEP) target of 100 million a total of 44.22 million were enrolled in adult education.
- GOI appointed a review committee by Dr.D.S.Kothari to assess the strengths and weakness of national adult education programme.
- Total literacy campaign (TLC) is a area specific time-bound, volunteer-based cost effective and outcome oriented.
- The TLC approach has large scale mobilisation through a multifaceted communication strategy it is implemented in a phased manner.
- NLM has launched the two year post lileracy programme (PLC) for neo-litarates after the conclusion of the total literacy campaign (TLC).
- PLC include a 50 hrs of guided learning through a voluntary teacher to enable the learner to reach a self reliant level of learning.
- The NLM has designed a scheme of continuing education for neo-literates on jan 1st, 1996.

Chapter 5

Developmental Efforts in a Chronological Order

Sl.No.	*Year*	*Developmental Efforts Initiated*
1	1885	Night school for first time started by M.K. Gandhi, Jyotirao Phule in Maharashtra.
2	1912	Dewan of Mysore established night schools for illiterates and vignyan magazine to create awareness about science.
		National leaders Lala Lajapatiroy, Balagangadhar Tilak and their efforts are identified in these years.
3	1921	Sriniketan attempt by Rabindranath Tagore.
4	1927	National Broadcasting services started.
5	1924	Marathandam Project in Kerala by Spencer Hatch
6	1930s	Wardha attempt, Sewagram by M.K. Gandhi
7	1936	All India Radio started
8	1937	Indian Adult Education Society started
9	1939	Indian Adult Education Association started as an NGO.
10	1948	Department of Social Education by Ministry of Education started to formulate policies on Adult education
11	1950	Free compulsory education in constitution (Article 45); aimed universalization of elementary education by 1960.

Sl.No.	*Year*	*Developmental Efforts Initiated*
12	1951-1956	☆ Social Education in connection with Community Development Program (CDP) started. ☆ Department of adult education (DAE) started
13	1953	☆ National Extension Service started ☆ UGC came into existence (1953 Dec 28), and became a statutory organization by an act of parliament in 1956.
14	1959	Grama Sikshan Mohim in Maharashtra
15	1962	Formation of all India women's association
16	1966	Akashwani started.
17	1968	Farmers Functional Literacy Program (FFLP) started in connection with High Yielding Varieties Program, Intensive Agriculture Development program (Green Revolution period)
18	Late 1960s	☆ Workers Education ☆ Non formal Education for Youth
19	1961	NCERT started; frames educational policy of primary education.
20	1962	Formation of All India Women's Association
21	1965	Regular T.V. telecasted from Delhi from Aug 15, 1965
22	1967	Shramika Vidya peeth started for vocational training. Polyvalent, multi facet Adult education
23	1968	☆ National Literacy Award was institutionalized ☆ Kothari commission
24	1970	National board of adult education
25	1974-1975	☆ Satellite instructed Television Education SITE initiated ☆ Training and Visit Program started. ☆ 1st Krishi Vignyan Kendra (KVK) started at Pondicherry for vocational training
26	1975-1976	Functional literacy program for Adult Women (FLAW)
27	1976	Jana Sikshan Nilayams started
28	1977	UGC introduced Extension into higher education.
29	1978	☆ National Adult Education Program (NAEP) started on Oct 2nd. ☆ State resource centers established. ☆ Integrated Rural Development Program IRDP started. (1978-79)

Sl.No.	*Year*	*Developmental Efforts Initiated*
30	1979	Training for Rural youth for Self Employment (TRYSEM) started
31	1982	☆ (16 point in) 20 point program. Govt of India introduced in 1983-1989 ☆ Continuing education program ☆ Dr. B.R. Ambedkar Open University (1st Open University) started in 1982 Aug 26.
32	1983	National Agricultural Extension Project
33	1987	☆ Operation black board; to improved facilities of learning in formal education. ☆ District Institutes of Education and Training started (DIET).
34	1985	☆ Rural Functional Literacy Program (RFLP) started by merging Functional literacy for youth (1979) and Farmers' training and Farmers' literacy project. ☆ Population Education clubs started (1984-85) ☆ IGNOU established (president of India is the chancellor., also called peoples university in India)
35	1986	Mass Program on Functional Literacy (MPFL) initiated
36	1986	New Education Policy
37	1988	☆ National Literacy Mission Started by Rajiv Gandhi ☆ Shramik Vidya Peeth turned to Jana Siksthan Samasthan; provide vocational training to the non literates. ☆ Mahila Samakhya started; for creating environment to promote girls' education.
38	1989	National Open School started.
39	1990-1997	Area based approach started that leads to Total literacy Campaign (TLC).
40	1992	☆ Bharat Gnyan Vignyan Jatha started to popularization of the science ☆ Lok Jumbish (peoples' movement) started in Rajasthan: sahaja siksha program for school dropouts, and for girls. ☆ National commission for women
41	1993-1994	☆ District primary Education Program (DPEP) started ☆ Library movement in KERALA ☆ Human Rights Act

Sl.No.	*Year*	*Developmental Efforts Initiated*
42	1995	☆ BGVJ started Lokshala Program for Universalization of elementory education under leadership of Prof. Asad Gopal. ☆ National Program for Nutritional Support (MID Day Meal)
43	1998	☆ NLM UNESCO award instituted ☆ ATMA started under NATP
44	2000	National population policy started and aimed to stabilize the population by 2045.
45	2000-2001	☆ Sarva Siksha Abhayan (SSA) for universalization of elementary education by 2010. ☆ National Policy on Women Empowerment (2001)
46	2003	Education guarantee Act
47	2004	Kasturba Gandhi Balika Vidyalaya (KGBV) started.
48	2005	Right to Information Act (RTI)
49	2009	Sakshara Bharat Mission
50	2010	Right to free and compulsory Education Act (2009 April 4th introduced and enforced from 2010 April 1st)
51	June 30, 2015	**e-Basta:** The platform, e-Basta, is merely not a library of books, but a collaborative platform where school Book publishers, School teachers, students and even various e-tailers can participate.
52	Jan 22, 2015	Beti Bachao, Beti Padhao: is a Government of India scheme that aims to generate awareness and improving the efficiency of welfare services meant for women started in Panipat (Haryana).
53	Jan, 2015	The National Institution for Transforming India (NITI AAYOG): Formerly called planning commission. **ICAR new schemes** (launched in July 25, 2015) **Farmer First,** The Farmer FIRST Programme (FFP) is an ICAR initiative to move beyond the production and productivity, to privilege the smallholder agriculture and complex, diverse and risk prone realities of majority of the farmers through enhancing farmers-scientists interface. **Attracting and Retaining Youth in Agriculture (ARYA):** Realizing the importance of rural youth in agricultural development especially from the point of view of food security of the country.

Chapter 6

Important Literacy Programmes and Schemes

- **Social Education:** This programme was implemented in the First Five Year Plan (1951-56). The major elements of this programme were literacy, extension, general education, leadership training and social consciousness of various development issues.
- **Gram Shikshan Mohim:** This movement for literacy in the rural areas was started in 1959 in Satara district of Maharashtra.
- **Farmer's Functional Literacy Project:** This inter-ministerial project was started in 1967-68 with two fold objective of farmer's training and functional literacy with the aim of popularization of high-yielding varieties of seeds through the process of adult education.
- **Non-Formal Education:** a programme of non-formal education for 15-25 age-group was launched IN 1975.
- **Polyvalent Adult Education Centres:** Workers' Social Education Institutes and Polyvalent Adult Education Centres were started in 1977.
- **Functional Literacy for Adult Women (FLAW):** This scheme was started in 1975-76 with the aim to enable illiterate adult women to acquire functional skills along with literacy in order to promote better awareness of health, hygiene, child-care practices and to bring about attitudinal changes.
- **Rural Functional Literacy Project (RFLP):** This was a major centrally sponsored scheme started in 1978 for rural areas.

- **State Adult Education Programme (SAEP):** The states also similarly took up centre based projects under the state plan funds on the lines of Rural Functional Literacy Projects.
- **Adult Education through Voluntary Agencies:** To ensure greater participation of voluntary agencies, the Central Scheme of Assistance to Voluntary Agencies was revived in April 1982.
- **Sakshara Bharat Mission:** This mission was launched on the International Literacy Day, 8th September 2009 with a focus on women in general and disadvantaged groups in particular.
- **Education for all:** In the year 2000, the world's governments adopted the six EFA goals and the eight Millennium Development Goals (MDGs), the two most important frameworks in the field of education.
- **UPE:** The need for universalization of primary education in India was pointed out a century ago by Sri Dadabhai Naoroji.
- **National Adult Education Programme (NAEP):** A massive programme of Adult Education called the National Adult Education Programme (NAEP) for removal of illiteracy in the 15-35 age group was introduced by the Government of India on 2nd October, 1978. The aim of this programme was to educate 100 million adults within a time frame of five years.
- **National Literacy Mission (NLM):** National Literacy Mission was launched on May 5, 1988 as a Technology Mission to impart functional literacy to non-literates in the country in the age group of 15-35 years in a time bound manner.
- **District Primary Education Programme (DPEP):** The Centrally-Sponsored Scheme of District Primary Education Programme (DPEP) (External website that opens in a new window) was launched in 1994 as a major initiative to revitalise the primary education system and to achieve the objective of universalization of primary education.
- **SSA:** Sarva Shiksha Abhiyan (SSA) has been operational since 2000-*2001*. It is Government of India's flagship programme for achievement of Universalization of Elementary Education (UEE) in a time bound manner, as mandated by 86th amendment to the Constitution of India making free and compulsory Education to the Children of 6-14 years age group, as a Fundamental Right.
- **JSN:** The scheme of Jana Sikshan Nilayam was launched by government of India in March 1998. Government decided to establish JSNs all over the country in a phased manner with basic objective to provide opportunities of continuing education to neo-literate to facilitate retention of their literacy skills.

☆ **Continuing Education Programme**: The new scheme continuing education programme which replaced the JSN scheme was launched on January 1, 1996 to meet the post literacy and continuing educational needs of the people.

☆ **JSS (SVP)**: Jan Shikshan Sansthan, (previously known as **Shramik Vidyapeeth**) is an institute of People's Education. This represents as an institutional frame-work for offering non-formal, adult and continuing education, vocational and skill development training to the disadvantaged groups.

☆ The Jan Shikshan Sansthan strives to improve the **"Living Standards"** of neo-literates and other target groups and in turn supporting their **"Livelihood".** The scheme of Jan Shikshan Sansthans or Institute of People's Education is a polyvalent or multi-faceted adult education programme aimed at improving the vocational skills and quality of life of its beneficiaries.

☆ **NIOS/NOS:** It is the Board of Education for Distance education, under the Union Government of India. It was established by the Ministry of Human Resource Development of Government of India in **1989** to provide education to remote areas under the motive to increase literacy and aimed forward for flexible learning.

☆ **Open basic education program:** The Open Basic Education is a programme providing Elementary Education at three levels, for children with special needs under its 'Sarva Shiksha Abhiyan (SSA).

☆ The National Institute of Open Schooling (NIOS) has launched the Open Basic Education (OBE) programme, as an alternative educational programme, equivalent to the Elementary Education programme of the formal education system.

☆ The OBE programme explores and makes use of the potentialities of Distance Education Mode (DEM) for reaching the unreached.

☆ **Population education Project:** Population Education Project was initially started in the year 1987 as an integral part of Adult Education Programme with the financial assistance of United Nations Fund for Population Activities (UNFPA).

☆ **National Book Trust, (NBT**) is an Indian publishing house, founded in 1957 as an autonomous body under the **Ministry of Education** within the Government of India

☆ **State Resource Centre (SRC):** started in 1976 and supported by the Ministry of HRD, Government of India, provides academic and technical resources to literacy and continuing education programme in the state of Rajasthan.

- ☆ **Directorate of Adult Education** originated from National Fundamental Education Centre (NFEC), which was set up by Govt. of India in the year 1956.
- ☆ National Fundamental Education Centre was renamed as Department of Adult Education.
- ☆ Functional Literacy for Adult Women (FLAW): The scheme of Functional Literacy for Adult Women (FLAW) was started in 1975-76 in the experimental ICDS project areas. It was gradually expanded along with the expansion of ICDS up to the year 1981-82.
- ☆ National Adult Education Programme (NAEP): The first nation-wide attempt at eradication of illiteracy was made through the National Adult Education Programme launched on October 2, 1978. It was a massive programme which aimed at educating 100 million non- literate adults in the age group of 15-35 years within a time frame of five years.
- ☆ Rural Functional Literacy Project (RFLP): This was a major centrally sponsored scheme started in 1978 for rural areas.
- ☆ **National literacy mission**: campaign mode was first started in Kottayam city in Kerala.
- ☆ The real breakthrough came with an experiment in mass literacy campaign initiated in 1989 and successfully completed in 1990 in Ernakulam district in Kerala.
- ☆ First fully literate district in country is Ernakulam.
- ☆ The total literacy campaign (TLC) was started in Feb15, 1994.
- ☆ Total literacy campaigns are area-specific, time-bound, volunteer-based, cost-effective and outcome oriented.
- ☆ Establishment of Continuing Education Centres (CECs) will be the principal mode of implementing continuing education programmes.
- ☆ Continuing education centres will essentially be community education centres (CECs).
- ☆ The National Literacy Mission was set up in 1988 with the goal of making 80 million people literate by 1995.
- ☆ A SAARC Conference of Voluntary Agencies working in the field of Literacy and Continuing Education was held from 14- 16 October, 1996 in New Delhi in which representatives from the countries of Nepal, Bangladesh, Pakistan and Sri Lanka participated.
- ☆ 4 The Total Literacy Campaign (TLC) is the principal strategy of the NLM for eradication of illiteracy in the country.

- The literacy campaigns under the Scheme are area-specific, time-bound, delivered through voluntarism, cost-effective and outcome-oriented, and are implemented by Zilla Saksharata Samitis usually headed by District Collectors.
- After completion of the TLC, Post Literacy Campaign (PLC) is launched to mop up the left-over illiterates to consolidate the gains of literacy acquired during TLC, and to enable the neo-literates to develop abilities for self-learning.
- The literacy campaigns are implemented through direct funding to the ZSS by the Central and State Governments in the ratio of 2:1.
- Scheme of Post Literacy and Continuing Education, launched in March 1988.
- National Literacy Resource Centre, Mussoorie.
- National Committee on the Education of Women under the chairmanship of Smt. Durga Bai Deshmukh.
- National Committee on Women's Education (1958-59).
- National Policy on Education (1986).
- The Programme of Action, (1992).
- The National Council of Educational Research and Training (NCERT) is an apex resource organisation set up by the Government of India, with headquarters at New Delhi, to assist and advise the Central and State Governments on academic matters related to school education.
- National Institute of Education (NIE), New Delhi
- Central Institute of Educational Technology (CIET), New Delhi.
- Pandit Sunderlal Sharma Central Institute of Vocational Education (PSSCIVE), Bhopal
- The Mahila Samakhya programme was launched in 1988 in pursuance of the goals of the New Education Policy (1986) and the Programme of Action as a concrete programme for the education and empowerment of women in rural areas, particularly of women from socially and economically marginalised groups.
- The government of india launched a new scheme in 2016 for Institutional capacity building is Swayam prabha.
- The government of india launched e-governance initiatives like ShaGun Portal, ePathshala, Shaala Siddhi etc.
- Right of Children to Free and Compulsory Education (RTE) Act, 2009.

- Kothari Commission Report - 1964-1966
- Woods Dispatch - 1854
- Radha Krishnan Education Report - 1978
- Secondary Education Report – 1948
- National Open School was renamed as National Institute of Open Schooling : 1989
- Gram Shikshan Mohim (Village education Campaign): 1959 (Satara distt, maharashtra)
- National Literacy Mission - 5 may 1988 (PM: Rajiv Gandhi)
- Sarva Shiksha Abhiyan -2001
- First Folk High School, Denmark -1844
- Non – Formal Education: 1975
- Sakshar Bharat Mission: 8 sep, 2009
- 16th Point in 20 Point Programme: 1982
- Area Development Approach 1988
- Mass Programme for Functional Literacy: 1stMay1986 (EOTO concept)
- Rural Functional literacy programme - 1978
- Each one teach one - 1986
- Prof. Ram Lal Parikh Review Committee Report.: 1983-85
- Farmers Functional Literacy Programme.: 1967
- Total Literacy Campaign: jan 1989
- Post Literacy: 1994
- Continuing Education: 1995
- Population Education Project was funded by UNFPA in the year: 1987discontinue - 2001
- Population education project: 1987
- Shramik vidyapeeth (1967)
- Jan Shikshan Sansthan (1stapril 2000)
- Jan Shikshan Nilayam : 1988
- State Resource Centre : 1976

- District Primary Education Programme (DPEP): 1994
- DIET: Oct, 1988
- Right to Free and Compulsory Education for age group of 6-14 year Act was notified on: 1st April, 2010
- Indian Adult education Association: 1939
- NCERT: 1961
- IGNOU: 1985
- NLM- UNESCO award instituted in: 1998
- Directorate of adult education: 1971
- NCTE: 17 aug,1995
- Domestic violence act:
- New educational policy: 1986
- Dowry prohibition amendment act: 1984
- Operation black board : 1987
- Mahila Samakhya yojana: 1989 (bottom up, 9 state)
- Accelerated female literacy centre: (top-down approach)
- Andragogy originated in : Europe,1950
- National book Trust: 1957
- National Education Association (NEA) created by Dept of adult education: 1857
- India adult education society: 1937, New delhi
- Ist All India Adult Education Conference: 1938, New delhi
- 2nd : mar, 1939 constituted indian adult education association
- Literacy House, (1953), lucknow (UP)
- National Fundamental Education Centre (1956)
- National Book Trust, Central Board of Workers Education (1957).
- Directorate of Adult Education (1971)
- National Institute of Adult Education :1991
- Jometian conference, Thailand 1990: Education for All

- Report of the UGC Working Group on Point No. 16 of the 20 Point Programme of the Government of India (1983)
- MPFL: 1st May, 1986
- Polyvalent education centre also called Shramik vidyapeeths
- UNESCO launched APPEAL (Asia Pacific Programme of Education for All) 1987
- Learning to be 1972
- Experimental world literacy programme 1964
- UNESCO report 'Learning to Be': Faure, 1972
- Ernakulum: Total literacy
- NCTE: Teacher's Education
- IGNOU: Higher Open Learning
- University : Higher Education
- NIOS: School Open Education
- UNESCO world assembly on adult education and life long learning was held at Hamburg in 1997
- Brazil in 2009.
- Tehran in 1965.
- Preparation of teaching learning material: SRC
- Universalization of primary education: SSA
- Open basic Education programme: NIOS
- Overseeing the education of primary level in village: VEC
- Anemateurs: NAEP
- Volunteers: TLC
- Extra-mural Lectures: United Kingdom
- Land Grant Colleges: USA
- Sakashara Bharat: female literacy
- Narmada movement: Gujarat
- Anti-Arrack movement: Nillore, Andhra Pradesh
- Chipko, 1973: Uttranchal

- Library movement: Kerala
- Education for all, 1990: NLM
- Frank Laubach's contribution : Each one Teach one
- World declaration education for all in: Thailand
- JSS: Vocational training
- JSN: Continuing education
- Nehru literacy award and Tagore literacy Award given by :IAEA
- NLM: total literacy campign
- NAEP: Centre based approach
- PLP: Follow up prog
- CEP: life long education
- Sakashar Bharat aim to reach - 70 million
- NLM: 80 million
- NAEP: 100 million
- CEC provides services for: equivalence and information window
- Dept of adult continuing edu and ext renamed as lifelong learning n ext in: XI plan
- **TLC:**'Literacy Campaigns in Operation Restoration'imparting basic literacy skill(non literates), 200 hours during 8-12 months
- **PLC:** application of literacy skill (neo-literates/sch dropouts)
- **CEC**: linking literacy with skill upgradation n improving quality of life; lifelong learning(neo-literates who completed PLC/TLC)
- **LIFE:** Literacy Initiative for Empowerment
- **LEAP:** lifelong education and awareness programme
- **IPCL:**Improved Pace and Content of learning
- **NEEM**: National Elementary Education Programme
- **DIET**: District Institute of Education and Training
- **DRU:** District Resource Unit
- **BGVS:** Bharat GyanVigyanSamiti
- **ALADIN**: Adult Literacy Documentation and Information Network

- **Fundamental Education (1950s-1960s):** imparting the basic literacy skills of reading and writing
- **Functional Literacy (1960s-1970s)**
- **Major Programmes of Adult Education during 1947-77**
- **Social Education Programme:**First Five Year Plan (1951-56), major thrust of Social Education Programme was to make illiterate citizens conscious of their rights and responsibilities
- **Farmers' Functional Literacy Project:**known as KisanSaksharataYojana, was launched as a centrally-sponsored scheme in the Fourth Plan (1969-74); components of the Farmers' Training and Functional Literacy Project (FI'FLP), focus of the FFLP was on upgrading the occupational skills of farmers and inculcating among them modem attitudes, values, and behaviours to attain self-sufficiency in food production.
- Scheme of Non-formal Education for Youth (15-25 years):who had missed schooling to provide them second chance for learning; The Fifth Plan (1974-79)
- NAEP integrated literacy, functionality and social awareness.
- Shramik vidyapeeths (polyvalent adult education centre)
- NLM also introduced a technocratic pedagogic approach, known as Improved Pace and Content of Learning (IPCL) to address the problems of slow pace and poor quality of learning among adult learners.
- 86th Constitutional Amendment Act (2002) makes free and compulsory education a justifiable fundamental right for all children in the age group 6-14 years.
- 72nd and 73rd Constitutional Amendments has paved the way to decentralisation of educational governance at the local level.
- **Learning by Association/**Operant or Instrumental conditioning.: E. L. Thorndike.; stressed the importance of reward in forming associations or connections, as he used to call them, between Stimulus (S) and Response (R).
- **Learning by Conditioning:** 2 types
- In Pavlov's experiment (1 960), the Natural stimulus was paired with the Un-conditioned or Natural Stimulus (UCS) and the natural stimulus got the properties of the UCS and became the Conditioned Stimulus (CS). This, according to B.F. Skinner, is the Respondent Conditioning.
- In Skinner's Operant Conditioning (OC), a response occurs spontaneously in the absence of any specifically correlated stimulus. The term 'operant'

means that behaviour operates upon the environment to generate its own consequences.

☆ In Classifiable or Respondent Conditioning (RC), the RC is due to a reinforcing stimulus, which forces the formation of the RC. In operant conditioning, the RC had to occur first at least once before it gets reinforced.

☆ Operant Conditioning (OC) is called instrumental learning.

☆ Learning by Insight: cognitive learning theories (Field Theories).

☆ Psycho-Analytic Theory: power that motivates the person

☆ Target of CEC: Equivalency Programmes (EPs),

☆ Quality of Life Improvement Programmes (QLIPs),

☆ (IGPs) Income Generating Programme and

☆ (IIPPs) Individual Interest Promotion Programmes

☆ Elements of TLC: Area, time, cost, output, volunteer

☆ Objectives of PLC: Remediation, continuation, Application, Communitization

Chapter 7

Important Facts about Teaching and Research

- ☆ The famous Air Force Central School is situated at –Delhi Cantt
- ☆ Tamil Nadu has a Sainik School at –Amrauathinagar
- ☆ The Sainik School in Orissa is at –Bhuvaneshwar
- ☆ The Sainik School in Karnataka is at –Bijapur
- ☆ Gandhi had which Educational Degree ? –Law
- ☆ Gandhi got his law Degree from –England
- ☆ Where did Gandhi as a teacher ? –South Africa
- ☆ Who said "A cowardly teacher cannot make his students valiant ? –M.K. Gandhi
- ☆ Effective teaching is a function of Teacher's methodology
- ☆ What should be the attitude of the teacher towards school authorities ? –Cordial
- ☆ The attitude of teacher towards new idea should be –Receptive
- ☆ Teachers should be made accountable for –Teaching
- ☆ An excellent teacher must be –Good guide
- ☆ As a teacher, you are never supposed to be angry –I am a human and can also be angry

- What is your Prime duty as a teacher ? –To help the student in understanding Physical and Social Environment
- What is the best Quality of the teacher ? –good human subject being
- The enthusiastic teachers generally ? –involve the students in learning–teaching process
- A teacher has better chances of succeeding if ? –he is properly trained for the profession
- Does the teachers enjoy the freedom to make their syllabus flexible ? –False
- A good teacher can overcome the defects of ? –System
- A quality teacher always reaches the school ? –Before the morning assembly is over
- Why you want to make teaching as a career ? –it make you eligible for the profession in ten months
- Generally a good number of students do not like to go to the class rooms because the curriculum is dull
- What is attitude –feeling
- As a teacher what means of recreation will you like to prefer – literary magazines and news papers
- A teacher always learns and he learns from – Students
- What enhances the status and respect of a teacher – community service
- Why a teacher fails in maintaining discipline in the class – because he lacks consistency in his approach to discipline
- What type behavior is expected from a teacher in the class room – calm, dignified and composed
- Why a teacher should be lover of sports – it encourages the students to take part in sports
- A good teacher priority in school is his –students
- People's attitude towards teaching is becoming positive because – perceiving teaching as a profession.
- Who can be creative teacher develop - thinking ability among the students
- Among the students faith in the human values can be generated through – Moral Education
- If as teacher you give too much liberty to students what will be result – indiscipline in the classroom

- If some one does not agree with you what will you do – polite explain your view point to him

International Level Conferences

- UNESCO world's assembly for ADULT EDUCATION held at TEHRAN in 1964.
- 4th International Conference on Adult Education held at PARIS in 1984.
- Conference on Education for ALL (EFA) held at JOMTEIN (THAILAND) in March 1990.
- UN conference on Environment and Development held at RIO in 1992.
- International Conference on Human rights held at Vienna (AUSTRALIA) in 1993.
- 5th International Conference on Population and Development held at CARIO in 1994.
- World Conference on Women held at BIEZING in 1995.
- UNESCO worlds assembly for ADULT EDUCATION held at HAMBURG (GERMANY) in 1997.
- (5TH INTERNATIONAL ADULT EDUCATION ASSEMBLY)
- UNESCO worlds assembly for ADULT EDUCATION and LIFELONG EDUCATION held at BRAZIL in 2009.
- 8TH WORLDS ASSEMBLY of International Council of Adult Education ICAE held at MOLMO (SWEEDEN) ON 14-17/JUNE/2011.
- 63rd international annual conference on Adult education about "Adult Educators: Making a Difference" held at Charleston, South Carolina (USA) by American Association for Adult and continuing education (AAACE) in NOV/2014.
- 4th International Conference on Educational and Information Technology (ICEIT 2015) held at Florence, Italy in March 2015.
- The World Conference on Education for All, convened in Jomtien, Thailand, in 1990, established goals and strategies to achieve Education for All (EFA).
- World Education Forum (Dakar, 2000).
- The Millennium Summit in 2000.
- The special session of the General Assembly on children in 2002.
- The Programme of Action of the International Conference on Population and Development (1994).

- ☆ In 1993, nine of the most populous developing countries of the world undertook the E-9 Initiative to attain the Education for All goals, both as a matter of fundamental human rights and as a strategy to curb population growth (United Nations Educational, Scientific and Cultural Organization (UNESCO), 1993).
- ☆ These nine countries — Bangladesh, Brazil, China, Egypt, India, Indonesia, Mexico, Nigeria and Pakistan have among the largest school-age populations in the world.
- ☆ On September 25th 2015, countries adopted a set of goals to end poverty, protect the planet, and ensure prosperity for all as part of a new sustainable development agenda. Each goal has specific targets to be achieved over the next 15 years.

Famous Quotations and Thoughts by Leaders

- ☆ Education is a manifestation of the perfection already in man. - Swamy Vivekananda.
- ☆ Education was a means to achieve perfection of individuality on the one hand and an instrument of service to the nation on the other. –**Gandhiji**
- ☆ "By education mean an all-round drawing out of the best in child and man-body, and spirit", -**Gandhiji.**
- ☆ Harmonious development of all the aspects of human personality such as physical, intellectual and spiritual was emphasized by him as an individual aim of education.-Gandhiji.
- ☆ The ultimate aim of education according to **Gandhi** is the **Self-Realization**.
- ☆ Gandhiji once wrote in Young India (1921) that "schools and colleges should become almost, if not wholly, self-supporting".
- ☆ Gandhi, emphatically, demanded that craft should be made the center of all education, centre of the school life.
- ☆ Gandhi's idea on education is a novel one. His idea of vocational education was unique which even now-a-days is being promoted by the government in India.
- ☆ **Gandhi's Sarvodaya:** Sarvodya is otherwise known as Gandhian Socialism. It is the around development of an individual. This idea came to the mind of Gandhi when he was translating John Raskin's book 'Unto the Last'. It includes the following features.
- ☆ **Upliftment of all:** Gandhian Sarvodya is a principle which is universal. It is a new approach of, socialism. It was against the principle that growth of majority in the society will improve the condition of the society.

☆ every human being is one who has potentialities of progressing towards the Super human being, the universal soul. –**Rabindranath tagore.**

Paulo Freire's Ideas on education

☆ Paulo Freire (1921-1997) was one of the best known and most influential radical education theorists in the 20th century; his impact upon peace education, adult education, non-formal education, and critical literacy has been incalculable. He brought the literacy to the third world countries. His ideology on education from his theories such as

1) Education as the Practice of Freedom (1967)
2) Pedagogy of the Oppressed (1970)
3) Paulo Freire's theory of human knowing and consciousness.
4) **Praxis:** Freire regarded praxis as a central concept in question. Praxis constitutes the means of gaining critical distance from one's world of action to engage in reflection geared toward transformative action.

List of National and International Days

International Days

☆ World Cancer Day-February 4.

☆ World Radio Day -13 February.

☆ International Mother Language Day -21 February.

☆ World Wildlife Day -3 March.

☆ International Women's Day -8 March.

☆ International Day of Happiness -20 March.

☆ International Day of Forests -21 March.

☆ World Water Day -22 March.

☆ World Meteorological Day -23 March.

☆ World Health Day -7 April.

☆ World Book and Copyright Day -23 April.

☆ English Language Day -23 April.

☆ World Press Freedom Day -3 May.

☆ International Day of Families -15 May.

☆ World Telecommunication and Information Society Day -17 May.

☆ World Day for Cultural Diversity for Dialogue and Development -21 May.

- ☆ International Day for Biological Diversity -22 May.
- ☆ World No-Tobacco Day -31 May.
- ☆ World Environment Day -5 June.
- ☆ International Day of Yoga -21 June.
- ☆ World Population Day -11 July.
- ☆ International Day of Friendship -30 July.
- ☆ International Youth Day -12 August.
- ☆ International Literacy Day -8 September.
- ☆ International Day of Democracy -15 September.
- ☆ International Day of Peace -21 September.
- ☆ World Tourism Day -27 September.
- ☆ International Day of Older Persons -1 October.
- ☆ International Day of Non-Violence -2 October.
- ☆ World Habitat Day -3 October.
- ☆ World Teachers' Day -5 October.
- ☆ International Day of the Girl Child -11 October.
- ☆ International Day of Rural Women -15 October.
- ☆ World Food Day -16 October.
- ☆ International Day for the Eradication of Poverty -17 October.
- ☆ United Nations Day 24 October.
- ☆ World Development Information Day 24 October.
- ☆ World Diabetes Day -14 November.
- ☆ World Philosophy Day -17 November.
- ☆ Universal Children's Day -20 November.
- ☆ World AIDS Day -1 December.
- ☆ International Day of Persons with Disabilities -3 December.
- ☆ World Soil Day -5 December.
- ☆ Human Rights Day -10 December.
- ☆ International Women's Day 8-Mar.

- ☆ World Disabled Day 15-Mar.
- ☆ World Forestry Day 21-Mar.
- ☆ International Day for the Elimination of Racial Discrimination 21-Mar.
- ☆ World Meteorological Day 23-Mar.
- ☆ Workers Day (International LaborDay) 1-May.
- ☆ International Friendship Day 3-Aug.
- ☆ Hiroshima Day 6-Aug.
- ☆ Quit India Day and Nagasaki Day 9-Aug.
- ☆ World Literacy Day 8-Sep.
- ☆ World Ozone Day 16-Sep.
- ☆ World Tourism Day 27-Sep.
- ☆ International day of the Elderly 1-Oct.
- ☆ World Food Day 16-Oct.
- ☆ UN Day, World development information Day 24-Oct.

National Days

- ☆ National Youth Day 12-Jan.
- ☆ Army Day 15- Jan.
- ☆ India's Republic Day and International Customs day 26-Jan.
- ☆ Martyrs' Day 30-Jan.
- ☆ Central Excise Day 24-Feb.
- ☆ National Science Day 28-Feb.
- ☆ National Technology Day 11-May.
- ☆ Anti-Tobacco Day 31-May.
- ☆ National Sports Day 29-Aug.
- ☆ Teachers' Day 5-Sep.
- ☆ Children's Day 14-Nov.
- ☆ Human Right Day 10-Dec.
- ☆ Kisan Divas Farmer's Day 23-Dec.
- ☆ National Science Day February-28.

- ☆ National press day Nov-16.
- ☆ Doctor's Day July-1.
- ☆ Engineers' Day September-15.
- ☆ National Post Day October-10.
- ☆ Mothers day – may,12
- ☆ National agriculture day –july,1
- ☆ World consumer rights day – march, 15
- ☆ National youth day – jan,12 (swami Vivekananda birthday)
- ☆ National girl child day – jan, 24
- ☆ Good governance day – dec, 25 (A.B. Vajpayee birthday)
- ☆ Civil service day – april, 21st

Chapter 8

Important Definitions and Terminologies

- **Adult Education:** May be a formal or non formal education where the learners are having age group more than 15 years generally known as adult education. NAEP targeted the people in the age group of 15-35years. It is an example for Non formal education.
- **Continuing Education:** Continuing education in the context of adult education in India means post literacy of neo literates, retention of literacy for school dropouts and application of this knowledge for improvement of living conditions.
- **Extension Education:** It is an applied science where it's content derived from the research and accumulated field experiences relevant principles drawn from the behavioral sciences synthesized with useful technology, in a body of philosophy, principles, content and methods focused on the problems of out of school education for adult and youth. **Agricultural Extension** Education is well known in Indian context. Where, it is one among the trinity (Research, Teaching and Extension) of university roles.
- **Literacy:** It is traditionally understood as the ability to read and write. The term's meaning has been expanded to include the ability to use language, numbers, images and other means to understand and use the dominant symbol systems of a culture.

- **Types of Literates**
  - **Neo literate:** an adult/adolescent who did not/could not make use of the available education opportunities on time, and who at later stage acquired the skills of literacy through formal and non formal approaches.
  - **Semi literates:** An adult/adolescent who require low level of formal education to became an literate; that means one who has received education earlier and later on he lost his literate skills.

    Ex: school dropouts
  - **Illiterate:** The one who cannot Read, write and comprehend is known as illiterate.
  - **Non literate:** illiterates, semi literates and the neo literates can be called as non literates.
  - **Scale of continuum from Literate to Illiterate**: Literate>Neo Literate>Semi Literate>Illiterate
- **Teaching:** Process of arranging situation where active learning takes place is nothing but teaching. In this process a series of steps will be there to transform learner from one level of comprehension to the next level of comprehension.
- **Learning:** Learning is a process by which sensations are perceived, understood and action undertaken resulting in desirable changes in knowledge, Skill and attitude.
- **3Rs of Education:** Reading, wRiting and aRithematic are considered as the 3Rs of Adult education. These are nothing but the "ability to read, write and doing small mathematical things like adding, subtracting, logic etc. is considered as education".
- **Training:** The process of improving one's knowledge, change in attitude and enhancement of skill through a communicational intervention is called training. In the training emphasis will be given to the improvement of the skill of the trainee and which has immediate application.
- **Empowerment:** empowerment is the act of improving social, economical, communicational strength of an individual and group of people. Empowerment will improve the confidence of individual with their own capacities and their own context.
- **Gender Mainstreaming:** Gender mainstreaming is the strategy to integrate men and women concerned experiences as an internal dimension of the planning, implementation, monitoring and evaluation of the policies, programmes so that equality will be generated and inequalities will not be perpetuated.

☆ **Gender blindness:** It is the inability to recognize the gender is an important dimension in the holistic development. It may also contribute for gender discrimination.

☆ **Population Education:** Population Education is an educational process which develops among learners an understanding of interrelationship between population and development, causes and consequences of population change and criticality of conditions of population stabilization. It includes in them the rationale attitude *and responsibility to population and development.*

☆ **Population studies:** Population Studies is a broad social science discipline concerned with the study of human populations in relation to their size, composition and geographical distribution, the changes which occur in these over time and the factors associated with these changes. The discipline emphasises the empirical investigation of population processes, including the conceptualisation and measurement of these processes and the study of their determinants and consequences. Population studies are also concerned with the broader nature of social and economic change, and with the impact of demographic change on the natural environment. The concepts of population studies have an important role to play in understanding of social change. Population Studies is an essential component of many activities, social and market research, physical and environmental use plans, administration, and in particular people-centred development planning.

☆ **Vocational training:** Training that emphasizes skills and knowledge required for a particular job function

☆ **Distance education:** is a mode of delivering education and instruction, often on an individual basis, to students who are not physically present in a traditional setting such as a classroom. Distance learning provides "access to learning when the source of information and the learners are separated by time and distance, or both."

☆ **Lifelong Education:** is the "ongoing, voluntary, and self-motivated" pursuit of knowledge for either personal or professional reasons. Therefore, it not only enhances social inclusion, active citizenship, and personal development, but also self-sustainability, rather than competitiveness and employability. The concept Lifelong Learning was introduced in Denmark as early as in 1971.

☆ **Night school:** A **night school** is an adult learning school that holds classes in the evening or at night to accommodate people who work during the day. It can also apply to a community college or university that hold classes for the aforementioned purpose, but also admits undergraduates.

☆ **Farmer field school:** is a group-based learning process that has been used by a number of governments, NGOs and international agencies to promote Integrated Pest Management (IPM). The first FFS were designed and managed by the UN Food and Agriculture Organisation in **Indonesia** in **1989** since then more than two million farmers across Asia have participated in this type of learning.

- ☆ **Research:** search of knowledge, scientific and systematic investigation for some pertinent information on a specific topic.
- ☆ **Social Research:** Scientific undertaking by means of logical and systematic techniques aims to discover / verify / test old facts and new facts, to analysis their inter relations as well as causal explanations and to develop new scientific tools, concepts through valid and reliable scientific methods.
- ☆ **Fundamental research/Basic research**: gathering of the knowledge for knowledge sake. Not used for the practical solving of problem but to discover the underling universal laws and theories.
- ☆ **Applied research:** gathering of knowledge that could aid in betterment of human destiny.
- ☆ **Adoptive research:** research conducted where people live and work. To make research relevant and understandable to the people. On farm research conducted by the agricultural scientists.
- ☆ **Action research:** form of social research, aims at better insight into practice by learning from experience to solve the problem.
- ☆ **Field Experiments:** manipulate one or more variable under NATUARL SETTING, realistic situation. Hence variables have strong effect that gives to sound generalization. Precision and accuracy not possible due to field. It is a most common tool for the sociologists, socio psychologists, and educationalists.
- ☆ **Descriptive/Non experiments:** here no manipulation of the variables taken place. It may be hypothesis testing type and can be done without hypothesis.
- ☆ **Ex-post facto research:** it is a systematic and empirical enquiry in which the scientists have direct control over the independent variable because their manifestation has already been occurred.
- ☆ **Survey research:** small, large populations by drawing samples to discover the relative incidence distribution and interrelations of the sociological and psychological variables.
- ☆ **Content analysis:** Document analysis, systematic examinations of the communications or current records / documents. Primary source of information includes letters, diaries, reports, photos, films etc.
- ☆ **Case studies:** one-way method of organizing social data for the purpose of viewing social reality

- ☆ **Ethnographic studies:** observation of the behaviour in a natural setting. To study the primitive group isolated with geographically, culturally.
- ☆ The gender parity index (GPI) is the ratio of the enrolment ratio for girls to that for boys.

Assertion Reason Type Questions

1. **Assertion (A): Learning needs of married and unmarried female learner are not same.**

   Reason (R): Married women have specific learning needs.

   Codes:

   (A) (A) and (R) are true and (R) is the correct explanation of (A).

   (B) (A) is true, but (R) is false.

   (C) (A) is false, but (R) is true.

   (D) Both (A) and (R) are true, but (R) is not correct explanation of (A).

2. **Assertion (A): Literacy and numeracy both are inbuilt components of Adult Education Programme.**

   Reason (R): An adult can manage with literacy only.

   Codes:

   (A) Both (A) and (R) are true, but (R) is correct explanation of (A).

   (B) Both (A) and (R) are true, but (R) is not the correct explanation of (A).

   (C) (A) is false, but (R) is true.

   (D) (A) is true, but (R) is false.

3. **Assertion (A): It has been reported that there is a huge gap between demand and supply of skilled workers.**

   Reason (R): National Skill Development Programme has been started to import skills in critical areas of production.

Codes:

(A) Both (A) and (R) are true and (R) is not the correct explanation of (A).
(B) Both (A) and (R) are false.
(C) Both (A) and (R) are true and (R) is the correct explanation of (A).
(D) (A) is true and (R) is false.

4. **Assertion (A): Health problems of villagers and slum dwellers are same.**

   Reason (R): Slum dwellers are unaware of health problem.

   Codes:

   (A) Both (A) and (R) are true and (R) is correct explanation of (A).
   (B) Both (A) and (R) are true, but (R) is not the correct explanation of (A).
   (C) (A) is true, but (R) is false.
   (D) (A) is false, but (R) is true.

5. **Assertion (A): Family life education is a part of population education.**

   Reason (R): Family life education is a specific components of population education.

   Codes:

   (A) Both (A) and (R) are true and (R) is correct explanation of (A).
   (B) Both (A) and (R) are true, but (R) is not the correct explanation of (A).
   (C) (A) is true, but (R) is false.
   (D) (A) is false, but (R) is true.

6. **Assertion (A): Rural Functional Literacy Programme was the core programme to cover rural population.**

   Reason (R): Farmer Functional Literacy is a part of RFLP.

   Codes:

   (A) (A) and (R) both are true, but (R) is the correct explanation of (A).
   (B) (A) and (R) both are true but (R) is not the correct explanation of (A).
   (C) (A) is false, but (R) is true.
   (D) Both (A) and (R) are false.

7. **Assertion (A): Functional Literacy for Adult Women provided holistic approach to women education.**

   Reason (R): FLAW was meant only for married woman.

   Codes:

   (A) (A) and (R) both are true and (R) is correct explanation of (A).
   (B) (A) and (R) both are true, but (R) is not correct explanation of (A).

(C) (A) is true, but (R) is false.

(D) (A) is false, but (R) is true.

8. **Assertion (A): Quality of life includes several development indication.**

Reason (R): Population education is help to achieve better quality of life.

Codes:

(A) (A) and (R) both are true and (R) is explanation of (A).

(B) (A) and (R) are true, but (R) is not an explanation of (A).

(C) (A) is false, but (R) is true.

(D) (A) and (R) both are false.

9. **Assertion (A): Adult Education leads to political awakening.**

Reason (R): Educated Adults can make a better political choice.

Codes:

(A) (A) and (R) both are true and (R) is an correct explanation of (A).

(B) (A) and (R) both are true, but (R) is not an correct explanation of (A).

(C) (A) is false, but (R) is true.

(D) (A) and (R) both are false.

10. **Assertion (A): Literacy learning has been reported to be slow among adult learners.**

Reason (R): Basic literacy learning suffers because of its excessive emphasis on 3Rs.

Codes:

(A) Both (A) and (R) are correct, but (R) is not the correct explanation of (A).

(B) Both (A) and (R) are correct and (R) is the correct explanation of (A).

(C) (A) is true and (R) is false.

(D) (A) is false and (R) is true.

11. **Assertion (A): Leaders are the products of a given situation.**

Reason (R): Leader emerges out of situation.

Codes:

(A) (A) is true, but (R) is wrong.

(B) (R) is true, but (A) is wrong.

(C) Both are true and (R)is correct explanation of (A).

(D) Both are correct, but (R) is not true explanation of (A).

12. **Assertion (A): Motivation is a hypothetical construct for learning.**

    Reason (R): Motivation can not do other than team work.

    Codes:

    (A) (A) and (R) both are true.

    (B) (A) and (R) both are false.

    (C) (A) is true, but (R) is false.

    (D) (A) and (R) both are true but (R) is not correct explanation of (A).

13. **Assertion (A): The Joint Family System has broken down in India.**

    Reason (R): Industrialization has created a great demand for working hands.

    Codes:

    (A) Both (A) and (R) is wrong.

    (B) (A) is correct, but (R) is wrong.

    (C) Both (A) and (R) are correct, but (R) is not correct explanation of (A).

    (D) Both (A) and (R) are correct and (R) is a correct explanation of (A).

14. **Assertion (A): The Hindu Marriage Act 1955 introduced a significant change in women status in India.**

    Reason (R): Polygamy let do increase the number of divorces.

    Codes:

    (A) (A) is correct, but (R) is false.

    (B) Both (A) and (R) are correct.

    (C) (A) is correct and (R) is not correct explanation of (A).

    (D) Both (A) and (R) are wrong.

15. **Assertion (A): Social education tries to make the adult ideal citizens.**

    Reason (R): Social education imparts the knowledge of the problems of the world of adults.

    Codes:

    (A) (A) is wrong, but (R) correct.

    (B) (R) is wrong, but (A) is correct.

    (C) Both (A) and (R) are correct and (R) is the correct explanation of (A).

    (D) Both (A) and (R) are correct and (R) is not correct explanation of (A).

16. **Assertion (A): Social, Political, and economic, equality is absolutely necessary for the success of democracy.**

    Reason (R): To some extent the problems of democracy can be solved through equality.

Codes:

(A) (A) is correct, but (R) is wrong.

(B) (R) is correct, but (A) is wrong.

(C) Both are correct, but (R) is not correct explanation of (A).

(D) Both are correct and (R) is correct explanation of (A).

17. **Assertion (A): The unemployment problems of the rural areas can be solved by economic reconstruction.**

Reason (R): There are many serious problems in rural areas and unemployment is one of them.

Codes:

(A) (R) is true, but (A) is false.

(B) (A) is true, but (R) is false.

(C) Both are true, but (R) is not correct explanation of (A).

(D) Both are true, and (R) is correct explanation of (A).

18. **Assertion (A): Community development is a process controlled by the community itself.**

Reason (R): Community development programmes are basically introduced and implemented by the community.

Codes:

(A) (A) is true, but (R) is false.

(B) Both are false.

(C) Both are true, but (R) is not correct explanation of (A).

(D) Both are true, and (R) is correct explanation of (A).

19. **Assertion (A): The panchayats are making considerable progress in the rural development in India.**

Reason (R): The rights of panchayats should be increased for rural development in India.

Codes:

(A) (A) is true, but (R) is false.

(B) (R) is true, but (A) is false.

(C) Both (A) and (R) are false.

(D) Both (A) and (R) are true, but (R) is not correct explanation of (A).

20. **Assertion (A): Extension as third dimension aims at promoting a meaningful and sustained rapport between the university and the community.**

Reason (R): **One of the goal of university grants commission is to transform the university system in an active instrument for social change.**

Codes:

(A) Both (A) and (R) are true and (R) is right explanation of (A).

(B) Both (A) and (R) are true and (R) is not right explanation of (A).

(C) (A) is true and (R) is false.

(D) (A) is false and (R) is true.

21. **Assertion (A):** **Formative evaluation is important for monitoring of adult education.**

Reason (R): **Adult teaching techniques are more important for adult education programme.**

Codes:

(A) (A) is correct, but (R) is wrong.

(B) Both (A) and (R) are correct, but (R) is not correct explanation of (A).

(C) (A) is wrong, but (R) is correct.

(D) (R) is wrong, but (A) is correct.

22. **Assertion (A):** **The development of higher education in India is a responsibility of central govt.**

Reason (R): **The higher education system of India is supported by each and every state government too.**

Codes:

(A) (A) is correct, but (R) is wrong.

(B) Both (A) and (R) are correct, but (R) is not correct explanation of (A).

(C) Both (A) and (R) are wrong.

(D) Both (A) and (R) are correct and (R) is a correct explanation of (A).

23. **Assertion (A):** **Computer application in adult education, is important for research and evaluation.**

Reason (R): **Information technology is helpful for adult learning.**

Codes:

(A) (A) is true, but (R) is wrong.

(B) Both (A) and (R) are wrong.

(C) Both (A) and (R) are correct and (R) is a correct explanation of (A).

(D) Both (A) and (R) are correct, but (R) is not correct explanation of (A).

24. **Assertion (A): Motivation implies any emotion or desire which so conditions one's will that individual is propelled in to action.**

Reason (R): Motivation means a process, by which peoples start to move to achieve goals.

Codes:

(A) (A) is correct, but (R) is wrong.

(B) (A) is wrong, but (R) is correct.

(C) Both (A) and (R) are correct and (R) is not correct explanation of (A).

(D) Both (A) and (R) are correct, and (R) is correct explanation of (A).

25. **Assertion (A): India is a developing nation with poor people.**

Reason (R): People of India are still under poverty.

Codes:

(A) (A) is correct, but (R) is wrong.

(B) (R) is correct, but (A) is wrong.

(C) Both (A) and (R) are correct, but (R) is not correct explanation of (A).

(D) Both (A) and (R) are correct, and (R) is explanation of A

26. **Assertion (A): Extension activities give an exposure to the university students and teachers.**

Reason (R): Extension is the 'Third important dimension of higher education'.

Codes:

(A) (A) is correct and (R) is false.

(B) (A) is false and (R) is correct.

(C) (A) and (R) are false.

(D) (A) and (R) are correct.

27. **Assertion (A): Adults learns from simple to complex.**

Reason (R): Adult learning is a rapid-process.

Codes:

(A) (A) is correct and (R) is false.

(B) (A) is false and (R) is correct.

(C) (A) and (R) are correct.

(D) (A) and (R) are false.

28. **Assertion (A): Education helps in developing human resource in a country.**

Reason (R): Literacy is the first step in educational process.

Codes:

(A) (A) is correct and (R) is false.

(B) (A) is false and (R) is correct.

(C) (A) and (R) are correct.

(D) (A) and (R) are false.

29. **Assertion (A): Trained man power is the biggest asset to an organisation.**

Reason (R): Training is a systematic process to improve the acquired abilities of the workers.

Codes:

(A) (A) is correct and (R) is false.

(B) (A) is false and (R) is correct.

(C) Both (A) and (R) are correct and (R) is the correct explanation of (A).

(D) Both (A) and (R) are correct, and (R) is not the correct explanation of (A).

30. **Assertion (A): Adoption of innovation is a mental process.**

Reason (R): Adoption rate of innovation is higher in communities favourable to change.

Codes:

(A) (A) is correct and (R) is false.
(B) (A) is false and (R) is correct.

(C) (A) and (R) are correct.
(D) (A) and (R) are false.

31. **Assertion (A): Media policy of NLM aims to create awareness among targeted people for literacy programmes.**

Reason (R): Media Policy of NLM aims to strengthen the delivery system for promoting literacy programmes.

Codes:

(A) Assertion (A) is true.

(B) Reason (R) is true.

(C) Assertion (A) and Reason (R) are true.

(D) Assertion (A) is true and Reason (R) is false.

32. **Assertion (A): The hypothesis may be tested through the use of one or more statistical tests, depending upon the nature and objective of a research problem.**

Reason (R): The result of the hypothesis-testing will only be acceptable and not rejected.

Codes:

(A) Assertion (A) is false.

(B) Reason (R) is true.

(C) Assertion (A) and Reason (R) are false.

(D) Assertion (A) is true, but Reason (R) is false.

33. Assertion (A): Good quality of practice in Adult Education is encouraging learner-instructor contact.

Reason (R): Good quality of practice encourages co-operation among adult learners.

Codes:

(A) Assertion (A) is false, but Reason (R) is true.

(B) Assertion (A) and Reason (R) are not correct.

(C) Assertion (A) and Reason (R) are correct.

(D) Assertion (A) is true and Reason (R) is false.

34. Assertion (A): Adult learning theories holds assumptions about how adults learn.

Reason (R): Andragogy emphasizes the value of process of adult learning.

Codes:

(A) Assertion (A) is false, but Reason (R) is true.

(B) Assertion (A) and Reason (R) are true.

(C) Assertion (A) and Reason (R) are false.

(D) Assertion (A) is true, but Reason (R) is false.

35. Assertion (A): Andragogy emphasizes the problem based and collaborative approaches of learning.

Reason (R): Andragogy emphasizes more equality between the instructor and learner.

Codes:

(A) Assertion (A) is false, but Reason (R) is true.

(B) Assertion (A) and Reason (R) are false.

(C) Assertion (A) and Reason (R) are true.

(D) Assertion (A) is true and Reason (R) is false.

36. Assertion (A): The possible motives for doing research may be desire to get a research degree along with its consequential benefits.

Reason (R): The possible motives for doing research may be desire to face the challenges in solving the unsolved problems.

Codes:

(A) Reason (R) is true.

(B) Assertion (A) and Reason (R) are true.

(C) Assertion (A) is false.

(D) Assertion (A) is true and Reason (R) is false.

37. **Assertion (A): Malcom Knowles identified the six principles of adult learning.**

Reason (R): Adults are internally motivated and self directed.

Codes:

(A) Reason (R) is true.

(B) Assertion (A) is false.

(C) Assertion (A) and Reason (R) are correct.

(D) Assertion (A) and Reason (R) are false.

38. **Assertion (A): Collection of research data can be done through observation method.**

Reason (R): Collection of research data can also be done through interview method.

Codes:

(A) Assertion (A) is false.

(B) Reason (R) is false and Assertion (A) is true.

(C) Assertion (A) is true and Reason (R) is false.

(D) Assertion (A) and Reason (R) are true.

39. **Assertion (A): UNESCO promotes adult literacy throughout the world.**

Reason (R): UNESCO has been playing a major role to increase the rate of literacy in each country.

Codes:

(A) Assertion (A) is true.

(B) Assertion (A) and Reason (R) are false.

(C) Assertion (A) is true and Reason (R) is also true.

(D) Assertion (A) is false and Reason (R) is true.

40. **Assertion (A): David Kolb published his Experimental Learning Theory [ELT] in 1984, along with a Learning System Inventory [LSI] building on the work of Carl Rogers, Jung and Piaget.**

Reason (R): ELT is closely related to theories such as Multiple Intelligences [MI] and Myers-Briggs Type Indicator [MBTI].

Codes:

(A) Assertion (A) is true.

(B) Assertion (A) and Reason (R) are true.

(C) Assertion (A) is true and Reason (R) is false.

(D) Assertion (A) is false and Reason (R) is true.

41. Assertion (A): Gardner, 1993 posited seven type of intelligences.

Reason (R): Linguistic intelligence is one of the seven types of intelligences posited by Gardener.

Codes:

(A) (A) is false.
(B) (A) is true, but (R) is false.
(C) (A) and (R) are false.
(D) (A) and (R) are true.

42. Assertion (A): According to Cross, 1981 approximately 70 percent of adult learning process is self directed.

Reason (R): According to Tough, 1971, 100 percent of adult learning process is self directed.

Codes:

(A) (A) is false.
(B) (A) is true and (R) is false.
(C) (A) and (R) are true.
(D) (A) and (R) are false.

43. Assertion (A): Self-directed learning is a process in which individuals take the initiative for adult learning.

Reason (R): Self-directed learning mutually helps both the instructors and learners for learning.

Codes:

(A) (A) is false.
(B) (R) is true.
(C) (A) and (R) are false.
(D) (A) and (R) are true.

44. Assertion (A): The states and Union Territories like Mizoram, Tripura, Goa, Kerala, Puducherry and Delhi have increased their literary rates above 80 percent as per 2011 census.

Reason (R): In the last one decade they have done extremely well in implementry literary programmes.

Codes:

(A) (A) is true.
(B) (A) and (R) are true.
(C) Both (A) and (R) are false.
(D) (R) is false.

45. Assertion (A): **In the seventh year of the Republic of India, UGC Act, 1956 was enacted by the Parliament.**

Reason (R): **It does not include the provision for co-ordination and determination of standards in Universities.**

Codes:

(A) Both (A) and (R) are true.
(B) Both (A) and (R) are false.
(C) (A) is true and (R) is false.
(D) (A) is false and (R) is true.

46. Assertion (A): **Life long learning involves all forms of Education.**

Reason (R): **Learning never ends is the major concept of Life Long Learning.**

Codes:

(A) Both (A) and (R) are false.
(B) (A) is false.
(C) Both (A) and (R) are true.
(D) (R) is true

47. Assertion (A): **The four characteristics of the life long learning are Learning to Do, Learning to Be, Learning to Know and Learning to Live together.**

Reason (R): **The characteristics of lifelong learning enhances the learner's overall skill set, if properly practiced.**

Codes:

(A) (R) is false.
(B) Both (A) and (R) are true.
(C) (A) is true.
(D) Both (A) and (R) are false.

48. Assertion (A): **The World Population has been increasing continuously for several decades despite adopting several population control measures.**

Reason (R): **The population of Third World Countries has been rapidly increasing due to poverty, illiteracy, high fertility rate etc.**

Codes:

(A) (R) is true.
(B) (A) and (R) are correct.
(C) (A) is false.
(D) (A) and (R) are not correct.

49. Assertion (A): **Every year 8th September has been celebrated as International Literacy Day by all the countries of the world.**

Reason (R): **International Literary Day is observed for creating awareness among the people on important of literary.**

Codes:

(A) (A) is not correct.
(B) (R) is correct.
(C) (A) and (R) are correct.
(D) (A) is correct.

50. Assertion (A): Learning needs of urban adults are different from rural adults.

Reason (R): Learning needs of adults are same in general for both urban and rural area.

Codes:

(A) (A) and (R) are not correct.

(B) Both (A) and (R) are correct.

(C) (A) is correct, but (R) is not correct.

(D) (A) is not correct, but (R) is correct.

51. Assertion (A): The major function of the Dept. of Adult and Continuing Education or Dept. of Lifelong Learning is undertaking field outreach activities.

Reason (R): Through the extension activities the Dept. of Adult and Continuing Education creates awareness among the rural people on different social issues.

Codes:

(A) (A) is not correct.

(B) (R) is correct.

(C) Both (A) and (R) are not correct.

(D) Both (A) and (R) are correct.

52. Assertion (A): Establishment of State Council of Higher Education in each state of India was emphasized in the National Policy of Education 1986 for promoting the Higher Education in massive scale.

Reason (R): The main purpose of establishing the State Council of Higher education in each state is to create networking with all higher educational institutions for providing quality education to students.

Codes:

(A) (A) is correct.

(B) Both (A) and (R) are correct.

(C) Both (A) and (R) are not correct.

(D) (R) is not correct.

53. Assertion (A): National Book Trust was founded in 1957 as an autonomous body by Govt. of India for publishing quality books in different fields.

Reason (R): National Book Trust gives award to authors of the book for encouraging their good and quality of writing.

Codes:

(A) (A) is not correct.

(B) (R) is correct.

(C) Both (A) and (R) are correct.

(D) Both (A) and (R) are not correct.

54. Assertion (A): **State Resources Centres are mandated to provide academic and technical resource support to adult education programmes.**

Reason (R): **State resources centres are developing and producing training modules for the functionaries of the adult education programmes.**

Codes:

(A) (A) is not correct. (B) (R) is correct.

(C) (A) and (R) are correct. (D) (A) and (R) are not correct.

55. Assertion (A): **India adds more people than any other country in the world in each decade.**

Reason (R): **Uttar Pradesh, State of India adds more people than any other state of India.**

Codes:

(A) (A) is correct. (B) (R) is not correct.

(C) (A) and (R) are not correct. (D) Both (A) and (R) are correct.

56. Assertion (A): **Continuing Education is one of the hallmark of learning society.**

Reason (R): **Continuing Education based on the premise that all adults should be entitled to continue a opportunities for education throughout their lives.**

Codes:

(A) (A) is true and (R) is false.

(B) (A) is false and (R) is true.

(C) (A) and (R) are true and (R) is the right explanation of (A).

(D) (A) and (R) are true and (R) is not the right explanation of (A).

57. Assertion (A): **Induction is an important technique of training.**

Reason (R): **Induction does not help the employee any way.**

Codes:

(A) Both (A) and (R) are true and (R) is correct explanation of (A).

(B) Both (A) and (R) are true, but (R) is not correct explanation of (A).

(C) (A) is true, but (R) is false.

(D) (A) is false, but (R) is true.

548. Assertion (A): Computer literacy should be an important component of continuing education programme.

Reason (R): Computer facility available in every part of country.

Codes:

(A) Both (A) and (R) are true and (R) is correct explanation of (A).

(B) (A) and (R) both are true, but (R) is not the correct explanation of (A).

(C) (A) is true, but (R) is false.

(D) (A) is false, but (R) is true.

549. Assertion (A): Rehabilitation ouncil of India (RCI) is responsible for education and training of differently abled persons.

Reason (R): Differently abled persons should have a specialised agency equipped to handle their specific need of education and training.

Codes:

(A) Both (A) and (R) are true and (R) is correct explanation of (A).

(B) Both (A) and (R) are true, but (R) is not correct explanation of (A).

(C) (A) is true, but (R) is false.

(D) (A) is false, but (R) is true.

60. Assertion (A): Illiteracy rate among minority group adults is still very high.

Reason (R): Education for all programme has not reached to all population.

Codes:

(A) Both (A) and (R) are correct and (R) is the correct explanation of (A).

(B) Both (A) and (R) are correct, but (R) is not the correct explanation of (A).

(C) (A) is true and (R) is false.

(D) (A) is false and (R) is true.

61. Assertion (A): NAEP was an adult education program.

Reason (R): Total literacy campaign is an improvement of NAEP.

Codes:

(A) Both (A) and (R) are correct and (R) is the correct explanation of (A).

(B) Both (A) and (R) are correct, but (R) is not the correct explanation of (A).

(C) (A) is true, but (R) is false.

(D) (A) is false, and (R) is true.

62. **Assertion (A): There is a positive co-relation between basic literacy and primary education.**

Reason (R): It has been a found that total literate districts have shown increase in enrolment at primary education.

Codes:

(A) Both (A) and (R) are true and (R) is the correct explanation of (A).

(B) Both (A) and (R) are true, but (R) is not the correct explanation of (A).

(C) (A) is true, but (R) is false.

(D) (A) is false, but (R) is true.

63. **Assertion (A): Mean in a distribution represent the whole data.**

Reason (R): Mean is not affected by extremities of data.

Codes:

(A) Both (A) and (R) are true and (R) is correct explanation of (A).

(B) Both (A) and (R) are true, but (R) is not correct explanation of (A).

(C) (A) is true and (R) is false.

(D) (A) is false and (R) is true.

64. **Assertion (A): Health care of rural population is one of the major concern of Government of India.**

Reason (R): N.R.H.M. has been implemented to provide health services to rural population.

Codes:

(A) Both (A) and (R) are true and (R) is a correct explanation of (A).

(B) Both (A) and (R) are true, but (R) is not a correct explanation of (A).

(C) (A) is true, but (R) is false.

(D) (A) is false, but (R) is true.

65. **Assertion (A): University Extension Services attempts to link university with community.**

Reason (R): Teaching and research in universities had a very low relevance to common people.

Codes:

(A) Both (A) and (R) are true and (R) is correct explanation of (A).

(B) Both (A) and (R) are true, but (R) is not a correct explanation of (A).

(C) (A) is true and (R) is false.

(D) (A) is false and (R) is true.

66. **Assertion (A): Leadership is the ability to exert interpersonal influence by means of communication towards the achievement of a goal.**

Reason (R): Integeration and direction create problem in leadership.

Codes:

(A) Both (A) and (R) are true and (R) is correct explanation.

(B) Both (A) and (R) are true, but (R) is not a correct explanation.

(C) (A) is true, but (R) is false.

(D) (A) is false, but (R) is true.

67. **Assertion (A): Literacy demand is low in adult illiterates.**

Reason (R): Environment building is done to increase awareness about literacy.

Codes:

(A) Both (A) and (R) are correct and (R) is correct explanation.

(B) Both (A) and (R) are correct and (R) is not a correct explanation.

(C) (A) is true, but (R) is false.

(D) (A) is false, but (R) is true.

68. **Assertion (A): Effective communication is bringing out the desired change through information sharing.**

Reason (R): Response to sharing of information is not a feed back.

Codes:

(A) Both (A) and (R) are true and (R) is correct explanation.

(B) Both (A) and (R) are true, but (R) is not a correct explanation.

(C) (A) is true, but (R) is false.

(D) (A) is false, but (R) is true.

69. **Assertion (A): Literacy relapse in to illiteracy in absence of follow up activities.**

Reason (R): Post literacy and continuing education programme has been started to continue and retain basic literacy skills of neoliterates.

Codes:

(A) (A) is true, but (R) is false.

(B) (R) is true, but (A) is false.

(C) Both (A) and (R) are true and (R) is the correct explanation of (A).

(D) Both (A) and (R) are false.

70. **Assertion (A):** **Extension has been included as third dimension of higher education in university system.**

Reason (R): **University should develop close and meaningful relations with the society.**

Codes:

(A) (A) is true, but (R) is false.

(B) Both (A) and (R) are true, but (R) is not the correct explanation of (A).

(C) Both (A) and (R) are false.

(D) Both (A) and (R) are true and (R) is the correct explanation of (A).

71. **Assertion (A):** **Educated parents are more aware about the education of their children.**

Reason (R): **Increase in literacy rate has positive impact on primary education.**

Codes:

(A) (A) is true, but (R) is false.

(B) (R) is true, but (A) is false.

(C) Both (A) and (R) are true and (R) is the correct explanation of (A).

(D) Both (A) and (R) are true, but (R) is not the correct explanation of (A).

72. **Assertion (A):** **In order to improve the quality of Higher Education autonomy should be given to the colleges.**

Reason (R): **Autonomy need not be given to the colleges as they are not competent to frame the curriculum and evaluation.**

Codes:

(A) (A) and (R) are true.

(B) (A) and (R) are not true.

(C) (A) is not true but (R) is true.

(D) (A) is true but (R) is not true.

73. **Assertion (A):** **The Adult Literacy Programmes are not attractive, as they are not need based.**

Reason (R): **The activities of the adult literacy centres are framed based on the needs of the learners.**

Codes:

(A) (A) and (R) are true.

(B) (A) is not true but (R) is true.

(C) (A) and (R) are not true.

(D) (A) is true but (R) is not true.

74. **Assertion (A):** **The participation of women in the Adult Literacy Centres are low because the men volunteers discriminate women learners.**

Reason (R): **More women volunteers are required to improve the participation of the women learners.**

Codes:

(A) (A) is not true but (R) is true.

(B) (A) and (R) are true.

(C) (A) and (R) are not true.

(D) (A) is true but (R) is not true

75 **Assertion (A): Non-formal education is out of school education.**

Reason (R): **Non-formal education is deliberate, planned, staffed financially supported like formal education and it has valid claim to reality.**

Code :

(A) Both (A) and (R) are true.

(B) Both (A) and (R) are true but (R) is not correct explanation.

(C) (A) is true but (R) is false.

(D) (A) is false but (R) is true.

76 **Assertion (A): Saakshar Bharat (2009) has been devised as the new variant of National literacy Mission.**

Reason (R): **A considerable demand for female literacy is reported by different stake holder.**

Code :

(A) Both (A) and (R) are true.

(B) Both (A) and (R) are true but (R) is not correct explanation of (A).

(C) (A) is true but (R) is false.

(D) (A) is false but (R) is true.

77. **Assertion (A): Friere's view of social reality is decidedly non-marxist.**

Reason (R): **Friere's analysis of social reality is both abstract and theoretical.**

Code :

(A) Both (A) and (R) are true.

(B) Both (A) and (R) are true but (R) is not correct explanation of (A).

(C) (A) is true but (R) is false.

(D) (A) is false but (R) is true.

78. **Assertion (A):** **Jana Shikshana Sansthan are engaged in promotion of skills of neoliterates and others.**

Reason (R): **Skill development is one of the key objectives of Saakshar Bharat Mission.**

Codes:

(A) Both (A) and (R) are true.

(B) Both (A) and (R) are true but (R) is not correct explanation of (A).

(C) (A) is true and (R) is false.

(D) (A) is false but (R) is true.

79. **Assertion (A):** **Non-formal education improves the participation of women in development.**

Reason (R): **All educational efforts improves the competency of individuals.**

Codes:

(A) Both (A) and (R) are true.

(B) Both (A) and (R) are true but (R) is not correct explanation.

(C) (A) is true, (R) is false.

(D) (A) is false, (R) is true.

80. **Assertion (A):** **Population education is intended to develop rational and responsible attitudes and behaviours towards population situation.**

Reason (R): **Population studies is related to family planning programme.**

Codes:

(A) Both (A) and (R) are true.

(B) Both (A) and (R) are true but (R) is not correct explanation of (A).

(C) (A) is true and (R) is false.

(D) (A) is false and (R) is true.

81. **Assertion (A):** **Planning, organising, motivating and controlling are all functions of management.**

Reason (R): **Each function of management is non-interating in nature.**

Codes:

(A) Both (A) and (R) are true.

(B) Both (A) and (R) are true but (R) is not correct explanation.

(C) (A) is true and (R) is false.

(D) (A) is false and (R) is true.

82. **Assertion (A):** **Agricultural extension grew because of it's close linkage of community with technology.**

Reason (R): **University extension grew because it is a replica of the agricultural extension.**

Codes:

(A) Both (A) and (R) are true.

(B) Both (A) and (R) are true but (R) is not correct explanation of (A).

(C) (A) is true and (R) is false.

(D) (A) is false and (R) is true.

83. **Assertion (A):** **Gross enrolment ratio in higher education is 40 per cent of total population.**

Reason (R): **Census report 2001 reports India's population structure as having 69 per cent of it's people below the age of 35 years.**

Codes:

(A) Both (A) and (R) are true.

(B) Both (A) and (R) are true but (R) is not correct explanation of (A).

(C) (A) is true and (R) is false.

(D) (A) is false and (R) is true.

84. **Assertion (A):** **It has been observed that there was an increase in voting percentage in general elections in the districts which achieved total literacy.**

Reason (R): **Total literacy programme worked in enhancing the literacy and generating more awareness to the social and political realities of the area.**

Codes:

(A) (A) and (R) are false.

(B) (A) is correct, (R) is false.

(C) (A) and (R) are correct.

(D) (A) is false, but (R) is correct.

85. **Assertion (A):** **All managers are not effective in their job.**

Reason (R): **Function of managers involves planning, organizing, controlling and motivating.**

Codes:

(A) (A) is correct and (R) is false.

(B) (A) and (R) are correct.

(C) (A) is false and (R) is correct.

(D) (A) and (R) are false.

86. **Assertion (A):** **Higher education students and teachers are engaged in awareness and development of society.**

Reason (R): **Extension is the 'Third Dimension' of the higher education.**

Codes:

(A) (A) is correct, and (R) is false. (B) (A) is false, and (R) is correct.

(C) (A) and (R) are false. (D) (A) and (R) are correct.

87. **Assertion (A): Continuing Education is becoming popular.**

Reason (R): Continuing Education offers need based innovative courses to a wide section of the population.

Codes:

(A) (A) and (R) are correct. (B) (A) is correct, and (R) is false.

(C) (A) is false, and (R) is correct. (D) (A) and (R) are false.

88. **Assertion (A): Radio talk is less reviewable than book.**

Reason (R): Radio talk is recorded first and then reviewed.

Codes:

(A) (A) is false, and (R) is correct. (B) (A) is correct, and (R) is false.

(C) (A) and (R) are correct. (D) (A) and (R) are false.

89. **Assertion (A): MGREGP is not working efficiently.**

Reason (R): Panchayat leaders are unable to monitor the programme effectively.

Codes:

(A) (A) and (R) are false. (B) (A) and (R) are correct.

(C) (A) is correct, and (R) is false. (D) (A) is false, and (R) is correct.

90. **Assertion (A): Several illiterates have been found to be using computer.**

Reason (R): Simple computer operations does not require formal educational skills.

Codes:

(A) (A) is correct, and (R) is false. (B) (A) and (R) are false.

(C) (A) is false, and (R) is correct. (D) (A) and (R) are correct.

91. **Assertion (A): Human Resource Development involves quality education and training and use of modern technology.**

Reason (R): Without a planned strategy Human Resource Development is not possible.

Codes:

(A) (A) is false, and (R) is true. (B) (R) is false, and (A) is true.

(C) (A) and (R) are false. (D) (A) and (R) are correct.

92. Assertion (A): Women empowerment is possible through legislation and education.

Reason (R): Social change is difficult to achieve.

Codes:

(A) (A) is false, and (R) is correct.
(B) (A) is correct, and (R) is false.
(C) (A) and (R) are correct.
(D) (A) and (R) are false

93. Assertion (A): Dialogue improves the learning.

Reason (R): Learning promotes action oriented dialogue.

Codes:

(A) (A) is correct, and (R) is false.
(B) (R) is correct, and (A) is false.
(C) (A) and (R) are correct.
(D) (A) and (R) are false.

94. Assertion (A): In Pedagogic approach communication is one way from teacher to learner.

Reason (R): Experience of the teacher is valued and viewed as primary source of Knowledge

Codes:

(A) Both (A) and (R) are correct.
(B) Only (R) is correct.
(C) Both (A) and (R) are false.
(D) (A) is correct and (R) is false.

95. Assertion (A): Mobile phone technology lies in between the face to face and mass communication

Reason (R): Mobile phone is an example of Interpersonal communication wherein here is no interpose of machine and organization.

Codes:

(A) (A) and (R) are correct.
(B) (A) is correct and (R) is false.
(C) (A) and (R) are false.
(D) (A) is false and (R) is correct.

96. Assertion (A): Interpersonal communication allows participants to participate completely in the process.

Reason (R): It gives you the advantage of hearing, seeing, touching etc. simultaneously.

Codes:

(A) (A) is false (R) is correct.
(B) (A) is correct (R) is false.
(C) (A) and (R) are correct.
(D) (A) and (R) are false.

97. **Assertion (A):** **In developing countries acquisition of literacy and skills is essential for people.**

Reason (R): **It is viewed as a means of improving their socio-economic status.**

Codes:

(A) (A) is false (R) is correct. (B) (A) is correct and (R) is false.

(C) (A) and (R) are correct. (D) (A) and (R) are false.

98. **Assertion (A):** **Poverty breeds illiteracy and vice versa.**

Reason (R): **Illiteracy creates a state of indecisiveness.**

Codes:

(A) (A) and (R) are false. (B) (A) is correct and (R) is false.

(C) (A) is false and (R) is correct. (D) (A) and (R) are correct.

99. **Assertion (A):** **Education and Training are different.**

Reason (R): **Education is a long term process while training meets the immediate needs.**

Codes:

(A) (A) is false but (R) is correct. (B) (R) is false and (A) is correct.

(C) (A) and (R) are false. (D) (A) and (R) are correct.

100. **Assertion (A):** **Adult learning is a problem solving approach.**

Reason (R): **It has no place for experience.**

Codes:

(A) (A) is false (R) is correct. (B) (A) and (R) are false.

(C) (A) and (R) are correct. (D) (A) is correct and (R) is false.

101. **Assertion (A):** **Adult Extension Education is a practical discipline.**

Reason (R): **It is not concerned with the factual elements.**

Codes:

(A) (A) is false and (R) is correct. (B) (A) and (R) are false.

(C) (A) is correct and (R) is false. (D) (A) and (R) are correct.

102. **Assertion (A):** **People in developed countries enjoy a better quality of life.**

Reason (R): **Literacy, income, nutrition, longevity etc. are the indicators of quality of life.**

Codes:

(A) (A) is false and (R) is correct.

(B) (A) is correct and (R) is false.

(C) (A) and (R) are correct.

(D) (A) and (R) are false.

103. Assertion (A): Inspite of a rapid economic development the standard of living of common people is low.

Reason (R): The accelerated rate of growth in population leads to use of maximum resources in meeting the basic needs of the people.

Codes:

(A) (A) and (R) are correct.

(B) (A) is correct and (R) is false.

(C) (R) is correct and (A) is false.

(D) (A) and (R) are false.

104. Assertion I: Media Policy of NLM aims at strengthening the delivery mechanism of the mission.

Assertion II: Media Policy of NLM aims at securing the programme from adverse publicity.

Codes:

(A) Assertion I is false

(B) Assertion II is true

(C) Assertion I is true and Assertion II is false

(D) Assertion I and Assertion II both are true

105. Assertion I: Chauraha is a forty-episode audio-visual material for promotion of literacy.

Assertion II: Chauraha is a 10 episode radio programme for promotion of post literacy.

Codes:

(A) Assertion I is false

(B) Assertion II is true

(C) Assertion I is true and Assertion II is false

(D) Assertion I and Assertion II both are false

106. Assertion I: Jan Shikshana Sansthan provides opportunity to neoliterates to acquire and upgrade vocational skills.

Assertion II: Jan Shikshana Sansthan provides opportunity to all adults to acquire and upgrade their vocational skills in their locality.

Codes:

(A) Assertion I is true
(B) Assertion II is false
(C) Assertion I and II are true
(D) Assertion I and II are false

107. Assertion I: **Evaluation of continuing education programme is both qualitative and quantitative in nature.**

Assertion II: **Total literacy programme evaluation has largely been quantitative in nature.**

Codes:

(A) Assertion I is true
(B) Assertion II is false
(C) Assertion I and II are true
(D) Assertion I and II are false

108. Assertion I: **Learning needs of adults of tribals urban and rural areas are same.**

Assertion II: **Learning needs of urban males are different from these of rural males.**

Codes:

(A) Assertion I is true
(B) Assertion II is false
(C) Assertion I is true and Assertion II is false
(D) Assertion I is false and Assertion II is true

109. Assertion I: **As per past census reports sex ratio in 1901 was 992 and 931 in 2001.**

Assertion II: **As per past census report sex ratio was 972 in 1901 and 933 in 2001.**

Codes:

(A) Assertion I is true
(B) Assertion II is false
(C) Assertion I is true and Assertion II is false
(D) Assertion I is false and Assertion II is true

110. Assertion I: **Health, nutrition, literacy, percapita income, life expectancy are the indicators of quality of life.**

Assertion II: **Quality of life of developed and developing countries are quite different.**

Codes:

(A) Assertion I is true
(B) Assertion II is false
(C) Assertion I and II are true
(D) Assertion I and II are false

111. Assertion I: **Sarva Shiksha Abhiyan aims at reducing dropout rate at the primary level of education.**

Assertion II: **Sarva Shiksha Abhiyan also aims that all girl children go to school.**

Codes:

(A) Assertion I is true
(B) Assertion II is false
(C) Assertion I and II are true
(D) Assertion I and II are false

112. Assertion I: **UNESCO world assembly on adult education was held at Tehran in 1964, and at Hamburg in 1997.**

Assertion II: **UNESCO world assembly on adult education and life long learning was held at Brazil in 2009.**

Codes:

(A) Assertion I is true
(B) Assertion II is false
(C) Assertion I and II are true
(D) Assertion I and II are false

113. Assertion I: **XI Plan UGC guidelines for the Department of Adult, Continuing Education and Extension suggest the promotion of integration between formal and non-formal education.**

Assertion II: **Department of Adult, Continuing Education and Extension are to conduct teaching, training and research like any other Department in University.**

Codes:

(A) Assertion I is true
(B) Assertion II is false
(C) Assertion I and II are false
(D) Assertion I and II are true

114. Assertion I: **The term 'Andragogy' was originally formulated by Alexander Kapp.**

Assertion II: **Rosenstock in a report used the term 'Andragogy'.**

Codes:

(A) Assertion I is true
(B) Assertion I is false
(C) Assertion II is true
(D) Both are true

115. Assertion I: **As a person matures the motivation to learn becomes internal.**

Assertion II: **As a person matures, his self concept becomes a dependent personality.**

Codes:

(A) Assertion I is true (B) Assertion II is true

(C) Assertion I is false (D) Assertion II is false

116. Assertion I: Learning experiences should not be based around experiences.

Assertion II: Learning programme organised around life application.

Codes:

(A) Assertion I is true (B) Assertion I is false

(C) Assertion II is true (D) Assertion II is false

117. Assertion I: The teacher knows everything and the students know nothing.

Assertion II: The teacher is one who himself taught in dialogue with the students.

Codes:

(A) Assertion I is false (B) Assertion I is true

(C) Assertion II is true (D) Both are true

118. Assertion I: Problem posing education is revolutionary futurity.

Assertion II: For the oppressors, 'human beings' refers only to themselves.

Codes:

(A) Assertion I is true (B) Assertion II is false

(C) Assertion I is false (D) Both are true

119. Assertion I: The Fotodialogo Method could be a powerful strategy for low literacy groups and minority women.

Assertion II: The Fotodialogo Method is aimed at building dialogue through the use of drawings.

Codes:

(A) Assertion I is true

(B) Assertion II is false

(C) Assertion I is false

(D) Both are true

120. Assertion I: Many of the adult education programmes are aimed at combating 'colonial mentalities'.

Assertion II: Education is an active supporter and faithful reflector of the status quo in society.

Codes:

(A) Assertion I is false
(B) Assertion I is true
(C) Assertion II is false
(D) Both are true

121. Assertion I: **Developing consciousness is to have the power to transform reality.**

Assertion II: **Adult education is for liberation.**

Codes:

(A) Assertion I is true
(B) Assertion II is true
(C) Assertion I is false
(D) Both are true

122. Assertion I: **Oppression and overwhelming control, is nourished by love of death, not life.**

Assertion II: **The problem posing method does dichotomize the activity of the teacher-student.**

Codes:

(A) Assertion I is true
(B) Assertion I is false
(C) Assertion II is true
(D) Both are false

123. Assertion I: **Education is the practice of domination.**

Assertion II: **Education is the practice of freedom.**

Codes:

(A) Assertion I is true
(B) Assertion I is false
(C) Assertion II is true
(D) Assertion II is false

124. Assertion I: **Literacy is an imposition of the modern world which damages traditional culture.**

Assertion II: **Literacy has brought about significant changes among people.**

Codes:

(A) Assertion I is true
(B) Assertion I is false
(C) Assertion II is true
(D) Assertion II is false

125. Assertion I: **The ideology of adult education is to meet the felt needs of the suffering communities.**

Assertion II: **The curriculum of the adult education has not been ameliorative.**

Codes:

(A) Assertion I is true
(B) Assertion I is false
(C) Assertion II is true
(D) Assertion II is false

126. Assertion I: The problem of street children in India is a very big social issue.

Assertion II: The problem of bonded labour in India is also a very big social issue.

Codes:

(A) Assertion I and II both are true
(B) Assertion I is true but Assertion II is false
(C) Assertion I is false but Assertion II is true only
(D) Both the Assertions are false

127. Assertion I: Application of Management Principles is applicable to the highly sophisticated system of Industries only.

Assertion II: Programmes of Extension Education do not require principles of management.

Codes:

(A) Assertion I is true
(B) Assertion II is true
(C) Assertion II is false
(D) Both the Assertions are true

128. Assertion I: Computer is a good instrument to create data base of Adult Education.

Assertion II: Use of computer for Adult Education is must Now-a-Days.

Codes:

(A) Both the Assertions are false
(B) Assertion I is false
(C) Assertion I is true
(D) Assertion II is false

129. Assertion I: Studies of population falls within the purview of Demography.

Assertion II: Adult Education is a part of Demography.

Codes:

(A) Both the Assertions are false
(B) Assertion II is true
(C) Assertion I is false
(D) Assertion I is true

130. Assertion I: To cater the learning needs of the learner is pre-requisite condition for continuing education.

Assertion II: Continuing education programmes have potentiality to cater the needs of industries.

Codes:

(A) Both the Assertions are true.

(B) Both the Assertions are false.

(C) Assertion I is true but Assertion II is false.

(D) Assertion II is true but Assertion I is false.

131. Assertion I: Kothari Commission's report on Education and New Education Policy are one and the same.

Assertion II: Kothari Commission's report recommended "Work Experience" in Education while New Education Policy recommended New Area Development Approach for Extension Education.

Codes:

(A) Both the Assertions are false.

(B) Assertion I is true but Assertion II is false.

(C) Assertion II is true but Assertion I is false.

(D) Both the Assertions are true.

132. Assertion I: Jan Siksha Sansthan is not the part of National open school.

Assertion II: Jan Siksha Sansthan is nothing else but Shramik Vidyapeeth.

Codes:

(A) Assertion II is true but Assertion I is false.

(B) Assertion I is true but Assertion II is false.

(C) Both the Assertions are true.

(D) Both the Assertions are false.

133. Assertion I: Sarva Shiksha Abhiyan aims at universalisation of primary education.

Assertion II: Sarva Shiksha Abhiyan ends with Adult Education.

Codes:

(A) Assertion I is false

(B) Assertion I is true

(C) Assertion II is false

(D) Both the Assertions are false

134. Assertion (A): Non-Formal Education is the out-of-school education.

Reason (B): Non-Formal Education is deliberate, planned, staffed, financially supported like formal education and it has its own valid claim to reality.

Codes:

(A) Both (A) and (B) are true

(B) Both (A) and (B) are true but (B) is not correct explanation

(C) (A) is true but (B) is false

(D) (A) is false but (B) is true

135. Assertion (A): One of the aims recently given to education, in most civilized countries, is to provide technical and professional training.

Reason (B): The recent remarkable developments in science and technology have led to important changes in human values.

Codes:

(A) Both (A) and (B) are true

(B) Both (A) and (B) are true but (B) is not correct explanation

(C) (A) is true but (B) is false

(D) (A) is false but (B) is true

136. Assertion (A): At present, some kind of educational qualification is essential for almost every job.

Reason (B): Very extensive educational qualifications become necessary for good jobs which carry big salaries.

Codes:

(A) Both (A) and (B) are true

(B) Both (A) and (B) are true but (B) is not correct explanation

(C) (A) is true but (B) is false

(D) (A) is false but (B) is true

137. Assertion (A): SRC provides information and supply proto-type materials on Adult Education.

Reason (B): SRC provides technical support to all the Adult Education Programmes.

Codes:

(A) (A) and (B) are true

(B) (A) is true and (B) is false

(C) (A) is false and (B) is true

(D) (A) and (B) are false

138. Radhakrishnan Commission focuses at higher education by :

Assertion (A): Encouraging Universities to play their part as organs of culture and the intellectual leaders of civilization.

Reason (B): **Discovering the innate qualities of individuals and developing them through suitable learning.**

Codes:

(A) (A) and (B) are true
(B) (A) is true and (B) is false
(C) (A) is false and (B) is true
(D) (A) and (B) are false

139. **Assertion (A):** **The literacy scenario is characterized by wide inequities among different groups of population.**

Reason (B): **Widespread illiteracy is found not only among aged, but also among younger boys and girls because of low enrolment of and high drop out rates and also the wide disparity among various social groups.**

Codes:

(A) Both (A) and (B) are true
(B) Both (A) and (B) are true but (B) is not correct explanation
(C) (A) is true but (B) is false
(D) (A) is false but (B) is true

140. **Assertion I:** **Formal and Non-Formal Education are coming under the broader category of education.**

Assertion II: **Teaching and Training is one of the major objective of higher education.**

Codes:

(A) Assertion I is true
(B) Both are true
(C) Assertion II is false
(D) Assertion I and II false

141. **Assertion I:** **Kothari Commission first articulated the concept of 'Extension and TRINITY' of teaching, research and extension.**

Assertion II: **Extension is essential for developing the educand a sense of responsibility towards society.**

Codes:

(A) Assertion I is False
(B) Assertion II is True
(C) Assertion I and II are true
(D) Both are False

142. **Assertion I:** **Preparation of the teaching/learning materials in adult education is need based and target specific.**

Assertion II: **Preparation of the teaching/learning materials in non-formal education should not be need based and target specific.**

Codes:

(A) Assertion II is true (B) Assertion I is false

(C) Assertion I and II are true (D) Assertion I is true

143. Assertion I: Shramik Vidyapeeth has been re-named into Jana Shikshan Sansthan.

Assertion II: Jana Shikshan Sansthan and Jana Shikshan Nilayam are the same

Codes:

(A) Assertion II is true (B) Assertion I is true

(C) Both are true (D) Assertion I and II are false

144. Assertion I: 'How Adult Learn' was written by Roby Kidd.

Assertion II: 'Cultural Action for freedom' was written by Paulo Freire

Codes:

(A) Assertion I is true (B) Assertion II is false

(C) Assertion both are true (D) Both Assertion are false

145. Assertion I: Human Rights and Child Rights are the same.

Assertion II: To empower Women, Knowledge of Human Rights is essential.

(A) Assertion I is false (B) Assertion II is true

(C) Both are true (D) Both are false

146. Assertion I: Management Information System is important for monitoring the Adult Education Programme.

Assertion II: Managerial Techniques and Technologies are being used for the effective implementation of the Adult Education Programme

Codes:

(A) Assertion I is false

(B) Assertion I and II are false

(C) Assertion II is true

(D) Assertion I and II are true

147. Assertion I: Andragogy deals with arts and science of helping adult to learn.

Assertion II: Pedagogy deals with arts and science of teaching children.

Codes:

(A) Assertion I and (II) true

(B) Assertion II true

(C) Both are false

(D) Assertion I is true and (II) is false

148. Assertion I: **Programmes were launched in India for the Eradication of illiteracy in India, the correct chronological order is Social Education Programme, Farmers Functional Literacy Programme, National Literacy Mission, National Adult Education Programme.**

Assertion II: **Programme were launched in India for the Eradication of illiteracy in India, the correct chronological order is Social Education Programme, Farmers Functional Literacy Programme, National Adult Education Programme, National Literacy Mission.**

Codes:

(A) Assertion I is false

(B) Assertion II is true

(C) Both are true

(D) Assertion I and I) are false

149. Assertion I: **Sarva Shiksha Abhiyan has been curb dropout rate at the primary level.**

Assertion II: **The rate of drop outs shall be minimised through active participation of the people.**

Codes:

(A) Assertion I is false

(B) Assertion II is true

(C) Both are false

(D) Assertion I and II are true

150. Assertion I: **Every evaluation programmes involve input process and output process.**

Assertion II: **There are two major type of evaluation *i.e.*, formative and summative evaluation.**

Codes:

(A) Assertion I is false

(B) Assertion II is false

(C) Assertion I and II are true

(D) Assertion I and II are false

151. Assertion I: **The development of higher education in India is the responsibility of Indian Government.**

Assertion II: **The development of higher education in the state is the responsibility of the state concern.**

Codes:

(A) Assertion I is true
(B) Assertion II is false
(C) Assertion I and II is true
(D) Both are false

152. **Assertion I:** **'WWW' being used to open a side is called World Wide Web.**

Assertion II: **Computer can be used to impact adult literacy.**

Codes:

(A) Assertion I and II are true
(B) Assertion I and II are false
(C) Assertion I is true
(D) Assertion II is true

153. **Assertion I:** **The development of higher education in India is the responsibility of Indian Government.**

Assertion II: **The development of higher education and its maintenance is the function of U.G.C.**

Codes:

(A) Assertion I true
(B) Both False
(C) Assertion II true
(D) Assertion I and II are true

154. **Assertion I:** **In virtual university the teaching is learner centered.**

Assertion II: **The base of virtual University is Internet**

Codes:

(A) Assertion I false
(B) Assertion II true
(C) Assertion I and II are false
(D) Assertion I and II are true

155. **Assertion I:** **University of Rajasthan is the first to initiate the Adult Education department in India.**

Assertion II: **Barkatullah University-Bhopal is the first University to initiate Adult Education department in India.**

Codes:

(A) Assertion I true
(B) Assertion II true
(C) Both Assertions are true
(D) Both Assertions are false

156. **Assertion I:** **One barrier to participate is the lack of continuity or post-follow up in planning and implementing educational programmes by agencies.**

Assertion II: **Participation is a very personal matter and free choice of the individual is fundamental right in a democratic society**

Codes:

(A) Assertion I and Assertion II are true

(B) Only Assertion I is true

(C) Assertion II is true and Assertion I is false

(D) Both Assertion I and Assertion II are false

157. Assertion I: **'Androgogy' is the art and science of helping adults to learn.**

Assertion II: **Pedagogy is the art and science of teaching children**

Codes:

(A) Assertion I true

(B) Assertion I and II are false

(C) Assertion II is true

(D) Assertion I and II are true

158. Assertion I: **The 'Window Period' is the period in which the person gets infected with virus of HIV/AIDS but does not show any sign in medical investigation.**

Assertion II: **The 'Window Period' first 5-7 months period in which the person gets infected with virus of HIV/AIDS but does not show any sign in medical investigation.**

Codes:

(A) Assertion I and II are true

(B) Assertion II is true

(C) Assertion I and II are false

(D) Assertion I is true

159. Assertion I: **Aristotle defined education as a creation of a sound mind in a sound body.**

Assertion II: **The Basic indicator of conscientization was made by Paulo-Frere**

Codes:

(A) Assertion I is true

(B) Assertion II is true

(C) Assertion I and II are true

(D) Assertion I and II are false

160. Assertion I: **According to Mc Donald, motivation is an energy change within the person**

Assertion II: **According to Mc Donald, motivation is a process of arousing movement in the person.**

Codes:

(A) Both Assertion I and II are true

(B) Assertion I is true But Assertion II is false

(C) Assertion I is false But Assertion II is true

(D) Assertion I and II are false

161. Assertion I: BGVS is a Non-Governmental Organisation

Assertion II: BGVS received funds from the Govt.

Codes:

(A) Assertion I is true

(B) Assertion II is true

(C) Both the Assertions (I) and (II) are true

(D) Both the Assertions (I) and (II) are false

162. Assertion (A): Motivation is a goal-directed and need-satisfying behaviour.

Reason (R): Motivation means a process, by which people start to move to achieve goals.

Codes:

(A) (A) is correct and (R) is false.

(B) (A) is false and (R) is correct.

(C) Both (A) and (R) are correct and (R) is correct explanation of (A).

(D) Both (A) and (R) are correct but (R) is not correct explanation of (A).

163. Assertion (A): Leadership concerns action more than position.

Reason (R): Success of extension education programmes depends more on positional leaders than the action leaders.

Codes:

(A) (A) is correct and (R) is false.

(B) (A) is false and (R) is correct.

(C) Both (A) and (R) are correct.

(D) Both (A) and (R) are false.

164. Assertion (A): Social change is a slow process.

Reason (R): Extension educator should develop programmes step-by-step.

Codes:

(A) (A) is correct and (R) is false.

(B) (A) is false and (R) is correct.

(C) (A) is correct and (R) is false and (R) is not correct explanation of (A).

(D) Both (A) and (R) are correct and (R) is the correct explanation of (A).

165. Assertion (A): Crimes against women are not a matter of concern to the development process.

Reason (R): Crimes against women restrict them from full participation in development efforts and this affects development.

Codes:

(A) (A) is correct and (R) is false.

(B) (A) is false and (R) is correct.

(C) Both (A) and (R) are correct and (R) is the correct explanation of (A).

(D) Both (A) and (R) are false.

166. Assertion (A): Early marriage is one of the responsible factors for population Growth in India.

Reason (R): Government has fixed the legal age of marriage for girls and boys.

Codes:

(A) (A) is correct and (R) is false.

(B) (A) is false and (R) is correct.

(C) Both (A) and (R) are correct and (R) is the correct explanation of (A).

(D) Both (A) and (R) are correct but (R) is not the correct explanation of (A).

167. Assertion (A): Participatory training is participated centred.

Reason (R): Training arises out of specific needs of participants.

Codes:

(A) Both (A) and (R) are true.

(B) (A) is true and (R) is the correct explanation of (A).

(C) (A) is true, but (R) is not the correct explanation of (A).

(D) Both (A) and (R) are false.

168. Assertion (A): There is a positive co-relation between literacy and primary education.

Reason (R): It has been found that total literate districts have shown increase in enrolment at primary level.

Codes:

(A) Both (A) and (R) are correct and (R) is the correct explanation of (A).

(B) Both (A) and (R) are correct, but (R) is not the correct explanation of (A).

(C) (A) is correct and (R) is false.

(D) (A) is false and (R) is correct.

169. Woman Commission is related to :

I. Woman health

II. Woman employment

III. Gender justice

IV. Gender equality

Code :

(A) I and II (B) II and III

(C) III and IV (D) I and IV

170. Assertion (A): Mortality is one of the basic elements of population change.

Reason (R): Death of human being causes change in population growth.

Codes:

(A) Both (A) and (R) are true.

(B) Both (A) and (R) are false.

(C) (A) is true, but (R) is not the correct explanation of (A).

(D) (R) is the correct explanation of (A).

171. Assertion (A): Extension is a means for making higher education relevant to the needs of the society.

Reason (R): Community linkages and engagements help the students to understand the social realities around him in better way.

Codes:

(A) (A) is Correct and (R) is false.

(B) (A) is false and (R) is correct.

(C) Both (A) and (R) are correct.

(D) Both (A) and (R) are false.

172. Assertion (A): Paulo Friere developed widely influential concepts for Adult Education for the urban and rural neo-literates.

Reason (R): Paulo Friere work on conscientisation reinforced the nation that economically marginalised people could be involved in the production of knowledge.

Codes:

(A) Both (A) and (R) are true.

(B) (A) is true and (R) is the correct explanation of (A).

(C) Both (A) and (R) are false.

(D) (A) is true, but (R) is not the correct explanation of (A).

173. Assertion (A): Distance education is indirect education as it is not centered on face to face communication.

Reason (R): Distance education is a system of mass communication.

Codes:

(A) (A) is correct and (R) is false.

(B) (A) is false and (R) is correct.

(C) Both (A) and (R) are correct.

(D) Both (A) and (R) are false.

174. Assertion (A): More NSS units were sanctioned in educational institutions Throughout the country.

Reason (R): Expansion of NSS scheme aims to provide certificates to the students of large number.

Codes:

(A) (A) is correct and (R) is false and (R) is not the correct explanation of (A).

(B) Both (A) and (R) are correct and (R) is the correct explanation of (A).

(C) (A) is false and (R) is correct.

(D) Both (A) and (R) are false.

175. Assertion (A): The lecture method is an effective way to introduce new information or concepts to a group of learners.

Reason (R): The learners always appreciate a concise, stimulating well delivered lecture.

Codes:

(A) Both (A) and (R) are true.

(B) (A) is true, but (R) is not the correct explanation of (A).

(C) (A) is true, (R) is the correct explanation of (A).

(D) Both (A) and (R) are false.

176. Assertion (A): Apprenticeship and practice are methods of paramount importance for skill training.

Reason (R): The difference between the two lies in that practice is done in uncontrolled situations while apprenticeship is done in real life situations.

Codes:

(A) Both (A) and (R) are true.

(B) (A) is true, (R) is false.

(C) (A) is true, (R) is the correct explanation of (A).

(D) (R) is false, but (R) is the correct explanation of (A).

177. **Assertion (A): The concept of extension was not properly understood by the teachers and administrators in higher education.**

Reason (R): Mere service, not learning is considered as the goal of extension in university.

Codes:

(A) (A) is correct and (R) is false.

(B) (A) is false and (R) is correct.

(C) Both (A) and (R) are correct and (R) is the correct explanation of (A).

(D) Both (A) and (R) are correct and (R) is not the correct explanation of (A).

Answers

1	(D)	20	(A)	39	(C)	58	(C)
2	(B)	21	(B)	40	(B)	59	(A)
3	(A)	22	(D)	41	(B)	60	(C)
4	(B)	23	(C)	42	(B)	61	(C)
5	(C)	24	(D)	43	(D)	62	(A)
6	(C)	25	(D)	44	(B)	63	(C)
7	(C)	26	(D)	45	(C)	64	(A)
8	(A)	27	(A)	46	(C)	65	(A)
9	(A)	28	(C)	47	(B)	66	(C)
10	(B)	29	(C)	48	(B)	67	(A)
11	(C)	30	(C)	49	(C)	68	(C)
12	(C)	31	(C)	50	(C)	69	(C)
13	(C)	32	(D)	51	(D)	70	(D)
14	(C)	33	(C)	52	(B)	71	(C)
15	(C)	34	(B)	53	(C)	72	(D)
16	(D)	35	(C)	54	(C)	73	(B)
17	(C)	36	(B)	55	(D)	74	(A)
18	(D)	37	(C)	56	(C)	75	(A)
19	(D)	38	(D)	57	(C)	76	(A)

77	(D)	103	(A)	129	(D)	155	(A)
78	(A)	104	(D)	130	(A)	156	(A)
79	(A)	105	(C)	131	(C)	157	(D)
80	(C)	106	(A)	132	(C)	158	(D)
81	(C)	107	(C)	133	(B)	159	(C)
82	(C)	108	(D)	134	(D)	160	(A)
83	(D)	109	(D)	135	(A)	161	(C)
84	(C)	110	(C)	136	(A)	162	(C)
85	(B)	111	(C)	137	(A)	163	(A)
86	(D)	112	(C)	138	(A)	164	(D)
87	(A)	113	(D)	139	(A)	165	(C)
88	(C)	114	(D)	140	(B)	166	(C)
89	(B)	115	(A)	141	(C)	167	(B)
90	(C)	116	(C)	142	(D)	168	(A)
91	(D)	117	(B)	143	(B)	169	(C)
92	(A)	118	(D)	144	(C)	170	(A)
93	(C)	119	(D)	145	(B)	171	(C)
94	(A)	120	(D)	146	(D)	172	(C)
95	(A)	121	(D)	147	(A)	173	(C)
96	(C)	122	(A)	148	(B)	174	(A)
97	(C)	123	(C)	149	(D)	175	(B)
98	(D)	124	(C)	150	(C)	176	(D)
99	(D)	125	(A)	151	(C)	177	(C)
100	(B)	126	(A)	152	(C)		
101	(C)	127	(C)	153	(A)		
102	(C)	128	(C)	154	(D)		

Matching Type Questions

1.

	List – I		**List – II**
a.	CAPART	i.	Women Empowerment
b.	NABARD	ii.	Dairy
c.	SEWA	iii.	Rural Technology
d.	NDDB	iv.	Agricultural Banking

Options	a	b	c	d
(A)	iv	iii	i	ii
(B)	iii	iv	ii	i
(C)	iii	i	ii	iv
(D)	iii	iv	i	ii

2.

	List – I		**List – II**
a.	Yes I can	i.	Tanzania
b.	Education is vital for rapid development.	ii.	Vietnam
c.	Community Learning Center	iii.	Ho Chi Minh
d.	Work oriented literacy.	iv.	J. Nyerere

Options	a	b	c	d
(A)	i	ii	iii	iv
(B)	ii	iv	i	iii
(C)	iii	iv	ii	i
(D)	iv	ii	iv	i

3. **List – I** / **List – II**

List – I	List – II
a. Fayole	i. Motivation
b. E. Mayo	ii. Principle of Management
c. Jucious	iii. Learning Theory
d. Ausbel	iv. Human change

Options	a	b	c	d
(A)	ii	i	iv	iii
(B)	ii	iv	i	iii
(C)	ii	iii	iv	i
(D)	i	ii	iii	iv

4. **List – I** / **List – II**

List – I	List – II
a. Work map	i. Man specification
b. Organizing	ii. Planning
c. PLP	iii. Resource mobilization
d. Staffing	iv. Literacy program

Options	a	b	c	d
(A)	iv	iii	ii	i
(B)	i	ii	iv	iii
(C)	iii	iv	ii	i
(D)	ii	iii	iv	i

5. **List – I (Literacy Rates)** / **List – II (State)**

List – I (Literacy Rates)	List – II (State)
a. 93.91	i. Maharashtra
b. 91.6	ii. Himachal Pradesh
c. 83.8	iii. Mizoram
d. 80.1	iv. Kerala

Options	a	b	c	d
(A)	iii	iv	ii	i
(B)	iv	i	ii	iii
(C)	iv	iii	ii	i
(D)	iv	ii	iii	i

6. **List – I** / **List – II**

List – I	List – II
a. PREAL	i. Learning software
b. Chauraha	ii. Residual Literacy
c. PRI	iii. Radio programme
d. CBFL	iv. Motivational software

Options	a	b	c	d
(A)	i	ii	iii	iv
(B)	iii	iv	ii	i
(C)	iii	ii	iv	i
(D)	iii	i	ii	iv

7. **List – I** | **List – II**

List – I	List – II
a. Right to Education	i. 2013
b. Sakshar Bharat	ii. 2010
c. Right to Food	iii. 1976
d. Fundamental Rights	iv. 2009

Options	a	b	c	d
(A)	i	ii	iii	iv
(B)	ii	i	iv	iii
(C)	iii	i	iv	ii
(D)	ii	iv	i	iii

8.

List – I	List – II
a. LCD	i. Multimedia
b. Kathputli	ii. Audio
c. Radio	iii. Audio-visual
d. Internet	iv. Folk media

Options	a	b	c	d
(A)	i	ii	iii	iv
(B)	iii	iv	ii	i
(C)	i	iii	iv	ii
(D)	ii	iv	iii	i

9.

List – I (Psychologist)	List – II (Personality Assessment Approach)
a. Freud	i. Life Span
b. Sheldon	ii. Humanistic
c. Maslow	iii. Constitutional
d. Erickson	iv. Psycho analytical

Options	a	b	c	d
(A)	iii	iv	i	iii
(B)	iv	iii	ii	i
(C)	i	ii	iii	iv
(D)	ii	i	iv	ii

10. List – I (Policy/ACT) List – II (Year)

a. National Curriculum Framework (NCF) — i. 2005

b. NCTE — ii. 2010

c. NPE — iii. 1993

d. RTE — iv. 1986

Options	a	b	c	d
(A)	i	iii	iv	ii
(B)	ii	i	iii	iv
(C)	iii	iv	ii	i
(D)	iv	ii	i	iii

11. List – I (HRM function) List – II (Stages)

a. Selection — i. II

b. Appointment — ii. III

c. Induction — iii. IV

d. Job assignment — iv. I

Options	a	b	c	d
(A)	ii	iv	i	ii
(B)	iii	i	ii	iv
(C)	ii	iii	iv	i
(D)	i	ii	iii	iv

12. List – I List – II

a. Right to Education — i. 2009

b. NLM — ii. 1978

c. Sakshar Bharat — iii. 1988

d. NAEP — iv. 2010

Options	a	b	c	d
(A)	iv	iii	i	ii
(B)	iii	i	ii	iv
(C)	i	iii	ii	iv
(D)	iv	ii	i	iii

13. List – I List – II

a. Print — i. Radio

b. Audio — ii. T.V.

c. Projected — iii. Slide

d. Audio/Video — iv. Newspaper

Options	a	b	c	d
(A)	i	ii	iii	iv
(B)	iv	i	iii	ii
(C)	iii	iv	ii	i
(D)	ii	iii	i	iv

14.

List – I	List – II
a. Rabindra Nath Tagore	i. Tolstoy Farm
b. Raja Ram Mohan Roy	ii. Arya Samaj
c. Daya nand Saraswati	iii. Brahma samaj
d. Mahatma Gandhi	iv. Shanti Niketan

Options	a	b	c	d
(A)	iv	ii	iii	i
(B)	iii	ii	i	iv
(C)	iv	iii	ii	i
(D)	i	ii	iii	iv

15.

List – I	List – II
a. Labour Day	i. 11 July
b. Population Day	ii. 1 May
c. Teacher's Day.	iii. 8 Sept
d. International Literacy Day	iv. 5 Sept.

Options	a	b	c	d
(A)	i	ii	iii	iv
(B)	ii	iii	iv	i
(C)	iv	iii	i	ii
(D)	ii	i	iv	iii

16.

List – I	List – II
a. Tilonia	i. Gujarat
b. Nilokheri	ii. West Bengal
c. Sri Niketan	iii. Rajasthan
d. Anand	iv. Haryana

Options	a	b	c	d
(A)	iii	iv	ii	i
(B)	iv	iii	i	ii

(C)	iii	i	ii	iv
(D)	i	ii	iii	iv

17. **List – I** **List – II**

a. H.N. Bahuguna — i. Maharashtra

b. Deen Dayal Upadhyaya — ii. Tamil Nadu

c. Gandhi Gram Rural Institute — iii. Uttarakhand

d. S.N.D.T — iv. UttarPradesh

Options	a	b	c	d
(A)	iv	iii	i	ii
(B)	iii	iv	ii	i
(C)	ii	i	iii	iv
(D)	i	ii	iv	iii

18. **List – I**

a. Traditional functions of higher education

b. Third dimension of higher education

c. Limitation of higher education in promoting extension

d. Human resources in higher education

List – II

i. Teachers, researchers and students

ii. Lack of extension culture in academic community

iii. Teaching and research

iv. Extension

Options	a	b	c	d
(A)	i	ii	iii	iv
(B)	iii	iv	ii	i
(C)	ii	iii	i	iv
(D)	iii	ii	iv	i

19. **List – I** **List – II**

a. Highest growth rate of population in 2011 — i. Bihar

b. Lowest growth rate of population in 2011 — ii. Nagaland

c. Highest density of population in 2011 — iii. Nagar Haveli

d. Lowest density of population in 2011 — iv. Arunachal

Options	a	b	c	d
(A)	iii	ii	i	iv
(B)	ii	iii	iv	i
(C)	i	ii	iii	iv
(D)	iii	ii	iv	i

20. **List – I** **List – II**

List – I	List – II
a. CDP	i. 1980
b. IRDP	ii. 1960-61
c. JRY	iii. 1989
d. IADP	iv. 1952

Options	a	b	c	d
(A)	i	ii	iii	iv
(B)	ii	i	iv	iii
(C)	i	iv	ii	iii
(D)	iv	i	iii	ii

21.

List – I	List – II
a. Albeat Mayer	i. Sriniketan Yojana
b. Ravindranath Tagore	ii. Sewagram Yojana
c. F.L. Broyne	iii. Ettawah Project
d. M.K. Gandhi	iv. Gurgaon Project

Options	a	b	c	d
(A)	ii	iii	i	iv
(B)	iii	ii	iv	i
(C)	iii	i	iv	ii
(D)	i	ii	iii	iv

22.

List – I	List – II
a. Trade Union	i. Maslow's
b. Theory of need hierarchy	ii. Research
c. Sampling	iii. Herzbergis
d. Theory of motivation hygiene	iv. Collective bargaining

Options	a	b	c	d
(A)	ii	iii	iv	i
(B)	i	ii	iii	iv
(C)	iv	iii	ii	i
(D)	iii	ii	i	iv

23. **List – I** | **List – II**

List – I	List – II
a. Programme of action	i. 1986
b. Centre model	ii. 1992
c. Each one teach one model	iii. 1998
d. Area development approach	iv. 1937

Options	a	b	c	d
(A)	ii	iv	i	iii
(B)	i	ii	iii	iv
(C)	iv	iii	ii	i
(D)	iii	ii	iv	i

24.

List – I	List – II
a. International literacy day	i. 1st December
b. World AIDS day	ii. 8th March
c. International women's day	iii. 8th September
d. International population day	iv. 11th July

Options	a	b	c	d
(A)	iii	i	ii	iv
(B)	iv	iii	ii	i
(C)	ii	iii	i	iv
(D)	i	ii	iii	iv

25.

List – I	List – II
a. Grass-root level democracy	i. PRA
b. Population related activities	ii. PEW
c. Women related education	iii. PRI
d. Methods of data collection	iv. PERC

Options	a	b	c	d
(A)	i	ii	iii	iv
(B)	iii	iv	ii	i
(C)	iv	iii	ii	i
(D)	ii	iii	iv	i

26.

List – I	List – II
a. Rabindranath Tagore	i. Nobel prize for economics
b. H.G. Khurana	ii. Nobel prize for physics
c. Chandra Sekar	iii. Nobel prize for literature
d. Amartya Sen	iv. Nobel prize for Biology

Options	a	b	c	d
(A)	i	ii	iii	iv
(B)	iv	ii	i	iii
(C)	iii	iv	ii	i
(D)	ii	iii	iv	i

27. **List – I** / **List – II**

List – I	List – II
a. Kiran Bedi	i. Magsaysay award for Environment
b. Rajendra Singh	ii. Water management
c. Ella Bhatt	iii. Women empowerment
d. Chandi Prasad Bhatt	iv. Social service

Options	a	b	c	d
(A)	ii	iii	iv	i
(B)	iii	iv	i	ii
(C)	i	iii	ii	iv
(D)	iv	ii	iii	i

Match the following List-I with List-II by using the codes given below

28.

List – I	List – II
a. Reading, Writing and Arithmetic	i. CE
b. Extension Education	ii. 3R
c. Continuing Education	iii. 3H
d. Head, Hand and Heart	iv. EE

Options	a	b	c	d
(A)	ii	iv	i	iii
(B)	iv	ii	iii	i
(C)	i	ii	iii	iv
(D)	i	iii	ii	iv

29.

List – I	List – II
a. Population education	i. UTA
b. National Service Scheme	ii. PERC
c. Adult Education	iii. DPEP
d. Primary Education	iv. NAEP

Options	a	b	c	d
(A)	i	ii	iii	iv
(B)	ii	i	iv	iii
(C)	ii	i	iii	iv
(D)	iii	ii	i	iv

30. **List – I** | **List – II**

List – I	List – II
a. NLM	i. Follow up programme
b. NAEP	ii. Life long education
c. PLP	iii. Center based approach
d. CEP	iv. Total literacy compaign

Options	a	b	c	d
(A)	i	ii	iii	iv
(B)	iv	iii	ii	i
(C)	iii	iv	i	ii
(D)	iv	iii	i	ii

31.

List – I	List – II
a. National Youth Day	i. 3 October
b. National Science Day	ii. 8 September
c. World Nature Day	iii. 12 January
d. International Literacy Day	iv. 28 February

Options	a	b	c	d
(A)	iv	iii	i	ii
(B)	iii	iv	i	ii
(C)	i	ii	iii	iv
(D)	ii	i	iii	iv

32.

List – I	List – II
a. Case study	i. Innovation
b. Flash card	ii. Teaching technique
c. Perceiving a new idea	iii. Method
d. Way of presentation	iv. Teaching aid

Options	a	b	c	d
(A)	iii	iv	i	ii
(B)	i	iii	ii	iv
(C)	i	iv	iii	ii

(D)	i	ii	iii	iv

33. **List – I** | **List – II**

List – I	List – II
a. Malcom Knowles	i. Motivation
b. Maslow	ii. Concept of conscientization
c. Robby Kidd	iii. Adult learning
d. Paulo Freire	iv. Andragogy

Options	a	b	c	d
(A)	iv	i	iii	ii
(B)	ii	iv	iii	i
(C)	iii	ii	iv	i
(D)	i	iv	iii	ii

34.

List – I	List – II
a. Universal Declaration of Human Rights	i. 1948
b. World Declaration on Higher Education for the 21 century	ii. 1998
c. UNESCO World Declaration Education for all	iii. 1990
d. Hamburg Declaration on Adult Learning	iv. 1997

Options	a	b	c	d
(A)	iv	iii	ii	i
(B)	iv	ii	iii	i
(C)	i	ii	iii	iv
(D)	ii	iv	iii	i

35.

List – I	List – II
a. Co-operative Method	i. Equal opportunity
b. Zero Method	ii. Symbols
c. Teacher dominated Method	iii. Lecture Demonstration/Counseling
d. Traditional Method	iv. Literacy Method

Options	a	b	c	d
(A)	iv	iii	ii	i
(B)	ii	iv	iii	i
(C)	i	ii	iii	iv
(D)	iv	ii	iii	i

36. **List – I** / **List – II**

List – I	List – II
a. Systematic sampling	i. Same chance for each element
b. Simple Random Sampling	ii. Random numbers
c. Population	iii. Growth
d. Sample size	iv. The number of elements in the obtained sample

Options	a	b	c	d
(A)	iv	iii	ii	i
(B)	i	ii	iii	iv
(C)	ii	iv	iii	i
(D)	iv	ii	iii	i

37. **List – I** / **List – II**

List – I	List – II
a. Strikes and Lockout	i. Democracy in Industries
b. Workers Participation in Mgt.	ii. Trade Union
c. Incentives, Promotion	iii. Elements of Motivation
d. Man Power Planning	iv. Human Resource Development

Options	a	b	c	d
(A)	i	ii	iii	iv
(B)	ii	i	iii	iv
(C)	iv	iii	ii	i
(D)	ii	i	iv	iii

38. **List – I** / **List – II**

List – I	List – II
a. Census	i. Population
b. Sampling	ii. Subset of individuals
c. Quota sampling	iii. Segmented into subgroups
d. Accidental sampling	iv. Convenience

Options	a	b	c	d
(A)	iv	iii	ii	i
(B)	i	ii	iii	iv
(C)	ii	iii	i	iv
(D)	iv	i	ii	iii

39. **List – I** / **List – II**

List – I	List – II
a. Electronic Media	i. Equivalency Programme
b. Continuing Education	ii. Television
c. National Policy on Education	iii. Social Awareness

d. Social Education — iv. MPFL

Options	a	b	c	d
(A)	i	ii	iii	iv
(B)	ii	iv	iii	i
(C)	ii	i	iv	iii
(D)	iv	i	iii	ii

40. **List – I** / **List – II**

List – I	List – II
a. S and T institution	i. IIT
b. NCERT	ii. School curriculum
c. NLMA	iii. Making policies on literacy
d. IGNOU	iv. Open learning system

Options	a	b	c	d
(A)	i	ii	iii	iv
(B)	ii	iii	iv	i
(C)	iv	iii	ii	i
(D)	i	iv	ii	iii

41.

List – I	List – II
a. Goal-setting Theory	i. Reward
b. Alderfer's ERG Theory	ii. Reward
c. Need Hierarchy Theory	iii. Reward
d. Incentive Theory	iv. Existence, relatedness and growth

Options	a	b	c	d
(A)	iii	iv	ii	i
(B)	i	ii	iii	iv
(C)	ii	iii	i	iv
(D)	iii	ii	iv	i

42.

List – I	List – II
a. Case Studies	i. Problem description
b. Small Group Tasks	ii. Opportunities to work together
c. Role playing	iii. Sharing with similar group
d. Interactive Lecture	iv. Siturational description

Options	a	b	c	d
(A)	i	iii	iv	ii

(B)	i	ii	iii	iv
(C)	ii	iv	iii	i
(D)	i	iv	ii	iii

43. **List – I** **List – II**

List – I	List – II
a. HIV/AIDS is more	i. Vienna
b. Environment conservation is part of	ii. Population education
c. Incidence of bounded labour	iii. Agricultural labourers
d. World conference on Human Rights held on	iv. Socio-medical problem

Options	a	b	c	d
(A)	ii	iii	iv	i
(B)	i	ii	iii	iv
(C)	iv	ii	iii	i
(D)	iii	iv	i	ii

44.

List – I	List – II
a. Basic Literacy	i. 15-35 age group
b. NAEP	ii. Income generating courses
c. Continuing Education	iii. 3 Rs
d. Non-formal Education	iv. 6-14 age group

Options	a	b	c	d
(A)	ii	i	iii	iv
(B)	iii	i	ii	iv
(C)	i	ii	iii	iv
(D)	iv	iii	ii	i

45.

List – I	List – II
a. Shriniketan Programme	i. 1942
b. Etawah Project	ii. 1952
c. Community Development Programme	iii. 1921
d. Grow more food campaign	iv. 1947

Options	a	b	c	d
(A)	iii	iv	ii	i
(B)	iii	iv	i	ii
(C)	iv	iii	ii	i

(D)	i	ii	iii	iv

46. **List – I** | **List – II**

List – I		List – II
a. Chipko Movement	i.	Charu Majumdar
b. Naxal Movement	ii.	Medha Patkar
c. Narmada Bachao Movement	iii.	Sunder Lal Bahuguna
d. Ganga Bachao Movement	iv.	G.D. Agarwal

Options	a	b	c	d
(A)	i	ii	iii	iv
(B)	iii	i	ii	iv
(C)	ii	iii	i	iv
(D)	iv	ii	i	iii

47.

List – I		List – II
a. New Education Policy	i.	1988
b. Dowry Prohibition Amendment Act	ii.	1987
c. National Literacy Mission	iii.	1984
d. Operation Black Board Scheme	iv.	1986

Options	a	b	c	d
(A)	iv	iii	ii	i
(B)	iv	ii	iii	i
(C)	iii	iv	i	ii
(D)	iv	iii	i	ii

48.

List – I		List – II
a. Youth Services	i.	NRHM
b. Agricultural Services	ii.	NLM
c. Literacy Services	iii.	NYK
d. Health Services	iv.	KVK

Options	a	b	c	d
(A)	iii	i	ii	iv
(B)	iii	iv	ii	i
(C)	iii	iv	i	ii
(D)	iii	ii	i	iv

49. **List – I** / **List – II**

List – I	List – II
a. Demonstration	i. Campaign
b. Selective contact	ii. Experimental section
c. Group Action	iii. Farmer's call
d. Individual contact	iv. New practices

Options	a	b	c	d
(A)	iii	iv	ii	i
(B)	iv	i	ii	iii
(C)	iv	iii	i	ii
(D)	iv	ii	i	iii

50. **List – I** / **List – II**

List – I	List – II
a. Andragogy	i. John Dewey
b. Praxis	ii. Ivan Ellich
c. Deschooling	iii. Paulo Friere
d. Pragmatism	iv. M. Knowles

Options	a	b	c	d
(A)	iv	iii	ii	i
(B)	iv	ii	i	iii
(C)	iv	iii	i	ii
(D)	iii	iv	i	ii

51. **List – I** / **List – II**

List – I	List – II
a. Motivation Theory	i. Malcom Knowles
b. Concept and Conscientization	ii. Maslow
c. Adult Learning	iii. Robby Kidd
d. Andragogy	iv. Paulo Freire

Options	a	b	c	d
(A)	iv	iii	i	ii
(B)	ii	iv	iii	i
(C)	iv	iii	ii	i
(D)	i	ii	iii	iv

52. **List – I** / **List – II**

List – I	List – II
i. Zero method	1. Symbols
ii. Teacher dominated method	2. Lecture and demonstrations
iii. Traditional method	3. Literary method
iv. Cooperative method	4. Equal oppurtunity

Options	i	ii	iii	iv
(A)	4	3	2	1
(B)	1	2	3	4
(C)	2	4	1	3
(D)	3	4	1	2

53. **List – I** | **List – II**

List – I	List – II
i. Hamburg declaration	1. 1997
ii. UNESCO worlds Declaration on Education	2. 1990
iii. World Declaration on Higher Education for the 21st Century	3. 1998
iv. Universal Declaration of Human Rights	4. 1948

Options	i	ii	iii	iv
(A)	4	3	2	1
(B)	4	1	2	3
(C)	3	4	2	1
(D)	1	2	3	4

54.

List – I	List – II
i. Social education	1. MPFL
ii. National policy on education	2. Social conciosness
iii. Mass media	3. income generating program
iv. Continuing education	4. Radio, TV and Film

Options	i	ii	iii	iv
(A)	1	2	3	4
(B)	4	3	2	1
(C)	2	1	4	3
(D)	1	2	4	3

55.

List – I	List – II
i. Syrvey	1. Cause and effect
ii. Observation method	2. Discriptive information
iii. Contact method	3. Behavioural social science
iv. Experimental method	4. Telephone

Options	i	ii	iii	iv

(A)	1	2	3	4
(B)	4	3	2	1
(C)	1	2	4	3
(D)	2	3	4	1

56.

List – I	**List – II**
i. Incentive theory	1. Human requirements
ii. Need hierarchy theory	2. Rewards
iii. Goal setting theory	3. Existence and growth
iv. ERG theory	4. Drive to reach

Options	i	ii	iii	iv
(A)	4	3	2	1
(B)	1	2	3	4
(C)	3	4	1	2
(D)	2	1	4	3

57.

List – I	**List – II**
i. SRC	1. Women literacy
ii. AFLP	2. State level program administration
iii. SLMA	3. Training material production
iv. ZSS	4. District level program administ.

Options	i	ii	iii	iv
(A)	4	3	2	1
(B)	3	1	2	4
(C)	1	4	3	2
(D)	2	3	1	4

58.

List – I	**List – II**
i. NLMA	1. Education, Planning and Administration
ii. NUPA	2. Resource support body
iii. JSS	3. Policy making body
iv. SRC	4. Vocational skill development

Options	i	ii	iii	iv
(A)	3	1	4	2
(B)	1	2	3	4

(C)	2	4	3	1
(D)	1	2	4	3

59. **List – I** | **List – II**

List – I	List – II
i. IPCL	1. Training of trainers
ii. PRI	2. Unit of Department of Adult and continuing education
iii. KEP	3. Method of teaching literacy
iv. PERC	4. Local self government

Options	i	ii	iii	iv
(A)	4	3	2	1
(B)	1	2	3	4
(C)	3	4	1	2
(D)	1	3	2	4

60.

List – I	List – II
i. Convergence	1. DVV Germany
ii. IJAE	2. IAEA, New Delhi education
iii. Adult Education and development	3. ICAE, UK
iv. university news	4. AIU, New Delhi

Options	i	ii	iii	iv
(A)	4	3	2	1
(B)	1	2	3	4
(C)	2	1	4	3
(D)	3	2	1	4

61.

List – I	List – II
i. DIET	1. Distance Education
ii. IGNOU	2. School education
iii. NCERT	3. Alternative education
iv. NIOS	4. Teacher education

Options	i	ii	iii	iv
(A)	4	3	2	1
(B)	4	1	2	3
(C)	1	2	3	4
(D)	4	2	1	3

62. **List – I** / **List – II**

i. SHGs — 1. Reproduction and Child health
ii. VECs — 2 Information window
iii. ICDS — 3. Women empowerment
iv. CECs — 4. Primary education

Options	i	ii	iii	iv
(A)	3	4	1	2
(B)	2	3	4	1
(C)	1	2	3	4
(D)	4	3	2	1

63. **List – I** / **List – II**

i. International Women's Day — 1. Dec 1
ii. International Population day — 2. Sept 8th
iii. AIDS day — 3. March 8th
iv. International Literacy Day — 4. July 11th

Options	i	ii	iii	iv
(A)	4	2	1	3
(B)	3	4	2	1
(C)	3	4	1	2
(D)	1	2	3	4

64. **List – I** / **List – II**

i. Formal Education — 1. Non academic
ii. Informal Education — 2. Both written and unwritten syllabi education
iii. Actual Curriculum — 3. Derived from other sources
iv. Hidden curriculum — 4. Syllabus

Options	i	ii	iii	iv
(A)	4	3	2	1
(B)	1	2	3	4
(C)	3	2	1	4
(D)	4	3	1	2

65. **List – I** / **List – II**

i. Role Playing — 1. Situational discription
ii. Small group discussions — 2. Sharing within the group
iii. Case studies — 3. Problem description

iv. Interactive lecture			4. Ties to work together	
Options	i	ii	iii	iv
(A)	4	3	2	1
(B)	2	1	3	4
(C)	1	2	3	4
(D)	4	1	2	3

66.

List – I	List – II
i. Social Education	1. 1951-1956
ii. Grama sikshan mohim	2. 1959
iii. FFLP	3. 1967-1968
iv. Functional Literacy for Women	4. 1975-1976

Options	i	ii	iii	iv
(A)	4	1	2	3
(B)	1	2	3	4
(C)	1	2	4	3
(D)	4	3	2	1

67.

List – I	List – II
i. Rigveda	1. Education is that whose end product is salvation
ii. Tagore	2. All round development and drawing out the best in the child mind, body and spirit
iii. Gandhiji	3. Enabling the mind to find out the ultimate truth.
iv. Upanishad	4. Education makes a man self-reliant and selfless

Options	i	ii	iii	iv
(A)	1	2	3	4
(B)	3	1	2	4
(C)	4	3	2	1
(D)	2	4	1	3

68.

List – I	List – II
a. Traditional Method	i. Simple charts representing a phrase, a word and the first letters of the same are used by the instructor.

b. Alphabetic Method	ii. Grouping of letters according to similarity of their shapes.
c. Lauback Method	iii. Letters are taught individually and then they are combined into words to form sentences.
d. Sythetic Method	iv. Letters having similar structure are grouped on each page of the primer.

Options	(a)	(b)	(c)	(d)
(A)	iii	ii	iv	i
(B)	iv	iii	i	ii
(C)	ii	iv	i	iii
(D)	i	ii	iii	Iv

69.

List – I (Program)	**List – II**
i. Gurgaon Experiment	1. 1976
ii. Etawah pilot project	2. 1978
iii. NAEP	3. 1920
iv. Firka development scheme	4. 1947

Options	i	ii	iii	iv
(A)	2	3	1	4
(B)	1	2	4	3
(C)	3	4	2	1
(D)	4	1	3	2

70.

List – I	**List – II**
i. Jan Sikshan Nilayam	1. All Children
ii. Continuing education Programme	2. School dropouts
iii. NIOS	3. Literate adults
iv. SSA	4. Neo Literate Adults

Options	i	ii	iii	iv
(A)	2	4	1	3
(B)	1	3	2	1
(C)	3	1	4	2
(D)	4	3	2	1

71. **List – I** **List – II**

List – I	List – II
i. Abraham Maslow	1. Achievement motivation
ii. C.L. HULL	2. Need Hierarchy theory
iii. Thorndike	3. Needs Reduction theory of Learning
iv. Maceland	4. Theory of Connectivism

Options	i	ii	iii	iv
(A)	1	2	3	4
(B)	2	3	4	1
(C)	3	4	1	2
(D)	4	3	2	1

Match the items given under List-I (Country) with those under List-II (year of literacy campaign) and select the right answer using the codes given below the items :

72.

List – I	List – II
i. China	1. 1945-77
ii. Viatnam	2. 1950-80
iii. Burma	3. 1967-80
iv. Brazil	4. 1960-80

Options	i	ii	iii	iv
(A)	1	2	3	4
(B)	3	2	1	4
(C)	4	1	3	2
(D)	2	3	1	4

Match the items given under List-I (States) with those in List-II (Literacy ranking) according to 2001 census and select the correct answer using the codes given below the list :

73.

List – I	List – II
i. GOA	1.
ii. Mizoram	2.
iii. Kerala	3.
iv. Delhi	4.

Options	i	ii	iii	iv
(A)	1	3	4	2
(B)	3	2	1	4

(C)	4	1	3	2
(D)	3	1	2	4

Match the items given under List-I (Training) with those under List-II (activity under taken) and select the right answer using the codes given below the items :

74. **List – I** / **List – II**

List – I	List – II
i. Need	1. Follow up
ii. Pre Training	2. Planning
iii. Training	3. Implementation
iv. Post Training	4. Assesment

Options	i	ii	iii	iv
(A)	3	2	1	4
(B)	1	2	3	4
(C)	4	2	3	1
(D)	2	3	1	4

75. **List – I** / **List – II**

List – I	List – II
i. Continuing education	1. Pollution
ii. Quality of life	2. Developmental indicator
iii. Environmental education	3. Exchange information
iv. Communication	4. Enhancing education

Options	i	ii	iii	iv
(A)	3	1	2	4
(B)	4	2	1	3
(C)	1	2	3	4
(D)	2	3	4	1

76. **List – I** / **List – II**

List – I	List – II
i. Audio	1. Television
ii. Video	2. Radio
iii. Audio-Video	3. Internet
iv. Multi media	4. Silent movie

Options	i	ii	iii	iv
(A)	1	2	3	4
(B)	2	4	1	3

(C)	3	4	1	2
(D)	4	3	2	1

77. **List – I** / **List – II**

List – I	List – II
i. NCTC	1. Teachers education
ii. IGNOU	2. Higher open learning
iii. University	3. School open education
iv. NIOS	4. Higher education

Options	i	ii	iii	iv
(A)	1	2	3	4
(B)	1	2	4	3
(C)	1	4	2	3
(D)	1	3	2	4

78.

List – I	List – II
i. Ontological view of education	1. Faure
ii. Self actualization	2. Evan Ellich
iii. Deschooling of society	3. Maslow
iv. Lifelong education	4. Paulo friere

Options	i	ii	iii	iv
(A)	4	1	3	2
(B)	4	3	2	1
(C)	2	3	1	4
(D)	1	2	3	4

79.

List – I	List – II
i. Reproductive and Child Health	1. Agriculture
ii. Awareness generation and education	2. Continuing education
iii. technology transfer to farmers	3. Community health
iv. Non credit courses	4. Extension

Options	i	ii	iii	iv
(A)	1	4	3	2
(B)	1	2	3	4
(C)	3	4	1	2
(D)	3	2	1	4

80. **List – I** / **List – II**

List – I	List – II
i. Indigenous learning	1. Modern economic phenomenon
ii. Identity politics	2. Cultural reality
iii. Experimental learning	3. Self recognition
iv. Globalization	4. Education in outside setting

Options	i	ii	iii	iv
(A)	(A) 2	3	4	1
(B)	(B) 2	4	1	3
(C)	(C) 1	2	3	4
(D)	(D) 3	4	2	1

81. **List – I** / **List – II**

List – I	List – II
i. Theriotical orientation	1. Training
ii. Broad perspective	2. Education
iii. Specific task	3. Education
iv. Application	4. Training

Options	i	ii	iii	iv
(A)	1	2	3	4
(B)	1	4	2	3
(C)	3	4	1	2
(D)	3	2	1	4

82. **List – I** / **List – II**

List – I	List – II
i. Present employees	1. Internal
ii. Advertisements	2. External
iii. Employment exchange	3. Internal
iv. Employees referral	4. External

Options	i	ii	iii	iv
(A)	2	1	3	4
(B)	4	3	2	1
(C)	1	2	4	3
(D)	1	3	2	4

83. **List – I** / **List – II**

List – I	List – II
i. Affiliation	1. Training
ii. Screening	2. orientation
iii. Simulation	3. Motivation

iv. Mobilization of resources — 4. Selection

Options	i	ii	iii	iv
(A)	1	2	3	4
(B)	3	4	3	2
(C)	4	3	2	1
(D)	2	3	4	1

84.

List – I	List – II
i. NYK	1. Jana sikshan samsthan
ii. SRC	2. District education committe
iii. JSS	3. Nehru yuvak kendras
iv. ZSS	4. State resource centres

Options	i	ii	iii	iv
(A)	4	3	2	1
(B)	3	4	2	1
(C)	1	2	3	4
(D)	2	1	4	3

85.

List – I	List – II
i. Adulthood	1. Psychological
ii. Right to vote	2. Social
iii. parenthood	3. Biological
iv. Self responsibility	4. Legal

Options	i	ii	iii	iv
(A)	4	3	2	1
(B)	1	4	3	2
(C)	3	4	2	1
(D)	4	1	3	2

86.

List – I (Word)	List – II (Origin)
i. Evaluation	1. Latin
ii. Andragogy	2. French
iii. Laissez Faire	3. Latin
iv. Extension	4 Greek

Options	i	ii	iii	iv
(A)	1	3	2	4
(B)	3	4	2	1

(C)	3	4	1	2
(D)	2	4	3	1

87. **List – I** | **List – II**

i. Less number of women — 1. Use condoms

ii. STD/HIV- AIDS — 2. Reproductive and child health

iii. ICDP — 3. Women empowerment

iv. Biejing Sex Confertence — 4. Declining ratio

Options	i	ii	iii	iv
(A)	4	1	2	3
(B)	3	2	1	4
(C)	2	3	4	1
(D)	1	2	3	4

88. **List – I (Type of Learning)** | **List – II (Proposed by)**

i. Learning through Connection — 1. Pavlov

ii. Discriminate operant — 2. Kimble

iii. Instrumental response — 3. Thorndike

iv. conditional learning — 4. Skinner

Options	i	ii	iii	iv
(A)	3	4	2	1
(B)	2	3	4	1
(C)	1	2	3	4
(D)	4	1	3	2

89. **List – I** | **List – II**

i. World Population Day — 1. Sept 8

ii. World Literacy day — 2. March 8

iii. International Women Day — 3. Sept 5

iv. Teachers day — 4. July 11

Options	i	ii	iii	iv
(A)	(4)	(1)	(2)	(3)
(B)	(2)	(3)	(4)	(1)
(C)	(3)	(2)	(4)	(1)
(D)	(1)	(2)	(3)	(4)

90. **List – I** | **List – II**

i. NLM — 1. 1994

ii. NAEP — 2. 1989

iii. TLC			3. 1978	
iv. PLP			4. 1988	
Options	i	ii	iii	iv
(A)	(3)	(2)	(1)	(4)
(B)	(2)	(1)	(3)	(4)
(C)	(4)	(1)	(3)	(2)
(D)	(4)	(3)	(2)	(1)

91. **List – I** / **List – II**

List – I	List – II
i. Reading, writing and arithmetic	1. CE
ii. Extension eduication	2. 3R
iii. Continuing education	3. 3H
iv. Head, Hand, Heart	4. EE

Options	i	ii	iii	iv
(A)	2	4	1	3
(B)	1	3	2	4
(C)	4	2	1	3
(D)	3	1	2	4

92. **List – I** / **List – II**

List – I	List – II
i. Tagore	1. Concentization
ii. Gandhiji	2. Sarvodaya
iii. Malcome Adisheshayah	3. Adult Education
iv. Pulo Friere	4. Self realization

Options	i	ii	iii	iv
(A)	(4)	(2)	(3)	(1)
(B)	(3)	(1)	(2)	(4)
(C)	(2)	(1)	(3)	(4)
(D)	(1)	(2)	(3)	(4)

93. **List – I** / **List – II**

List – I	List – II
i. Projected	1. Film Aids
ii. Non-projected aids	2. Models
iii. Projected aids	3. Slides
iv. Non projected	4. Chart Aids

Options	i	ii	iii	iv
(A)	(4)	(3)	(2)	(1)

(B)	(1)	(4)	(3)	(2)
(C)	(3)	(2)	(4)	(1)
(D)	(1)	(2)	(4)	(3)

94. **Assertion I:** **Media policy of NLM is to create awareness among potential beneficiaries of the literacy programme to bring them in their reach.**

Assertion II: **Media policy of NLM intends to take the achievements of the 'mission' to the people, decision makers and society at large with a view to solicit their active support, cooperation and participation in the endeavour of the mission**

(A) Assertion I is true (B) Assertion II is false.

(C) Assertion I and II are false. (D) Assertion I and II are true.

95. **Assertion I:** **Chauraha is a very popular motivational print material of literacy programme**

Assertion II: **Chauraha is a popular audio-visual advocacy material of literacy programme**

(A) Assertion I is true. (B) Assertion II is false.

(C) Assertion I is false (II) is true. (D) Assertion I and II are false.

96. **Assertion I:** **Jan Shikshan Sansthan, also known as Shramik Vidya Peeth provides opportunity to all sections of society to acquire and upgrade their skills**

Assertion II: **Jan Shikshan Sansthan, also known as Shramik Vidya Peeth provides opportunity to acquire and upgrade the vocational skills of neoliterates only.**

(A) Assertion I is true. (B) Assertion II is false.

(C) Assertion I and II are false. (D) Assertion I and II are true

97. **Assertion I:** **Total literacy programme evaluation is qualitative in nature.**

Assertion II: **Continuing Education programme evaluationis quantitative in nature.**

(A) Assertion I is true. (B) Assertion II is false.

(C) Assertion I and II are true. (D) Assertion I and II are false.

98. **Assertion I:** **Learning needs of urban male illiterate are different from those of urban female illiterates.**

Assertion II: **Learning needs are free from gender, social and cultural differences. Assertion I is true.**

(A) Assertion I is true. (B) Assertion II is false.

(C) Assertion I is true, Assertion II is false (D) Assertion I and II are false.

99. Assertion I: **According to Census reports, sex ratio was 972 in 1901 and 933 in 2001**

Assertion II: **Sex ratio was 990 in 1901 and 930 in 2001.**

(A) Assertion I is true. (B) Assertion II is false.

(C) Assertion I and II are false. (D) Assertion I and II are true.

100. Assertion I: **Quality of life indicators are symptoms of status of development of a country.**

Assertion II: **Literacy is not part of the indicators to measure quality of life.**

(A) Assertion I is false. (B) Assertion II is true.

(C) Assertion I is true, Assertion II is false. (D) Assertion I and II are false.

101. Assertion I: **SSA aims that all girl children goes to school.**

Assertion II **SSA aims at reducing dropout rate at the primary level of education.**

(A) Assertion I is true. (B) Assertion II is false.

(C) Assertion I and II are false. (D) Assertion I and II are true.

102. Assertion I: **UNESCO world assembly on adult education and life long learning was held at Hamburg in 1997 and at Brazil in 2009.**

Assertion II: **UNESCO world assembly on adult education was held at Tehran in 1965**

(A) Assertion I is true (B) Assertion II is false.

(C) Assertion I and II are true. (D) Assertion I and II are false.

103. Assertion I: **Focus of XIth plan guidelines for Department of Adult, Continuing Education and Extension are to reach out to the larger sections of the community especially the deprived groups.**

Assertion II: **The Department of Adult, Continuing Education and Extension strives to contribute to the generation of new knowledge through extension and research.**

(A) Assertion I is true. (B) Assertion II is false.

(C) Assertion I and II are true. (D) Assertion I and II are false.

104.

List – I	**List – II**
(a) Conscientization	(i) Maslow
(b) Motivation	(ii) Malcom Knowles
(c) Androgogy	(iii) Robby Kidd

(d) How adults learn (iv) Paulo Freire

Options	a	b	c	d
(A)	ii	iii	i	iv
(B)	iv	ii	iii	i
(C)	iv	i	ii	iii
(D)	i	ii	iii	Iv

105. List – I **List – II**

(a) Preparation of teaching learning material — i. VEC

(b) Universalization of Primary education — ii. SRC

(c) Open basic education program — iii. SSA

(d) Overseeing the education of primary level in village code: — iv. NIOS

Options	a	b	c	d
(A)	i	ii	iii	iv
(B)	ii	iii	iv	i
(C)	iii	iv	ii	i
(D)	iv	i	ii	Iii

106. List – I **List – II**

(a) Non Projected — i. CDs aids

(b) Projected aids — ii. Microphone

(c) Audio aids — iii. Films

(d) Computer aids — iv. Charts

Options	a	b	c	d
(A)	iv	ii	i	iii
(B)	iii	ii	iv	i
(C)	iv	iii	ii	i
(D)	i	ii	iii	iv

107. List – I **List – II**

(a) 15-59 years of age population — i. Skill training provider

(b) Senior Citizens — ii. NCVT

(c) NGO, Public Pvt. Partners — iii. NPOP

(c) Skill Training Certificate — iv. Demographic Divident

Options	a	b	c	d
(A)	i	iii	ii	iv
(B)	ii	iv	iii	i
(C)	iv	iii	i	ii
(D)	ii	iv	i	iii

108. **List – I** **List – II**

List – I	List – II
(a) Right to Education	i. Right to Life and Liberty
(b) Fundamental Rights	ii. Right to Life with Dignity
(c) Human Rights	iii. Free and Compulsory Education
(d) Consumer Rights	iv. To be informed

Options	a	b	c	d
(A)	ii	iii	iv	i
(B)	i	ii	iii	iv
(C)	iii	i	ii	iv
(D)	iv	iii	ii	i

109. **List – I** **List – II**

List – I	List – II
(a) iAY	i. TLC
(b) Anemateurs	ii. SHG
(c) Micro Credit	iii. BPL
(d) Volunteers	iv. NAEP

Options	a	b	c	d
(A)	iv	ii	iii	i
(B)	i	iii	ii	iv
(C)	ii	i	iv	iii
(D)	iii	iv	ii	i

110. **List – I** **List – II**

List – I	List – II
(a) Inbreeding	i. Selection
(b) Pre-Service and In-service	ii. Controlling
(c) Picking right people for right job	iii. Internal recruitment
(d) Setting standards	iv. Staff training

Options	a	b	c	d
(A)	i	ii	iv	iii
(B)	iii	iv	i	ii

	a	b	c	d
(C)	i	iii	iv	ii
(D)	ii	i	iii	iv

111. **List – I** | **List – II**

(a) Library movement — i. Kerala
(b) Chipko movement — ii. Gujarat
(c) Narmada movement — iii. AP
(d) Anti arrack Movement — iv. Uttaranchal

Options	a	b	c	d
(A)	iii	i	ii	iv
(B)	iv	ii	i	iii
(C)	i	iv	ii	Iii
(D)	ii	iii	i	iv

112. **List – I** | **List – II**

(a) 1953 — i. NAEP
(b) 1978 — ii. CEP
(c) 1982 — iii. CDP
(d) 1952 — iv. NEP

Options	a	b	c	d
(A)	iv	i	ii	iii
(B)	i	ii	iv	iii
(C)	ii	i	iii	iv
(D)	i	iv	ii	iii

113. **List – I** | **List – II**

(a) Extra Mural Lectures — i. Female literacy
(b) Land grant colleges — ii. Finland
(c) Folk school — iii. USA
(d) Sakshar Bharat — iv. UK

Options	a	b	c	d
(A)	iii	iv	ii	i
(B)	iv	iii	ii	i
(C)	i	ii	iii	iv
(D)	iv	iii	i	ii

114. **List – I** | **List – II**

(a) Motivation theory — i. Malcom knowles

(b) Concentization — ii. Maslow

(c) Adult learning — iii. Robby kidd

(d) Andragogy — iv. Paulo Friere

Options	a	b	c	d
(A)	ii	iv	iii	i
(B)	iii	ii	iv	i
(C)	iv	iii	ii	i
(D)	i	iv	iii	ii

115.

List – I	List – II
(a) Overseeing the education at the village level	i. SRC
(b) Universalization of Primary Education	ii. NIOS
(c) Preparation of teaching-learning materials	iii. SSA
(d) Open Basic Education Programme	iv. VEC

Options	a	b	c	d
(A)	iv	iii	ii	i
(B)	iii	iv	ii	i
(C)	iii	i	ii	iv
(D)	iv	iii	i	ii

116.

List – I	List – II
(a) Projected aids	i. Microphone
(b) Non Projected aids	ii. Films
(c) Computers	iii. CDs
(d) Audio Aids	iv. Charts

Options	a	b	c	d
(A)	iv	iii	ii	i
(B)	i	ii	iii	iv
(C)	ii	iv	iii	i
(D)	iv	ii	iii	i

117.

List – I	List – II
(a) Senior citizens	i. NCVT
(b) Skill training certification	ii. Skill training Providers

(c) 15-59 years Age group — iii. Demographi dividend

(d) NGO public private partners — iv. NPOP

Options	a	b	c	d
(A)	ii	iii	iv	i
(B)	iv	i	iii	ii
(C)	i	ii	iii	iv
(D)	iv	ii	i	iii

118. **List – I** / **List – II**

List – I	List – II
(a) Consumer rights	i. Free Compulsory education
(b) Fundamental Rights	ii. Freedom of speech
(c) Education rights	iii. Right to life with dignity
(d) Human rights	iv. Right to be informed

Options	a	b	c	d
(A)	i	iv	ii	iii
(B)	iv	iv	i	iii
(C)	i	ii	iii	iv
(D)	iv	iii	ii	i

119.

List – I	List – II
(a) Anemateures	i. BPL
(b) Micro Credit	ii. TLC
(c) Volenteers	iii. NAEP
(d) IAY	iv. SHGs

Options	a	b	c	d
(A)	iv	iii	ii	i
(B)	iii	iv	ii	i
(C)	iii	iv	i	ii
(D)	i	ii	iv	iii

120.

List – I	List – II
(a) Setting the standerds	i. Staff training
(b) Picking right people for right job	ii. Internal recruitment
(c) Pre service and inservice	iii. Controlling
(d) Inbreeding	iv. Selection

Options	a	b	c	d

(A)	iii	i	ii	iv
(B)	iii	ii	i	iv
(C)	iii	ii	iv	i
(D)	iii	iv	i	ii

121. **List – I** **List – II**

(a) Narmada movement i. Uttaranchal

(b) Anti Arrack movement ii. Gujarat

(c) Chipko iii. AP

(d) Library movement iv. Kerala

Options	a	b	c	d
(A)	ii	iv	i	iii
(B)	ii	iii	i	iv
(C)	ii	i	iii	iv
(D)	ii	iii	iv	i

122. **List – I** **List – II**

(a) 1982 i. NES

(b) 1953 ii. NAEP

(c) 1952 iii. CEP

(d) 1977 iv. CDP

Options	a	b	c	d
(A)	iv	i	iii	ii
(B)	ii	iv	i	iii
(C)	iii	i	iv	ii
(D)	iii	iv	ii	i

123. **List – I** **List – II**

(a) Folk high school i. Female Liyteracy

(b) Land grant colleges ii. United Kingdom

(c) Extra mural lectures iii. USA

(d) Sakshar Bharat iv. Finland

Options	a	b	c	d
(A)	iv	iii	ii	i
(B)	iv	i	iii	ii

(C)	iv	ii	i	iii
(D)	iv	iii	ii	i

124. List – I **List – II**

(a) Decentralization i. Low Male-female Ratio

(b) Quality of life ii. Conservation and Development

(c) Sustainable environment iii. Panchayati Raj Institutions

(d) Gender inequality iv. Development Indicator

Options	a	b	c	d
(A)	(iv)	(i)	(iii)	(ii)
(B)	(i)	(ii)	(iii)	(iv)
(C)	(ii)	(iii)	(i)	(iv)
(D)	(iii)	(iv)	(ii)	(i)

125. List – I **List – II**

a. HIV/AIDS i. PERC

b. Improved Mother and Child Health ii. Sex workers

c. Environmental Protection iii. I.C.D.S.

d. UNFPA iv. Conservation of Natural Resources

Options	a	b	c	d
(A)	(i)	(ii)	(iii)	(iv)
(B)	(ii)	(iv)	(i)	(iii)
(C)	(ii)	(iii)	(iv)	(i)
(D)	(iii)	(iv)	(i)	(ii)

126. List – I (Name of Author) **List – II (Name of Book)**

a. Paulo Freire i. Budiam Talim

b. Ivan Illich ii. Culture action for freedom

c. Mahatma Gandhi iii. Pedagogy of the oppressed

d. Roby Kidd iv. How adults can learn

Options	a	b	c	d
(A)	(i)	(iii)	(ii)	(iv)
(B)	(ii)	(iv)	(i)	(iii)
(C)	(iii)	(ii)	(i)	(iv)
(D)	(iii)	(i)	(iv)	(ii)

127. **List – I** / **List – II**

List – I	List – II
a. Virtual University	i. Planning and Organization
b. Field Surveys	ii. Need Assessment
c. Project Management	iii. Internet
d. Voluntary Work	iv. NGOs

Options	a	b	c	d
(A)	(ii)	(i)	(iii)	(iv)
(B)	(iii)	(ii)	(i)	(iv)
(C)	(iii)	(iv)	(i)	(ii)
(D)	(ii)	(i)	(iv)	(iii)

128. **List – I** / **List – II**

List – I	List – II
a. Recorder	i. A.V. Aids
b. Chalk Board	ii. Visual Aods
c. Cinema	iii. Audio Aids
d. FM Channel	iv. Audio Aids

Options	a	b	c	d
(A)	(i)	(iii)	(ii)	(iv)
(B)	(iv)	(i)	(iii)	(ii)
(C)	(iv)	(ii)	(i)	(iii)
(D)	(ii)	(iii)	(i)	(iv)

129. **List – I** / **List – II**

List – I	List – II
a. Vinoba Bhave	i. Buniyadi Shiksha
b. Rabindranath Tagore	ii. Culture of Silence
c. Pulao Freire	iii. Self- realization
d. Mahatma Gandhi	iv. Sarvodaya

Options	a	b	c	d
(A)	(i)	(ii)	(iii)	(iv)
(B)	(ii)	(iii)	(iv)	(i)
(C)	(iii)	(iv)	(i)	(ii)
(D)	(iv)	(iii)	(ii)	(i)

130. **List – I** / **List – II**

List – I	List – II
a. Formal Education	i. 6-14
b. Sarva Shiksha Abhiyan	ii. ITI, Polytechnic
c. Vocational Education	iii. 15-35

d. Age Group of Adult Education Primary to Higher education	iv. Primary to higher education

Options	a	b	c	d
(A)	(ii)	(i)	(iii)	(iv)
(B)	(iv)	(i)	(ii)	(iii)
(C)	(i)	(iii)	(iv)	(ii)
(D)	(iii)	(ii)	(i)	(iv)

131.

List – I (Name of Author)	List – II (Name of Book)
a. Roby Kid	i. Bunyadi Talim
b. Ivan Illich	ii. Padagogy of the Oppressed
c. Paulo Freire	iii. How Adults Learn
d. Mahatma Gandhi	iv. Cultural Action for Freedom

Options	a	b	c	d
(A)	(iii)	(i)	(ii)	(iv)
(B)	(iii)	(ii)	(i)	(iv)
(C)	(iii)	(i)	(iv)	(ii)
(D)	(iii)	(iv)	(ii)	(i)

132.

List – I (Programmez)	List – II (Age Group)
a. Elementary Primary Education	i. 15 to 35 yrs.
b. National Adult Education Programme	ii. Neo Literatre from any age group
c. Post Literacy Programme	iii. All age group
d. Continuing Education Programme	iv. 6 to 14 yrs.

Options	a	b	c	d
(A)	(i)	(iii)	(ii)	(iv)
(B)	(iv)	(i)	(ii)	(iii)
(C)	(iii)	(ii)	(iv)	(i)
(D)	(ii)	(i)	(iii)	(iv)

133.

List – I	List – II
a. Primary data	i. Research Methodology
b. Interview	ii. Sample
c. Standard Deviation	iii. Data Collection
d. Respondent	iv. Statistical Method

Options	a	b	c	d
(A)	(i)	(ii)	(iii)	(iv)
(B)	(iii)	(i)	(iv)	(ii)
(C)	(iv)	(iii)	(ii)	(i)
(D)	(ii)	(i)	(iv)	(iii)

134. **List – I** / **List – II**

List – I	List – II
a. Story telling	i. Research Methodology
b. Charts	ii. Sample
c. Participatory Approach	iii. Data Collection
d. Computer	iv. Statistical Method

Options	a	b	c	d
(A)	iii	iv	ii	i
(B)	ii	iv	iii	i
(C)	ii	iii	iv	i
(D)	ii	i	iv	iii

135.

List – I	List – II
a. Reliability	i. Testing of hypothesis
b. Geometric Mean	ii. Sample selection
c. Null hyphothesis	iii. Level of confidence
d. Card Method	iv. Statistical average

Options	a	b	c	d
(A)	(iii)	(iv)	(i)	(ii)
(B)	(iii)	(ii)	(i)	(iv)
(C)	(iii)	(i)	(ii)	(iv)
(D)	(iii)	(iv)	(ii)	(i)

This consists of two list of statements, terms or symbols and the candidate, has to match with Item in List - I with Item in List – II

136.

List – I	List – II
a. Panto Freire	i. Teheran
b. Mobral System of Adult Education	ii. Sri Lanka
c. International Institute of Adult Literacy Methods	iii. Conscientization
d. Asian South Pacific Bureau of Adult Education	iv. Brazil

Options	a	b	c	d
(A)	(iv)	(iii)	(i)	(ii)
(B)	(ii)	(i)	(iv)	(iii)
(C)	(iii)	(i)	(iv)	(ii)
(D)	(iv)	(i)	(ii)	(iii)

137. **List – I** **List – II**

List – I	List – II
(a) Environmental day	i. Oct 2nd
(b) Worlds AIDS day	ii. March 8th
(c) Non violence day	iii. June 5th
(d) Women's day	iv. Dec 1st

Options	a	b	c	d
(A)	(iii)	(iv)	(i)	(ii)
(B)	(iv)	(iii)	(ii)	(i)
(C)	(ii)	(i)	(iii)	(ii)
(D)	(iv)	(i)	(ii)	(iii)

138. **List – I** **List – II**

List – I	List – II
a. Domestic violence Act	i. 2002
b. Panchayatiraj Act	ii. 2006
c. Right to Information Act	iii. 1986
d. Consumer Protection Act	iv. 2005

Options	a	b	c	d
(A)	iii	i	ii	iv
(B)	i	iv	iii	ii
(C)	iv	i	ii	iii
(D)	ii	iv	i	iii

139. **List – I** **List – II**

List – I	List – II
a. Individual Interest Promotion Programme	i. Small Family Norm
b. Equivalence Programme	ii. Self Help Group
c. Income Generation Programme	iii. Story Telling/Drama
d. Quality of Life Improvement	iv. Open Basic Education program

Options	a	b	c	d
(A)	iv	i	ii	iii

(B)	i	iv	iii	ii
(C)	iv	i	ii	iii
(D)	ii	iv	i	iii

140. List – I **List – II**

a. Nodal Continuing Education Centre — i. Preak

b. Continuing Education Centre — ii. Animator

c. Adult Edcatopm Cemtre — iii. Coordinator

d. TLC at the District level — iv. Nodal Prerak

Options	a	b	c	d
(A)	iv	i	ii	iii
(B)	i	iv	iii	ii
(C)	iv	i	ii	iii
(D)	ii	iv	i	iii

141. List – I **List – II**

a. Rabindranath Tagore — i. Satya – graham

b. Zakir Hussain — ii. Teacher's Day

c. MahatmaGandhi — iii. Visva – Bharati

d. Dr. Radhakrishnan — iv. Adult Education

Options	a	b	c	d
(A)	iv	iii	ii	i
(B)	iii	iv	i	ii
(C)	ii	iii	i	iv
(D)	iv	ii	i	Iii

142. List – I **List – II**

a. Folk High School — i. UNPF

b. Adult Basic Education — ii. UNESCO

c. Lifelong Education — iii. Denmark

d. Population Education — iv. USA

Options	a	b	c	d
(A)	ii	iii	iv	i
(B)	i	ii	iii	iv
(C)	i	ii	iv	iii
(D)	iii	iv	ii	i

143. List – I **List – II**

List – I		List – II
a. International literacy day	i.	1st Dec
b. Population day	ii.	8th March
c. AIDS day	iii.	8th Sept
d. Womens day	iv.	12th Oct

Options	a	b	c	d
(A)	i	ii	iii	iv
(B)	ii	iii	iv	i
(C)	iii	iv	i	ii
(D)	iv	i	ii	iii

This consists of two lists of organisations, statements, terms or activities and the candidates have to match an item in one list with an item in the other :

144. List – I **List – II**

List – I		List – II
a. State Resource Centre	i.	To develop teaching, learning and training materials for all types of education
b. Population Education Resource	ii.	To develop resource materials and skill Centre based primers for neo-literates
c. Population Education Club	iii.	To provide resource support to Population Education
d. National Council for Educational Research and Training	iv.	To create Population awareness

Options	a	b	c	d
(A)	i	ii	iii	iv
(B)	ii	iii	iv	i
(C)	iii	iv	i	ii
(D)	iv	i	ii	iii

This consists of two lists of organisations, statements, terms or activities and the candidates have to match an item in one list with an item in the other :

145. List – I **List – II**

List – I		List – II
a. NAEP	i.	Promotion of literacy
b. NLM	ii.	To enquire into the financial needs of the University

c. University Grants Commission	iii. Imparting Vocational, Occupational and Professional competence
d. Continuing Education	iv. To impart functional literacy with follow-up programme

Options	a	b	c	d
(A)	i	ii	iii	iv
(B)	ii	iii	iv	i
(C)	iii	iv	i	ii
(D)	iv	i	ii	iii

This consists of two lists of organisations, statements, terms or activities and the candidates have to match an item in one list with an item in the other :

146.

List – I	List – II
a. Prof. Ramlal Parikh Review Committee	i. 1953
b. Dr. Radha Krishna Report	ii. 1983-85
c. Kothari Commission	iii. 1978-79
d. UGC	iv. 1964-66

Options	a	b	c	d
(A)	i	ii	iii	iv
(B)	ii	iii	iv	i
(C)	iii	iv	i	ii
(D)	iv	i	ii	iii

147.

List – I	List – II
a. DAE	i. 1961
b. NCERT	ii. 1988
c. JSN	iii. 1976
d. SRC	iv. 1992

Options	a	b	c	d
(A)	i	ii	iii	iv
(B)	ii	iii	iv	i
(C)	iii	iv	i	ii
(D)	iv	i	ii	iii

This consists of two lists of organisations, statements, terms or activities and the candidates have to match an item in one list with an item in the other

148. **List – I** / **List – II**

List – I	List – II
a. Abraham Maslow	i. Theory of Connectionism
b. Sigmund Freud	ii. Theory of Connectionism
c. E.L. Thorndike	iii. Theory of Hierarchy of Needs
d. McCleland	iv. Psycho-Analytic Theory

Options	a	b	c	d
(A)	i	ii	iii	iv
(B)	ii	iii	iv	i
(C)	iii	iv	i	ii
(D)	iv	i	ii	iii

149. **List – I** / **List – II**

List – I	List – II
a. I. P. Pavlov	i. Classical Conditioning
b. B.F. Skinner	ii. Operant Conditioning
c. John B. Watson	iii. Behavioural Theory
d. E. R. Gurthrie	iv. Theory of Contiguity

Options	a	b	c	d
(A)	i	ii	iii	iv
(B)	ii	iii	iv	i
(C)	iii	iv	i	ii
(D)	iv	i	ii	iii

150. **List – I** / **List – II**

List – I	List – II
a. Gandhiji	i. Malcolm Adisheshiah
b. Rabindranath Tagore	ii. Self- realization
c. Paulo Friere	iii. Sarvodaya
d. Doyen of Adult Education in India	iv. Conscientization

Options	a	b	c	d
(A)	i	ii	iii	iv
(B)	ii	iii	iv	i
(C)	iii	iv	i	ii
(D)	iv	i	ii	iii

151. List – I **List – II**

a. Non-Formal Education — i. Physically Challenged

b. Informal Education — ii. School Children

c. Formal Education — iii. Illetrates

d. Special Education — iv. Drop outs

Options	a	b	c	d
(A)	i	ii	iii	iv
(B)	ii	iii	iv	i
(C)	iii	iv	i	ii
(D)	iv	iii	ii	i

Match the concept/term in List-I with the name in List-II

152. List – I **List – II**

a. Andragogy — i. Maslow

b. Conscientization — ii. Malcome Knowles

c. How Adult Learn — iii. Roby Kidd

d. Motivational Theory — iv. Paulo Freire

Options	a	b	c	d
(A)	iii	iv	ii	i
(B)	i	ii	iii	iv
(C)	iv	iii	ii	i
(D)	ii	iii	iv	i

153. List – I **List – II**

a. Projected Aids — i. Film

b. Non-projected Aids — ii. Models

c. Projected Aids — iii. Slides

d. Non-projected aids — iv. Charts

Options	a	b	c	d
(A)	ii	iv	i	iii
(B)	iii	i	ii	iv
(C)	i	iv	iii	ii
(D)	iv	i	ii	iii

154. List – I **List – II**

a. HIV Aids is more — i. Viena

b. Environment Conservation is part of — ii. Population education

c. Incidence of bounded labour is high among — iii. Agricultural Labour

d. World conference of human rights was held in — iv. Socio medical problem

Options	a	b	c	d
(A)	ii	iii	iv	i
(B)	i	ii	iii	iv
(C)	iv	ii	iii	i
(D)	iii	iv	i	ii

Answers

1	(D)	20	(D)	39	(C)	58	(A)
2	(C)	21	(C)	40	(A)	59	(C)
3	(B)	22	(C)	41	(A)	60	(D)
4	(D)	23	(A)	42	(A)	61	(B)
5	(C)	24	(A)	43	(C)	62	(A)
6	(B)	25	(A)	44	(B)	63	(C)
7	(D)	26	(B)	45	(A)	64	(A)
8	(B)	27	(C)	46	(B)	65	(C)
9	(B)	28	(A)	47	(D)	66	(B)
10	(A)	29	(B)	48	(B)	67	(C)
11	(C)	30	(D)	49	(D)	68	(B)
12	(A)	31	(B)	50	(A)	69	(C)
13	(B)	32	(A)	51	(B)	70	(B)
14	(C)	33	(C)	52	(B)	71	(B)
15	(D)	34	(C)	53	(D)	72	(A)
16	(A)	35	(C)	54	(C)	73	(B)
17	(B)	36	(C)	55	(D)	74	(C)
18	(B)	37	(B)	56	(D)	75	(B)
19	(A)	38	(B)	57	(B)	76	(B)
77	(B)	97	(C)	117	(B)	137	(A)
78	(B)	98	(A)	118	(B)	138	(C)
79	(C)	99	(A)	119	(B)	139	(A)
80	(A)	100	(C)	120	(D)	140	(A)
81	(D)	101	(D)	121	(B)	141	(B)
82	(C)	102	(A)	122	(C)	142	(D)

83	**(B)**	**103**	**(C)**	**123**	**(A)**	**143**	**(C)**
84	**(B)**	**104**	**(C)**	**124**	**(D)**	**144**	**(B)**
85	**(B)**	**105**	**(B)**	**125**	**(C)**	**145**	**(D)**
86	**(B)**	**106**	**(C)**	**126**	**(C)**	**146**	**(B)**
87	**(A)**	**107**	**(C)**	**127**	**(B)**	**147**	**(D)**
88	**(A)**	**108**	**(C)**	**128**	**(C)**	**148**	**(C)**
89	**(A)**	**109**	**(D)**	**129**	**(D)**	**149**	**(A)**
90	**(D)**	**110**	**(B)**	**130**	**(B)**	**150**	**(B)**
91	**(A)**	**111**	**(C)**	**131**	**(B)**	**151**	**(D)**
92	**(A)**	**112**	**(A)**	**132**	**(B)**	**152**	**(A)**
93	**(B)**	**113**	**(B)**	**133**	**(B)**	**153**	**(C)**
94	**(D)**	**114**	**(B)**	**134**	**(D)**	**154**	**(C)**
95	**(C)**	**115**	**(D)**	**135**	**(A)**		
96	**(D)**	**116**	**(C)**	**136**	**(C)**		

Memory Based Questions

1. **Distance Education is recognised by**
   (A) UGC (B) NCERT
   (C) NIOS (D) DEC
2. **Population Education in colleges is imported through**
   (A) Women Development Cells
   (B) NSS
   (C) Population Education Clubs
   (D) Dramatic Society
3. **The Chairman of First Higher Education Commission was**
   (A) Maulana Azad (B) Zakir Hussain
   (C) Radha Krishnan (D) D.S. Kothari
4. **Male/Female Sex Ratio in India has increased from 2001 to 2011**
   (A) 933-943 (B) 933-946
   (C) 930-943 (D) 930-946
5. **Main functions of GRC is**
   (A) Gender equality (B) Child care
   (C) Empowering woman (D) All of the above
6. **Functions of CEC are**
   (A) Income generation (B) Equivalency
   (C) Individual Interest promotion (D) All of them

7. **Median does the following :**
   (A) Gives the average size of data.
   (B) Shows the maximum frequency.
   (C) Divides the whole distribution into two equal parts.
   (D) Shows variation among the data.

8. **'Range' shows the following :**
   (A) The differences between the maximum and minimum number
   (B) The number with maximum frequency.
   (C) The number which divide the whole distribution in two equal part.
   (D) None of the above.

9. **PEC's in institution function under**
   (A) UNFPA (B) UNICFE
   (C) UNDP (D) WHO

10. **Sulabh International is engaged in**
   (A) Food Security (B) Legal Awareness
   (C) Remedial Adult Education (D) Sanitation

11. **Evaluation of extension programme should be**
   (A) Quantitative (B) Qualitative
   (C) Both Qualitative and Quantitative (D) None of the above

12. **Learning needs of Adults in rural and urban areas are**
   (A) Quite difference (B) Same
   (C) Some what different (D) Cannot say

13. **NIOS offers**
   (A) Open Basic Education (B) Academic Programmes
   (C) Vocational Programmes (D) All of the above

14. **The learning material for Adult Education is produced by**
   (A) National Book Trust (B) State Resource Centre
   (C) Non-Governmental Organization (D) All of the above

15. **Each one teach one model is suitable for**
   (A) Urban Area
   (B) Rural Area
   (C) Scantly distributed population area
   (D) None of the above

16. Conditioning, imitation, memorising, skill training and exploring are stages for adult learning theory by

(A) Bloom (B) Belbin

(C) Skinner (D) Pavlov

17. Adult learning should be

(A) Learner-centred (B) Process-centred

(C) Content-centred (D) All of the above

18. Training of Prerak at CEC should have

(A) Group work (B) Field visits

(C) Presentation by expert (D) Above all

19. Which one of the following is the result of Adult Literacy Programme ?

(A) Chipko movement (B) Bachapan Bachao Andolan

(C) Anti-arrack agitation (D) Bhoodan movement

20. Leadership style in extension programme should be

(A) Autocratic (B) Democratic

(C) Participatory (D) None of above

21. First evaluation of Continuing Education Programme is done after

(A) One year (B) Two years

(C) Three years (D) Four years

22. Constitutional Amendment 73 is not related to

(A) Power to people (B) Democracy at grassroot

(C) Literacy to people (D) Local Self Government

23. 'Angootha Chhap' is a

(A) Literacy Learning Sheet (B) Literacy Radio Programme

(C) Literacy Primer (D) Literacy Film

24. Sakshar Bharat programme completed how many years on 8th September 2013 ?

(A) Four (B) Five

(C) Six (D) Seven

25. Meeting the current development needs of today without compromising the future needs is known as

(A) Distribution development (B) Democratic development

(C) Sustainable development (D) Equitable development

26. Most widely used method in social research is

(A) Case Study (B) Interview

(C) Participant Observation (D) Survey

27. Term 'Praxis' was coined by

(A) Petarson (B) Knox

(C) Friere (D) Knowles

28. Literacy rate increased from 2001 to 2011

(A) 64.8 per cent – 73 per cent (B) 64.8 per cent – 75 per cent

(C) 64.8 per cent – 77 per cent (D) 64.8 per cent – 78 per cent

29. 'Convergence' journal is published by

(A) ICAE (B) IUACE

(C) IAEA (D) DUV International

30. 'Delegation' means

(A) Transferring specified resources to people

(B) Transferring specified powers to sub-ordinates

(C) Transferring specified powers to superiors

(D) Garnering maximum benefits from resources

31. Who coined the term 'extension' ?

(A) Charles McCarthy (B) Triebel

(C) Rogers (D) Belanger

32. Which one of the following is a centre of polyvalent education ?

(A) Jan Shikshan Sansthan (B) Lok Shikshan Sansthan

(C) State Resource Centre (D) None of the above

33. The World Education Forum adopted EFA goals at Dakar in year

(A) 1997 (B) 1998

(C) 1999 (D) 2000

34. According to which author 'adult's life situation is central to learning ?

(A) Skinner (B) Ausbel

(C) Thorndike (D) Knox

35. Training focuses on

(A) Long-term issues of significance (B) Immediate concerns

(C) Extended concerns (D) None of the above

36. Which one is not correct about education and empowerment ?

(A) It helps people coming together and act as a collective.

(B) It inculcates the value of Superiority.

(C) It helps improve productivity.

(D) It enables a person to negotiate better.

37. What is not true about Mahila Samkhya Programme ?

(A) It was not initiated by Government

(B) It was intended to enable women to organize

(C) Government cannot mobilize women

(D) It was formulated in 1988

38. The size of sample for external evaluation of literacy programme was prescribed as

(A) 2 per cent of the universe subject to maximum of 5000 learners

(B) 3 per cent of the universe subject to maximum of 6000 learners

(C) 4 per cent of the universe subject to maximum of 8000 learners

(D) 5 per cent of the universe subject to maximum of 10000 learners

39. Which one is not a required skills of a manager ?

(A) Mind reading skills

(B) Technical skills

(C) Conceptual skills

(D) Human skills

40. Social factors of personality are

i. Physical appearance

ii. Parents

iii. Home environment

iv. Nervous system

Codes:

(A) i is true

(B) Both ii and iii are true.

(C) Both i and iii are true.

(D) Both ii and iii are false

41. Living and learning for a viable future : The power of adult learning, was the slogan of World Conference held in

(A) Canada

(B) Brazil

(C) Germany

(D) France

42. Work Oriented Literacy Project was conducted in

(A) Vietnam

(B) China

(C) Germany

(D) None of the above

43. Which country adopted the model of 'Yes I Can' in promotion of adult literacy ?

(A) China (B) India

(C) Tanzania (D) Vietnam

44. Which international organization coordinates the 'Education for All' programme at global level ?

(A) UNDP (B) UNESCO

(C) IMF (D) UNFP

45. When was National Literacy Mission Launched ?

(A) 5 May, 1988 (B) 5 September, 1988

(C) 5 December, 1988 (D) 5 March, 1988

46. Education Commission was established under Chairmanship of Prof. D.S. Kothari in the year

(A) 1952-54 (B) 1964-66

(C) 1962-64 (D) 1965-67

47. International Literacy Day celebrated on

(A) 8 September (B) 8 March

(C) 8 December (D) 8 June

48. The third dimension of higher education is

(A) Teaching (B) Research

(C) Extension (D) Evaluation

49. The University Grants Commission was established in the year

(A) 1952 (B) 1957

(C) 1950 (D) 1948

50. Which one of the following educational philosophies had its origin in social, political and educational movements of the time?

(A) Humanistic (B) Analytic

(C) Progressive (D) Behaviouristic

51. Folk High Schools concept was developed by

(A) Pavlov (B) Grundtwig

(C) Piaget (D) John Dewey

52. Millenium Development has

(A) 8 goals (B) 10 goals

(C) 12 goals (D) 16 goals

53. A tentative answer to a proposed enquiry is known as

(A) Inference (B) Appraisal

(C) Conclusion (D) Hypothesis

54. Which one of the following is not a core function of Continuing Education Centre ?

(A) Recreation (B) Personal Interest Promotion

(C) Income Generation (D) Sectarian Teaching

55. Self concept, Readiness to learn, orientation to learn and experience are the features of Adult learners according to

(A) Paulo Friere (B) Malcolm Knowles

(C) Alexander Kapp (D) Chris Dukes

56. Pilot survey is conducted

I. After completion of research

II. In the beginning of the research

III. Before conducting the action research

IV. In the middle of the research Codes:

Codes:

(A) I and IV are correct (B) II and IV are correct

(C) III and IV are correct (D) II and III are correct

57. Sakshar Bharat Mission intends to

I. Make 70 million adults literate.

II. Make 60 million adult womensliterate.

III. Make 30 million adults skilled person.

IV. Make 30 million adult womansliterate.

Codes:

(A) I and II are correct (B) II and III are correct

(C) III and IV are correct (D) II and IV are correct

58. The issues related to extension education and services are

I. Mahila Samakhya II. Extramural

III. Benevolent IV. Smith-lever Act

Codes:

(A) I and II are correct (B) II and III are correct

(C) III and IV are correct (D) II and IV are correct

59. Popular audio-visuals (films) for promotion of adult literary are

1. Padhna-Badhna
2. Akhar Sankranti
3. Angootha Chhap
4. Nai Duniya
5. Agla Kadam

Codes:

(A) 1, 2, 3 are correct
(B) 2, 3, 4 are correct
(C) 3, 4, 5 are correct
(D) 1, 3, 5 are correct

60. The characteristics of Rapid Rural Appraisal are

1. Rapid
2. Inter disciplinary
3. Holistic
4. Territorial
5. Discriminatory

Codes:

(A) 1, 2 and 3 are correct
(B) 2, 3 and 4 are correct
(C) 3, 4 and 5 are correct
(D) 1, 3 and 5 are correct

61. A learning society have the following stages in its development :

1. Autonomous learner
2. Neo literate
3. Post literate
4. Non-literate

Codes:

(A) 1, 2 and 4 are correct
(B) 1, 3 and 4 are correct
(C) 2, 3 and 4 are correct
(D) 1, 2 and 3 are correct

62. Advocates of Radical Philosophy of Education are

1. Paterson
2. Evan Illich
3. Paulo Friere
4. Thomson Codes

Codes:

(A) 1 and 2 are correct
(B) 2 and 3 are correct
(C) 3 and 4 are correct
(D) 2 and 4 are correct

63. Primary motives are

1. Protection
2. Sleep
3. Food
4. Esteem Codes

Codes:

(A) 1 and 2 are correct
(B) 1 and 3 are correct
(C) 2 and 3 are correct
(D) 3 and 4 are correct

64. The component of communication are

1. Rejection
2. Interference
3. Feed back
4. Channel Codes

Codes:

(A) 1 and 2 are correct
(B) 2 and 3 are correct
(C) 3 and 4 are correct
(D) 1 and 4 are correct

65. Arrange the following in order of their placement from basic to higher as per Maslow's postulate:

(A) Esteem
(B) Food
(C) Self Actualisation
(D) Shelter and Safety
(E) Love and Belonging

Codes:

(A) (a) (b) (c) (d) (e)
(B) (b) (c) (d) (a) (e)
(C) (c) (d) (b) (e) (a)
(D) (b) (e) (d) (a) (c)

66. Arrange the stages of curriculum in order of their usage :

(A) Events
(B) Evaluation
(C) Content
(D) Context
(E) Frame work

Codes:

(A) (a) (b) (c) (d) (e)
(B) (a) (e) (c) (b) (a)
(C) (e) (d) (c) (a) (b)
(D) (c) (d) (b) (a) (e)

67. Arrange the stages of planning as per their place from beginning to completion using the correct code :

(A) Furnishing standards of control
(B) Identifying people to work
(C) Setting the work map
(D) Knowing the structure
(E) Kind of leadership needed

Codes:

(A) (b) (c) (e) (d) (a)
(B) (c) (d) (e) (b) (a)
(C) (c) (d) (b) (e) (a)
(D) (d) (b) (c) (e) (a)

68. Arrange the stages of Post Literacy Programme in order of their functioning using the correct code

(A) Remediation
(B) Consolidation
(C) Social development awareness
(D) Guided learning

Codes:

(A) (c) (a) (b) (d)
(B) (a) (c) (d) (b)
(C) (a) (b) (c) (d)
(D) (b) (a) (c) (d)

69. **Arrange the stages of research in order of their being undertaken and choose the answer using code :**

(A) Data Collection
(B) Problem Identification
(C) Sampling
(D) Tabulation and Analysis
(E) Review of earlier work

Codes:

(A) (b) (d) (e) (c) (a)
(B) (b) (e) (c) (a) (d)
(C) (b) (c) (d) (e) (a)
(D) (b) (c) (a) (d) (e)

70. **Arrange the following programmes as they were introduced in Adult Education in ascending order. Use the codes given below :**

(i) National Adult Education Programme
(ii) Mass Programme for Functional Literacy
(iii) Post Literacy
(iv) Total Literacy Campain

Codes:

(A) (i) (ii) (iii) (iv)
(B) (i) (iii) (ii) (iv)
(C) (i) (iii) (iv) (ii)
(D) (i) (iv) (iii) (ii)

71. **Arrange the stages of communication in order of their placement**

(A) Decoding
(B) Environment
(C) Feedback
(D) Source

Codes:

(A) (d) (b) (a) (c)
(B) (d) (b) (c) (a)
(C) (b) (d) (a) (c)
(D) (b) (a) (d) (c)

72. **Arrange the institution of Open University Chronologically :**

(A) Indira Gandhi National Open University
(B) Rajasthan Kota Open University
(C) Andhra Pradesh Open University
(D) Y.B. Chauhan Open University
(e) R. Tandon Uttar Pradesh Open University

Codes:

(A) (b) (a) (c) (d) (e)
(B) (c) (a) (b) (d) (e)
(C) (a) (b) (c) (d) (e)
(D) (c) (b) (a) (d) (e)

73. Arrange the stages of Bloom's 'Affective' learning in its hierarchy :

(A) Receiving
(B) Responding
(C) Valuing
(D) Conceptualising
(E) Organising

Codes:

(A) (a) (b) (c) (d) (e)
(B) (c) (b) (a) (d) (e)
(C) (d) (b) (c) (a) (e)
(D) (b) (d) (c) (A)(e)

74. Arrange the venues of World Conference on Adult Education chronologically :

(A) Germany
(B) Brazil
(C) Canada
(D) Denmark

Codes:

(A) (d) (b) (a) (c)
(B) (d) (c) (b) (a)
(C) (b) (d) (a) (c)
(D) (d) (c) (a) (b)

75. The government of India conducts census after every ten years. The method of research used in this process is

(A) Case study
(B) Developmental study
(C) Survey
(D) Experimental

76. Extension education originated in 1873 in

(A) Cambridge University
(B) Oxford University
(C) Manchester University
(D) Kent University

77. Which one of the following principles is not related to effective communication ?

(A) Clarity
(B) Attention
(C) Co-ordination
(D) Hierarchy

78. Which one of the following states registered negative population growth between 2001-2011 ?

(A) Tamil Nadu
(B) Goa
(C) Karnataka
(D) Nagaland

79. The National Bank of Agriculture and Rural Development (NABARD) was set up in :

(A) 1980
(B) 1981
(C) 1982
(D) 1984

80. The principal aim of the first five year plan was

(A) to check prices
(B) to solve the food problem
(C) to rehabilitate the Indian economy
(D) None of the above

81. E-mail refers to

(A) Electrical mail
(B) Electronic mail
(C) Elastic mail
(D) None of the above

82. Each one teach one was a part of the scheme :

(A) National Adult Education Programme (NAEP)
(B) Area Development Approach (ADA)
(C) Mass Prgramme for Functional Literacy (MPFL)
(D) None of these

83. Green revolution was initiated in

(A) 1947
(B) 1951
(C) 1965
(D) 1972

84. The beneficiaries of continuing education programmes are

(A) Neo-literates
(B) School dropouts
(C) All the members of the community
(D) All of the above

85. Which programme was launched by the prime minister of India on 8th September 2009 ?

(A) Sakshar Bharat Mission
(B) National Literacy Mission
(C) Functional Literacy Compaign
(D) None of the above

86. The medium that has widest reach in India is

(A) Print
(B) Radio
(C) Television
(D) Internet

87. Mandal panchayats were recommended by

(A) Balwant Rai Mehta Committee
(B) Narsimhan Committee
(C) Ashok Mehta Committee
(D) Vengal Rao Committee

88. Which of the following schemes is an effort to improve medical services in rural India?

(A) IRDP
(B) SEWA
(C) Bharat-Nirman
(D) ASHA

89. The Shannon and weaver model of communication is

(A) Modular
(B) Circular
(C) Linear
(D) Non-linear

90. Basic education has another name

(A) Non-formal education
(B) Vocational education
(C) Nai-Talim education
(D) Informal education

91. Which of the following books written by Paulo Friere ?

(A) Decentralized society
(B) Deschooling society
(C) Demoralized society
(D) Democratic society

92. International Women's Day is celebrated on

(A) 8th October
(B) 8th April
(C) 15th March
(D) 8th March

93. Who funded to establish PERCs in India ?

(A) UNESCO
(B) UNFPA
(C) ILO
(D) UNDP

94. 'My life is a message' this is written by whom ?

(A) Rajiv Gandhi
(B) Indira Gandhi
(C) Mahatma Gandhi
(D) Kanakmal Gandhi

95. Which of the following three R's is the concept of life long education is one well suited to our times and conditions ?

(A) Relevance-RelatednessRenewal
(B) Redefine-Reference-Redeploy
(C) Reading-Rereading-Retaining
(D) Reading-Reducing-Retraining

96. Right to Information Act was enforced in which year ?

(A) 2009
(B) 2008
(C) 2007
(D) 2005

97. Which one of the following centres functions as continuing education centres ?

(A) Community centre
(B) Youth centre
(C) Political centre
(D) Cultural centre

98. Quality of life improvement programme is part of which National Programme ?

(A) Adult literacy programme
(B) Post literacy programme
(C) Continuing education programme
(D) Basic literacy programme

99. Continuing education provides

(A) Second chance to drop-outs
(B) Learning opportunities affer basic literacy
(C) Skill development guidance and training
(D) All the above

100. Choose the correct Institution, which publishes journal of adult education.

(A) I.U.A.C.E. (B) I.A.E.A.

(C) I.C.S.S.R. (D) I.C.A.R.

101. Which of the following State was motivated to fight against arrack shop through adult education centre ?

(A) Kerala (B) Andhra Pradesh

(C) Tamil Nadu (D) Karnataka

102. Who was the first education minister of India after Independence ?

(A) Dr. Radha Krishnan (B) Dr. Zakir Hussain

(C) Maulana Azad (D) Dr. Rajendra Prasad

103. Which of the following centre provides training and reading materials for literacy and continuing education programmes ?

(A) UGC (B) DCC

(C) TLC (D) SRC

104. What is the main aim of the Sarva Shiksha Abhiyan, is one of the flagship programmes of Government of India ?

(A) to bring all the children who are not going to school to enrol them and teach them.

(B) to bring all the children to provide food and accommodation.

(C) to bring all the children who are going to schools

(D) to bring all the children to play and dance

105. Purpose of training is

(A) To develop human qualities (B) To develop reading habits

(C) To develop healthy habits (D) To develops writing habits

106. Meaning of workers participation in management is

(A) sharing the decision making power

(B) sharing the marketing policies

(C) Sharing the profit part

(D) Sharing the financial involvement

107. Meaning of motivation is

(A) This is a process (B) This is a result

(C) This is a need (D) This is a search

108. Objectives of questionnaire in social research is

(A) To collect authentic data (B) To find out authentic result

(C) To find out authentic source (D) To find out authentic process

109. Curriculum development is a need of
(A) Training (B) Teaching
(C) Research (D) All above

110. Population density is related with
(A) Population and resources (B) Population and roads
(C) Population and land (D) Population and politics

111. Population education includes
(A) Quality of like improvement programme
(B) Quality of skill improvement programme
(C) Quality of research improvement programme
(D) Quality of teaching improvement programme

112. Padagogy is a teaching techniques to
(A) Teaching adults (B) Teaching women
(C) Teaching childrens (D) Teaching teachers

113. Vocational education focused on
(A) Knowledge improvement (B) Life status improvement
(C) Skill improvement (D) Health improvement

114. Agricultural production improvement is a result of
(A) Economic factors (B) Social factors
(C) Technological factors (D) Natural factors

115. Environmental pollution is a result of
(A) Uncontrolled human activities (B) Natural activities
(C) Uncontrolled social activities (D) Increase poverty

116. National Council for Teacher Education was established in
(A) 17 Aug., 1994 (B) 17 Aug., 1995
(C) 17 Aug., 1996 (D) 17 Aug., 1997

117. Primary data collection is a
(A) Personal source (B) Documentary source
(C) Biographic source (D) Structural source

118. Arrange the following activities of the department of adult continuing education and extension in order by which these programmes were implemented in Indian Universities by using the Codes:
(i) Field out reach (ii) Population education
(iii) Continuing education (iv) Eradication of illiteracy

Codes:

(A) (i), (ii), (iii), (iv) (B) (iv), (i), (iii), (ii)

(C) (ii), (i), (iii), (iv) (D) (iii), (ii), (iv), (i)

119. Arrange the following programmes that were introduced by Government of India in ascending order by using the Codes:

(i) Post literacy programme (ii) Total literacy programme

(iii) National Adult Education Programme (iv) National literacy mission

Codes:

(A) (iii), (ii), (i), (iv) (B) (i), (ii), (iii), (iv)

(C) (iv), (i), (ii), (iii) (D) (ii), (i), (iii), (iv)

120. Arrange the following in the order of Maslow's hierarchical needs by using the codes given below

(i) Love and belonging (ii) Shelter and safety

(iii) Food (iv) Self esteem

Codes:

(A) (i), (ii), (iii), (iv) (B) (iii), (ii), (i), (iv)

(C) (ii), (i), (iii), (iv) (D) (iv), (ii), (iii), (i)

121. Arrange the following steps in research in proper order by using the codes given below:

(i) Analysis (ii) Tools preparation

(iii) Problem identification (iv) Tabulation and classification of data

Codes:

(A) (iv), (ii), (i), (iii) (B) (iii), (ii), (iv), (i)

(C) (i), (ii), (iii), (iv) (D) (ii), (iii), (i), (iv)

122. Arrange the following in the order in which they appeared by using the codes given below :

(i) Key resource persons (ii) Village level co-ordinator

(iii) Volunteer (iv) Resource persons

Codes:

(A) (iv), (ii), (i), (iii) (B) (ii), (i), (iii), (iv)

(C) (i), (ii), (iii), (iv) (D) (iii), (ii), (iv), (i)

123. Arrange the following open universities by year wise their establishment. Use the codes given below :

(i) Nalanda State Open University (ii) Kota Open University

(iii) Bhoj Open University

(iv) Indira Gandhi National Open University

Codes:

(A) (i), (iii), (ii), (iv)

(B) (ii), (i), (iii), (iv)

(C) (iv), (ii), (i), (iii)

(D) (iii), (ii), (i), (iv)

124 Arrange the steps in writing report in ascending order by using the codes given below:

(i) Interpretation of data

(ii) Sampling technique

(iii) Objective

(iv) Hypothesis

Codes:

(A) (ii), (i), (iii), (iv)

(B) (iii), (iv), (ii), (i)

(C) (i), (ii), (iii), (iv)

(D) (iv), (iii), (ii), (i)

125. Which of the following is not the objective of universalization of primary education ?

(A) Universal Provision

(B) Universal Supervision

(C) Universal Enrolment

(D) Universal Relention

126. One of the social objectives of extension education is

(A) Restoration of caste and culture harmony

(B) Increase income

(C) Training of artisans

(D) None of the above

127. Provision of 'Right to Equality' has been incorporated in Indian Constitution under the articles

(A) 16 to 20

(B) 15 to 19

(C) 14 to 18

(D) 13 to 17

128. Which of the following is an example of a community ?

(A) Family

(B) Marriage

(C) Village

(D) Refugee camp

129. As per 2011 census (Final data) the literacy rates in rural and urban areas of the country stands at

(A) 70.3 per cent and 83.1 per cent respectively

(B) 67.8 per cent and 84.1 per cent respectively

(C) 65.3 per cent and 82.6 per cent respectively

(D) 69.2 per cent and 78.9 per cent respectively

130. 'Nirman Bharat Abhiyan' Yojana is associated with
(A) Development of villages
(B) Community toilets in slum areas
(C) Construction of houses for low income groups
(D) None of the above

131. Adult learning process includes :
I. From whole to part
II. From simple to complex
III. From direct to indirect
IV. From invisible to visible

Codes:
(A) I, II, IV are correct
(B) I, II, III are correct
(C) II, III, IV are correct
(D) I, III, IV are correct

132. The main objective of "Education for all" is to be
(A) Promote to learning society
(B) Promote to economic development
(C) Promote to health facilities development
(D) Promote to child education

133. Main objective of the National Policy on Women Empowerment 2001 was
(A) Women's progress development and empowerment
(B) Education for women
(C) Economic development of women
(D) Health facilities development for women

134. Education technology is
(A) use of books
(B) use of material
(C) use of learning theories
(D) use of teaching techniques

135. Training is treated as
I. Two sided process
II. One sided process
III. Systematic process
IV. Planned process

Choose right code given below :
(A) I, II, IV are correct
(B) II, III, IV are correct
(C) I, II, III are correct
(D) I, III, IV are correct

136. Population education deals with
I. Death rate
II. Population situation
III. Quality of life
IV. Economic growth

Choose right code given below :

(A) I, II, IV are correct
(B) I, II, III are correct
(C) II, III, IV are correct
(D) I, III, IV are correct

137. Which of the following were included in five technology missions in 1988 ?

I. Immunization
II. Literacy
III. Energy
IV. Communication

Choose right code given below :

(A) I, II, III are correct
(B) II, III, IV are correct
(C) I, II, IV are correct
(D) I, III, IV are correct

138. Which of the following components are essential in any type of communication ?

I. A communicator
II. A massage
III. A sentence
IV. A receiver

Choose right code given below :

(A) I, III, IV are correct
(B) I, II, III are correct
(C) II, III, IV are correct
(D) I, II, IV are correct

139. The four pillars of 'Sakshar Bharat' are

I. Functional Literacy
II. Moral Education
III. Basic Education
IV. Vocational Skill Development
V. Continuing Education Programmes

Choose right code given below :

(A) I, III, IV, V are correct
(B) I, II, III, IV are correct
(C) II, III, IV, V are correct
(D) I, II, IV, V are correct

140. Pilot survey is conducted

I. After finishing research
II. In the beginning of a research
III. In the middle of a research
IV. Before conducting of a research

Codes:

(A) I and II are correct
(B) II and III are correct
(C) III and IV are correct
(D) II and IV are correct

141. Which of the following are more closer to extension education ?

I. Need based education

II. Formal education

III. Flexible education

IV. Multidimensional education

V. School education

Codes:

(A) I, III and IV are correct
(B) I, IV and V are correct
(C) II, III and V are correct
(D) V, I and II are correct

142. Quality education means

I. Improvement of education system

II. Improvement of teacher students relationship

III. Improvement of transport facility to all

IV. Improvement of teaching technology

Codes:

(A) I, III and IV are correct
(B) I, II and IV are correct
(C) II, I and III are correct
(D) I, II and III are correct

143. Skills of a leader include

I. Humanistic skills
II. Conceptual skills
III. Employment skills
IV. Efficiency skills

Codes:

(A) I and III are correct
(B) I and II are correct
(C) III and IV are correct
(D) II and III are correct

144. Characteristics of adult learner include

I. Remediation attitude
II. Motivation attitude
III. Experience attitude
IV. Indolence attitude

Codes:

(A) I and II are correct
(B) II and IV are correct
(C) III and IV are correct
(D) I and IV are correct

145. Arrange the following in correct order of their implementation.

(i) MNP
(ii) Community Development
(iii) IRDP
(iv) Total literacy campaign

Codes:

(A) (ii), (iii), (i), (iv) (B) (i), (ii), (iv), (iii)

(C) (iv), (ii), (i), (iii) (D) (iii), (iv), (ii), (i)

146. Arrange the following programmes in order of their implementation.

(i) Saakshar Bharat (ii) CEC

(iii) PLC (iv) TLC

Codes:

(A) (i), (ii), (iii), (iv) (B) (ii), (i), (iii), (iv)

(C) (iii), (ii), (i), (iv) (D) (iv), (iii), (ii), (i)

147. Arrange the following in order they appeared :

(i) Non formal education (ii) Extension education

(iii) Continuing education (iv) Social education

Codes:

(A) (i), (ii), (iii), (iv) (B) (iv), (i), (iii), (ii)

(C) (iii), (ii), (iv), (i) (D) (ii), (iii), (i), (iv)

148. Arrange the following stages of communication in order of the best sequence :

(i) Receiver (ii) Source

(iii) Coding (iv) Decoding

Codes:

(A) (i), (ii), (iv), (iii) (B) (iii), (i), (ii), (iv)

(C) (ii), (iii), (vi), (i) (D) (iv), (iii), (ii), (i)

149. Arrange the following as they appeared in ascending order by using the code given below :

(i) Open Schooling (ii) Adult literacy centre

(iii) Continuing education centre (iv) Post literacy centre

Codes:

(A) (i), (ii), (iii), (iv) (B) (ii), (i), (iii), (iv)

(C) (ii), (iv), (iii), (i) (D) (iv), (iii), (ii), (i)

150. Arrange the following programme implemented in order by using the code given below :

(i) FFLP (ii) MPFL

(iii) NAEP (iv) NLM

Codes:

(A) (ii), (i), (iii), (iv) (B) (iii), (ii), (i), (iv)

(C) (i), (ii), (iii), (iv) (D) (iv), (iii), (i), (ii)

151. Arrange the following media in order in which they are popularly used in adult education. Use the codes given below :

(i) Radio (ii) Folk arts, Kalajatha

(iii) Print media (iv) Television

Codes:

(A) (iv), (ii), (iii), (i) (B) (ii), (i), (iii), (iv)

(C) (i), (ii), (iii), (iv) (D) (iii), (ii), (i), (iv)

152. Put the correct sequence of Hierarchical theory of needs :

(i) Social needs (ii) Self actualization

(iii) Physiological needs (iv) Basic need

Codes:

(A) (i), (ii), (iii), (iv) (B) (ii), (iv), (i), (iii)

(C) (iv), (i), (ii), (iii) (D) (iv), (iii), (i), (ii)

153. Choose the correct sequence of growth of educational and communication technologies.

(i) Visual (ii) Audio-visual

(iii) Interactive (iv) Audio

Codes:

(A) (i), (ii), (iii), (iv) (B) (ii), (iii), (iv), (i)

(C) (iv), (ii), (i), (iii) (D) (iii), (iv), (i), (ii)

154. Arrange the following management steps in order by using the code given below:

(i) Implementation (ii) Planning

(iii) Evaluation (iv) Monitoring

Codes:

(A) (i), (ii), (iii), (iv) (B) (ii), (i), (iv), (iii)

(C) (iii), (ii), (i), (iv) (D) (i), (iii), (iv), (ii)

155. Andragogy is

(A) Teaching children to learn

(B) Making adults literate

(C) Teaching adults to learn

(D) Arts and Science of helping adults to learn

156. Pedagogy means

(A) Advising children (B) Talking with children
(C) Leading children (D) Making the children to learn

157. "Where the mind is without fear, and the head is held high, where the word is not broken up into fragments by narrow domestic walls" said by

(A) Rajaji (B) Rabindranath Tagore
(C) Mahatma Gandhi (D) Bharathidasan

158. Pedagogy can also be thought of as

(A) Principal centered (B) Department centered
(C) Teacher centered (D) Playing centered

159. The capacities needed by the every thinking adult are developing by ________

(A) Liberal education (B) Moderate education
(C) Restricted education (D) Compulsory education

160. Andragogy was originated in

(A) Europe in 1950's (B) America in 1970's
(C) Both (A) and (B) are correct (D) Both (A) and (B) are incorrect

161. ________ mind development is emphasized by the Adult Education Liberal Philosophy.

(A) Intellectual power (B) External event
(C) Basic needs (D) Physical requirements

162. The primary concern of behaviourism is

(A) Internal values behaviour (B) Observable behaviour
(C) Living behaviour (D) All the above are correct.

163. The inability of reading and writing associated with the persons is a condition of

(A) Meagre literacy (B) Illiteracy
(C) Literacy (D) Partial literacy

164. As per Census of India 2011 the literacy rate of India was

(A) 75.00 per cent (B) 74.04 per cent
(C) 79.50 per cent (D) 74.09 per cent

165. The distance mode of school education is provided by

(A) IGNOU (B) NIOS
(C) UGC (D) DEC

166. Continuing Education Programme (CEP) is being organized in the form of

(A) Open and In-house programme
(B) Close and Open programme
(C) Both (A) and (B) are correct
(D) Both (A) and (B) are wrong

167. The first district was declared as totally literate district in India.

(A) Thiruvananthapuram
(B) Kanyakumari
(C) Kottayam
(D) Ernakulam

168. The Folk School was started in

(A) United Kingdom
(B) Germany
(C) China
(D) Denmark

169. Total literacy campaign was aimed at

(A) to improve andragogy
(B) to emphasis on learning outcome
(C) to introduce child vaccination
(D) to generate awareness

170. One of the major programmes under Continuing Education Scheme is

(A) Education for all
(B) Equivalency programme
(C) Income Oriented Programme
(D) Environmental Education Programme

171. Which expansion for SRC is correct ?

(A) State Research Centre
(B) State Reorganisation Centre
(C) State Rehabilitation Centre
(D) State Resource Centre

172. The Department of Adult Continuing Education and Extension has been renamed as Lifelong Learning and Extension from which plan period ?

(A) XI Plan
(B) IX Plan
(C) X Plan
(D) XII Plan

173. The Indian Adult Education Association was started in which year

(A) 1939
(B) 1839
(C) 1933
(D) 1937

174. What are the elements in order to make curriculum ?

(A) Philosophical
(B) Context
(C) Content
(D) All the above

175. Evaluation is an important process of making

(A) Personal Assessment
(B) Decision about achievements
(C) Expectations and Effectiveness
(D) All the above

176. Arrange the following steps in Research process by using the following Codes:

(i) Decide on a topic
(ii) Determine the information requirements
(iii) Collection the information
(iv) Analyse and evaluate the information

Codes:

(A) (i), (ii), (iii), (iv)
(B) (iii), (iv), (i), (ii)
(C) (iv), (iii), (ii), (i)
(D) (ii), (i), (iii), (iv)

177. Arrange the following historical events Adult Education Development in USA with the help of codes given below:

(i) The National Education Association (NEA) created by the Department of Adult Education.
(ii) American Association of Adult Education (A.A.A.E)
(iii) The Federal Emergency Relief Administration (FERA)
(iv) The Works Progress Administration (WPA) and FERA

Codes:

(A) (iii), (iv), (i), (ii)
(B) (iv), (iii), (ii), (i)
(C) (i), (ii), (iii), (iv)
(D) (ii), (i), (iv), (iii)

178. Arrange the following provisions of adult education programmes on the basis of meaningful order with the help of codes given below :

(i) Adult Education in India was provided at Night schools, these are situated in almost all the Indian cities and villages. The provision for imparting education has been made at night because most of the people are engaged during the day.
(ii) Apart from the Night schools, the government of India had also setup some libraries so that the adults can study more to become educated, not just literate.
(iii) The government launched the programmes of Social Education, under the Community Development in 1952 as part of the first Five Year Plan.
(iv) The government has launched the programme called National Literacy Mission (NLM) for spreading adult education in India.

Codes:

(A) (iii), (iv), (i), (ii) (B) (i), (ii), (iii), (iv)

(C) (iv), (iii), (ii), (i) (D) (ii), (i), (iv), (iii)

179. Arrange the following Adult Education Programmes on the basis of its period of introduction by using the codes given below :

(i) Social Education (ii) Gram Shikshan Muhim

(iii) Farmers' functional literacy project (iv) Workers' education

Codes:

(A) (iii), (iv), (i), (ii) (B) (iv), (iii), (ii), (i)

(C) (i), (ii), (iii), (iv) (D) (ii), (i), (iv), (iii)

180. Arrange the Participatory Research Methods by its order of development by using the codes given below :

(i) Participatory Rural Appraisal (PRA)

(ii) Participant Observer (PO)

(iii) Participatory Action Research (PAR)

(iv) Rapid Rural Appraisal (RRA)

Codes:

(A) (iii), (iv), (i), (ii) (B) (iv), (iii), (ii), (i)

(C) (ii), (iv), (i), (iii) (D) (ii), (i), (iv), (iii)

181. Identify the order in which four types of Media come into view in India by using the codes given below :

(i) Print, Radio, Television, Film (ii) Radio, Print, Film, Television

(iii) Television, Film, Print, Radio (iv) Film, Print, Radio, Televisio

Codes:

(A) (i), (ii), (iii), (iv) (B) (ii), (i), (iv), (iii)

(C) (i), (iii), (ii), (iv) (D) (iv), (i), (iii), (ii)

182. Arrange the order of events happened in the Paulo Freire life by using the codes given below:

(i) Paulo Freire enrolled at law school at the University of Recife.

(ii) Freire was appointed Director of the Department of Education and Culture of the Social Service in the State of Pernambuco.

(iii) Freire was appointed Director of the Department of Cultural Extension of Recife University.

(iv) Freire was imprisoned as a traitor for 70 days.

Codes:

(A) (iii), (i), (ii), (iv) (B) (i), (ii), (iii), (iv)

(C) (ii), (iv), (i), (iii) (D) (i), (iv), (iii), (ii)

183. Arrange the literacy programmes in India in order by using the codes given below :

(i) Total Literacy Campaigns (TLC)

(ii) Sakshar Bharat Programme (SBP)

(iii) Continuing Education Programme (CEP)

(iv) Post Literacy Campaigns (PLC)

Codes:

(A) (i), (ii), (iii), (iv) (B) (iii), (i), (ii), (iv)

(C) (iv), (ii), (iii), (i) (D) (i), (iv), (iii), (ii)

184. Arrange the following commissions in the order in which they appeared. Use the codes given below :

(i) Radha Krishnan Commission (ii) Mudaliyar Commission

(iii) Kothari Commission (iv) Hunter Commission

Codes:

(A) (i), (ii), (iii), (iv) (B) (ii), (i), (iii), (iv)

(C) (iv), (i), (ii), (iii) (D) (i), (iii), (ii), (iv)

185. Arrange the following steps of management in the order in which they should by using the codes given below :

(i) Planning (ii) Organising

(iii) Implementing (iv) Monitoring and Evaluation

Codes:

(A) (iv), (i), (ii), (iii) (B) (i), (ii), (iii), (iv)

(C) (ii), (iii), (iv), (i) (D) (iii), (ii), (i), (iv)

186. Arrange the following in order of their introduction:

(i) NPOP (ii) NPE

(iii) POA (iv) TLC

Codes:

(A) (ii), (iv), (iii), (i) (B) (i), (iv), (iii), (ii)

(C) (iv), (i), (iii), (ii) (D) (ii), (iii), (iv), (i)

187. Arrange the following in the order which they appeared. Use the codes given below:

(i) Mahabharat (ii) Geeta

(iii) Ramayan (iv) Kamaya

Codes:

(A) (i), (ii), (iv), (iii) (B) (iii), (i), (ii), (iv)

(C) (ii), (i), (iv), (iii) (D) (iv), (i), (iii), (ii)

188. Arrange the following tasks of the Department of Adult Continuing Education and Extension in the order which they are being implemented with the help of given codes.

(i) Teaching/Training (ii) Extension work

(iii) Field out reach (iv) Research work

Codes:

(A) (iv), (iii), (ii), (i) (B) (i), (ii), (iii), (iv)

(C) (iii), (ii), (i), (iv) (D) (ii), (iv), (iii), (i)

189. Arrange the following in the order in which they appeared with the help given Codes:

(i) University Grants Commission

(ii) Population Education Club

(iii) Population Educators

(iv) Population Education

Codes:

(A) (i), (ii), (iii), (iv) (B) (iv), (iii), (ii), (i)

(C) (ii), (i), (iii), (iv) (D) (i), (iv), (ii), (iii)

190. What are the correct informations about literacy programme of Vietnam ?

I. Ho Chi Minh

II. Literacy rate more than 90 per cent

III. Learning in short term activity

IV. Popular learning centre

Codes:

(A) I, II are correct (B) II, IV are correct

(C) III, IV are correct (D) I, IV are correct

191. Arrange the stages of group formation as per their occurrence from initial to last:

(A) Performing (B) Storming

(C) Norming (D) Forming

(E) Informing

Codes:

(A) (B) (C) (D)(A)(E) (B) (E) (B) (D) (C) (A)

(C) (D) (E) (B) (C) (A) (D) (D) (B) (E) (C) (A)

192. Arrange the stages of agricultural growth in part as per from initial to final stage :

(A) Sedentary cultivation (B) Commercial cultivation

(C) Shifting cultivation (D) Subsistence cultivation

Codes:

(A) (D) (B) (C) (A) (B) (A) (B) (D) (C)

(C) (C) (A) (D) (B) (D) (A) (C) (D) (B)

193. Arrange the following countries in order of their hosting the World Conference of Adult Education ?

(A) Canada (B) France

(C) Germany (D) Denmark

Codes:

(A) (D) (C) (B) (A) (B) (D) (B) (C) (A)

(C) (D) (A) (B) (C) (D) (A) (B) (C) (d)

194. Arrange the following stages of staffing in order of their use :

(A) Induction (B) Screening

(C) Interview (D) Application

Codes:

(A) (D) (C) (A) (B) (B) (D) (B) (C) (A)

(C) (D) (A) (B) (C) (D) (D) (C) (B) (A)

195. Arrange the following programme of education according to their implementation :

(A) DPEP (B) POA

(C) NPE (D) Mahila Samakhya

Codes:

(A) (A) (B) (C) (D) (B) (D) (C) (A) (B)

(C) (C) (D) (B) (A) (D) (B) (C) (D) (A)

196. Third important dimension of higher education is

(A) Sports (B) Research

(C) Extension (D) Teaching

197. Basic concept of extension education is

(A) Dissemination of useful information

(B) Development of positive attitude

(C) Development of life skills

(D) All the above

198. ZSS stands for

(A) Zila Sewa Samiti (B) Zila Sadbhawna Samiti

(C) Zila Samanwaya Samiti (D) Zila Saksharta Samiti

199. Sakshar Bharat Mission was launched on

(A) 8th March, 2008 (B) 2nd October, 2008

(C) 8th September, 2009 (D) 2nd October, 2009

200. According to 2011 Census, the literacy rate of India is now

(A) 62 percent (B) 74 percent

(C) 80 percent (D) 82 percent

201. Millenium Development Goals have

(A) 8 goals (B) 10 goals

(C) 12 goals (D) 20 goals

202. New name of Shramik Vidyapeeth is

(A) Labour Education Group (B) Jana Shikshan Sansthan

(C) Vanasthali Vidyapeet (D) None of the above

203. Folk High School were created on the concept of

(A) Piaget (B) Paulo Friere

(C) John Dewey (D) N.F.S. Grundtwig

204. 'How Adults Learn' book was written by

(A) Alan Rogers (B) Malcolm Knowles

(C) Roby Kidd (D) Peter Jarvis

205. Sakshar Bharat programme have aimed to impart literacy to how many people?

(A) 40 million (B) 50 million

(C) 60 million (D) 70 million

206. Which of the following are more closer to extension education ?

I. Need based II. Formal

III. Flexible IV. Multidimensional

V. Teacher oriented

Codes:

(A) I, II and III
(B) I, II and IV
(C) I, III and IV
(D) II, IV and V

207. Adult Education includes

I. Functional Literacy

II. Social Awareness

III. Women Studies and Research

IV. Skill Development

Codes:

(A) I, II and IV are correct
(B) I, II and III are correct
(C) I, III and IV are correct
(D) II, III and IV are correct

208. The process of social research involves the following steps :

I. Collection of data

II. Statement of objectives

III. Selecting the problem

IV. Methodology

V. Analysis and interpretation of data

VI. Reporting the results

Codes:

(A) III, II, IV, I, V, VI
(B) I, III, II, V, VI, IV
(C) III, II, IV, I, VI, V
(D) III, II, V, I, VI, IV

209. Adults learn

I. From whole to part

II. From simple to complex

III. From direct to indirect

IV. From invisible to visible

Codes:

(A) I, II, IV are correct
(B) I, II, III are correct
(C) II, III, IV are correct
(D) I, III, IV are correct

210. Pilot Survey is conducted :

I. After finishing a research

II. In the beginning of a research

III. In the middle of a research

IV. Before conducting a research

Codes:

(A) I and II
(B) II and III
(C) III and IV
(D) II and IV

211. UNESCO World Adult Education Conference were held at

I. India | II. China
III. Brazil | IV. Germany

Codes:

(A) I and III | (B) II and III
(C) III and IV | (D) II and IV

212. Continuing Education Center provides services :

I. Equivalency | II. Secondary School Services
III. Information Window | IV. Senior School Certificate

Codes:

(A) I and II | (B) I and III
(C) I and IV | (D) II and IV

213. A tentative answer to a proposed research enquiry is

I. Hypothesis | II. Inference
III. Generalisation | IV. Hunch

Codes:

(A) I and II | (B) II and III
(C) I and IV | (D) II and IV

214. The programme in the National Literacy Missions were :

I. Remedial Education | II. Para Legal Training
III. Human Rights Education | IV. Mopping up operation

Codes

(A) I and II | (B) II and III
(C) I and IV | (D) II and IV

215. Alwyin Toffler wrote which of the books ?

I. Pedagogy of the Oppressed | II. Deschooling Society
III. Third Wave | IV. Future Shock

Codes:

(A) I and II | (B) I and III
(C) II and III | (D) III and IV

216. Which agencies are provider of Nonformal Education?

I. NIOS | II. IGNOU
III. NICD | IV. IIMC

Codes:

(A) I and II (B) II and III

(C) I and III (D) II and IV

217. Factors of Learning are :

I. Engagement II. Activity

III. Repulsion IV. Withdrawl

Codes:

(A) I and III (B) II and III

(C) III and IV (D) I and IV

218. Characteristics of adult learner include :

I. Remediation II. Motivation

III. Experience IV. Indolence

Codes:

(A) I and II (B) II and III

(C) III and IV (D) I and I

219. Arrange the following stages of communication in order of the best sequence, use codes given below :

(A) Message (B) Channel

(C) Source (D) Receiver

Codes:

(A) (C) (A) (B) (D) (B) (A) (C) (D) (B)

(C) (C) (A) (D) (B) (D) (D) (A) (B) (C)

220. Arrange the following functionaries of total literacy campaign in respect of their role from lower to higher, use the codes given below :

(A) Resource Person (B) Master Trainer

(C) Volunteer (D) Key Resource Person

Codes:

(A) (D) (A) (B) (C) (B) (A) (B) (C) (D)

(C) (C) (B) (A) (D) (D) (B) (C) (D) (A)

221. Arrange the steps of extension programme planning in which they are performed. Use the codes given below :

(A) Collection of Data (B) Analysis of Situation

(C) Determination of Objectives (D) Identification of Problems

Codes:

(A) (A) (B) (C) (D)
(B) (A) (B) (D) (C)
(C) (B) (A) (C) (D)
(D) (C) (A) (B) (D)

222. Arrange the following programmes/schemes according to the year of their launch, use codes given below :

(A) Jawahar Rojgar Yojna
(B) DPEP
(C) Revised 20 point programme
(D) MNREGA

Codes:

(A) (B) (C) (D) (A)
(B) (C) (A) (D) (B)
(C) (C) (A) (B) (D)
(D) (A) (C) (B) (D)

223. Arrange the stages of research in order of their being performed :

(A) Universe
(B) Statement of the problem
(C) Hypothesis testing
(D) Sampling

Codes:

(A) (A) (D) (C) (b)
(B) (A) (B) (D) (C)
(C) (B) (A) (C) (d)
(D) (B) (A) (D) (C)

224. Arrange the stages of communication in correct order:

(A) Noise
(B) Feedback
(C) Source
(D) Channel

Codes:

(A) (C) (D) (A) (B)
(B) (C) (D) (B) (A)
(C) (C) (B) (D) (A)
(D) (D) (C) (A) (B)

225. Arrange the following programme in order of their implementation :

(A) National Extension Service
(B) National Adult Education Program
(C) Mahila Samakhya
(D) National Literacy Mission

Codes:

(A) (A) (B) (C) (D)
(B) (A) (C) (B) (D)
(C) (A) (D) (C) (B)
(D) (A) (C) (D) (B)

226. Arrange the popular hierarchies in behaviourist learning

(A) Insightful learning
(B) Social learning
(C) Trial and Error
(D) Conditioning

Codes:

(A) (A) (B) (C) (d)
(B) (B) (C) (D) (A)
(C) (C) (A) (B) (D)
(D) (D) (C) (A) (B)

227. Liberal philosophy of Adult Education stresses development in

(A) Vocational skills
(B) Intellectual power
(C) Physical power
(D) Empowerment

228. Behaviourism is primarily concerned with

(A) Learning
(B) Observable Behaviour
(C) Personality
(D) Intelligence

229. Andragogy as a study of adult learning originated from

(A) America in 1970's
(B) Europe in 1950's
(C) Asia in 1980's
(D) Latin America in 1960's

230. Andragogy is known as

(A) Science of teaching children
(B) Arts and science of helping adults to learn
(C) Science of behavioural study of adult
(D) None of the above

231. Inability to read, write and with simple calculations of a person is enumerated as

(A) Literate
(B) Uneducated
(C) Semi-literate
(D) Illiterate

232. "Where the mind is without fear, and the head is held high, where the world is not brokenup into fragments by narrow domestic walls" was said by

(A) Arbindo
(B) Tagore
(C) Gandhi
(D) Patel

233. The Distance Mode of School Education is provided by

(A) IGNOU
(B) DEC
(C) NIOS
(D) UGC

234. TLC was launched primarily to

(A) Eradicate illiteracy
(B) Child vaccination
(C) Eradicate child labour
(D) Empower women folk

235. The expansion of SRC is

(A) State Reorganisation Committee
(B) State Reorganisation Commission

(C) State Research Centre

(D) State Resource Centre

236. is the audio-visual aid

(A) Poster (B) Radio

(C) Film (D) None of the above

237. The outreach activities has led to

(A) University-community interaction

(B) Increased enrolment of students

(C) Democratization of Institution

(D) All the above

238. NBT stands for

(A) National Bank for Tribes (B) National Book Trust

(C) National Bureau of Trustees (D) National Bus Transport

239. Seva Mandir, which is based at Udaipur of Rajasthan State, is a

(A) Governmental Institution (B) Bank

(C) NGO (D) Quasi Govt. Institution

240. A research study intended to study the relative effectiveness of two medicines for fever can be labelled as

(A) Experimental study (B) Qualitative study

(C) Quantitative study (D) None of the above

241. The first district was declared as totally literate district in India

(A) Elluru (B) Kottayam

(C) Ernakulam (D) Kanyakumari

242. Maulana Azad, the first Education Minister of India, re-named the various schemes of Adult Education as

(A) Further Education (B) Social Education

(C) Non-formal Education (D) Out of School Education

243. The National Policy of Education was approved by the Government of India in the year

(A) 1986 (B) 1985

(C) 1984 (D) 1983

244. The major function of the SRC is

(A) Teaching and Research

(B) Distributing Funds to NGOs

(C) Training and Materials Development

(D) None of the above

245. The basic feature of the TLC is

(A) Centre based approach (B) No time frame

(C) Voluntarism and area specific (D) None of the above

246. Concurrent evaluation will be taken up only

(A) Before launching the programme (B) During the programme

(C) End of the programme (D) None of the above

247. The concept of Folk School is connected with

(A) Germany (B) United Kindom

(C) China (D) Denmark

248. "Education for All" is sponsored by

(A) UNESCO (B) UNO

(C) UNICEF (D) ILO

249. The proposed nomenclature of the 'Dept of Adult and Continuing Education an Extension' is

(A) Continuing Education and Extension

(B) Lifelong Learning and Extension

(C) Lifelong Learning

(D) Extension Education

250. LEAP stands for

(A) Lifelong Education and Awareness Project

(B) Lifelong Education and Action Programme

(C) Lifelong Education and Action Project

(D) Lifelong Education and Awareness Programme

251. Assertion (A): Vocational education plays a crucial role in the socio and economic development of the nation.

Reason (R): Vocational skills promote productivity

(A) (A) is true but (R) is false (B) (A) and (R) are true

(C) (A) is false but (R) is true (D) (A) and (R) are false

252. Assertion (A): The possible motives for undertaking research is to get a research degree along with its consequential benefits.

Reason (R): The UGC provides research fellowships for promoting research.

(A) (A) and (R) are true
(B) (A) and (r) are not true
(C) (A) is true
(D) (r) is not true

253. Assertion (A): Collection of data can be done through observation techniques.

Reason (R): Collection of data can be done even without using a tool.

(A) (A) and (R) are true
(B) (A) is false but (R) is true
(C) (A) is true but (R) is false
(D) (A) and (R) are false

254. Assertion (A): Lifelong learning has a provision for using non-formal and formal learning.

Reason (R): Lifelong learning is not a systematic study.

(A) (A) and (R) are true
(B) (R) is true but (A) is not true
(C) (A) and (R) are not true
(D) (A) is true but (R) is not true

255. Assertion (A): Learning needs of Adults from rural, tribal and urban areas are same.

Reason (R): Adults of various regions are in the same age group with similar needs.

(A) (A) is true
(B) (A) and (R) are false
(C) (R) is true
(D) (A) and (R) are true

256. Assertion (A): Extension Education accelerate the pace of rural development

Reason (R): Extension Education programmes empower the rural masses.

(A) Both (A) and (R) are true
(B) (A) is true but (R) is not true
(C) (A) and (R) are not true
(D) (A) is not true but (R) is true

257. Assertion (A): The human resource development of the country depends upon the level of education possessed by its population.

Reason (R): Half of the women in India are illiterates.

(A) (A) and (R) are not true
(B) (A) is not true but (R) is true
(C) (A) is true but (R) is not true
(D) (A) and (R) are true

258. Assertion (A): UGC has established PERCs in Indian Universities for promoting population consciousness among youth.

Reason (R): Awareness need to be created among youth about the population explosion.

(A) (A) is correct but (R) is not correct
(B) (A) and (R) are not correct
(C) (A) is not correct but (R) is correct
(D) (A) and (R) are correct

259. Assertion (A): The Teaching/Learning materials in adult education should be need based and area specific.

Reason (R): The Teaching/Learning materials have no role in retaining the adult learning's in the literacy centres.

(A) (A) and (R) are true
(B) (A) is true but (R) is false
(C) (A) and (R) are false
(D) (A) is not true but (R) is true

260. Assertion (A): Monitoring is generally not intended to determine the impact of the programme.

Reason (R): Monitoring is required to know the progress of the programme

(A) (A) is false but (R) is true
(B) (A) and (R) are false
(C) (A) is true but (R) is not true
(D) (A) and (R) are true

261. Assertion (A): SRCs play a prominent role in preparation and distribution of Teaching/Learning materials.

Reason (R): SRCs provide technical support to all the Adult Education Programme.

(A) (A) is true but (R) is not true
(B) (A) is not true but (R) is true
(C) Both (A) and (R) are true
(D) Both (A) and (r) are not true

262. Assertion (A): Exploration of natural resources is one of the reasons for environmental degradation

Reason (R): Natural resources are being used extensively.

(A) Both (A) and (R) are not true
(B) (A) is true but (R) is not true
(C) (A) is not true but (R) is true
(D) Both (A) and (R) are true

263. Assertion (A): The State Councils of Higher Education have been established in the States based on the National Policy on Education.

Reason (R): State level institute is required to co-ordinate the higher educational programmes effectively.

(A) (A) is not correct but (R) is correct
(B) (A) and (R) are correct
(C) (A) is correct but (R) is not correct
(D) (A) and (R) are not correct

264. Assertion (A): JSS promotes vocational skills among the neo-literates.

Reason (R): The human resource development of the country depends upon the vocational skills possessed by its population.

(A) (A) and (R) are true
(B) (A) and (R) are not true
(C) (A) is true but (R) is not true
(D) (A) is not true but (R) is true

265. Assertion (A): The failure of the adult literacy programme is due to lack of proper followup programme.

Reason (R): The followup programme is not mandatory for retaining the level of literacy.

(A) (A) and (R) are true
(B) (A) and (R) are false
(C) (A) is true but (R) is false
(D) (A) is not true but (R) is true

266. Assertion (A): Income generating programme forms part of the Continuing Education Centres.

Reason (B): One of the aims of the Continuing Education Centres is to promote vocational skills.

(A) (A) is correct but (R) is not correct
(B) (A) is not correct but (R) is correct
(C) (A) and (R) are not correct
(D) (A) and (R) are correct

267. Arrange the following media in the order in which they come into view in India :

(A) Print, Radio, TV, Film
(B) TV, Film, Print, Radio
(C) Radio, Print, Film, TV
(D) Film, Print, Radio, TV

268. Arrange the following programmes in the order of implementation by using the code given below :

I. Gram Shikshan Muhim

II. Farmer's Functional Literacy Programme

III. Social Education.

IV. Non-formal Education

Code

(A)	I	II	III	IV
(B)	III	I	II	IV
(C)	III	II	IV	I
(D)	IV	III	II	I

269. Arrange the following in the order for writing a research report.

I. Deciding the research methodology

II. Formulating the research objectives

III. Formulating the research problem

IV. Extensive literature survey

Code :

(A)	III	II	IV	I

(B)	I	II	III	IV
(C)	IV	III	II	I
(D)	I	II	IV	III

270. Arrange the following programmes by the order of its implementation by using the codes given below :

I. Income Generating programmes
II. Post Literacy Programmes
III. Continuing Education Programmes
IV. Total Literacy Programmes

Codes:

(A)	IV	III	II	I
(B)	I	II	III	IV
(C)	IV	II	III	I
(D)	IV	I	II	III

271. Arrange the objectives of training in the order :

(A) Organisational objectives, individual objectives, social objectives, functional objectives.

(B) Individual objectives, organizational objectives, functional objectives, social objectives.

(C) Social objectives, organisational objectives, individual objectives, functional objectives.

(D) Functional objectives, organisational objectives, social objectives, individual objectives.

272. Arrange the following functions of the Dept. of Adult and Continuing Education in order by using the codes given below:

I. Teaching
II. Training
III. Extension
IV. Research

Codes:

(A)	I	III	IV	II
(B)	IV	III	II	I
(C)	I	II	III	IV
(D)	III	II	IV	I

273. Arrange the following in the order in which they appeared by using the codes given below :

I. Volunteer
II. Village level co-ordinator
III. Key Resource person
IV. Resource person

Codes:

(A)	III	II	I	IV
(B)	I	II	IV	III
(C)	IV	III	II	I
(D)	II	III	IV	I

274. Arrange the following in correct order for receiving the message.

(A) Sender, Message, Medium Receiver

(B) Receiver, Sender, Message, Medium

(C) Medium, Sender, Message, Receiver

(D) Receiver, Message, Medium, Sender

275. Arrange the following types of Education in order by using the Codes:

I. Informal education
II. Non-formal education
III. Formal education
IV. Incidental education

Codes:

(A)	I	IV	III	II
(B)	I	II	III	IV
(C)	III	II	I	IV
(D)	IV	III	II	I

276. The national legal literacy day is celebrated on

(A) 9th November
(B) 8th November
(C) 10th November
(D) 5th November

277. Right to free and compulsory elementary education for all children in the age group of 14 in India was implemented in the year

(A) 2007
(B) 2010
(C) 2008
(D) 2009

278. Which of the following programmes was launched in 1994 with the objective of Universalization of primary education?

(A) National Adult Education Programme (NAEP)

(B) District Primary Education Programme (DPEP)

(C) Sarva Shiksha Abhiyan (SSA)

(D) National Literacy Mission (NLM)

279. Which of the following programme was designed to develop effective linkage between literacy and primary education?

(A) Sarva Shiksha Abhiyan (SSA)

(B) Jeevanshala

(C) National Adult Education Programm

(D) Lokshala

280. Kalajathas campaign conducted in all corners of India since 1992 was organized by

(A) B G V S (B) I A E A

(C) I U A C E (D) None of the above

281. NEEM stand for

(A) National Extension Education Movement

(B) National Elementary Education Mission

(C) National Elementary Education Movement

(D) None of the above

282. The first International Conference on Adult Education organised by UNESCO was held in

(A) Tehran (B) Hamburg

(C) Rio de Jenerio (D) Kualalampur

283. The state which has the lowest literacy rate in India, as per 2001 census is

(A) Bihar (B) Madhya Pradesh

(C) Tamil Nadu (D) Orissa

284. Interpersonal communication is also known as

(A) Mass communication (B) Face to face communication

(C) Dyadic communication (D) Virtual communication

285. Who distinguished 'andragogy' with 'pedagogy'?

(A) Lindeman (B) Malcolm Knowles

(C) Alaxander kapp (D) Richard A. Swanson

286. Who coined the term 'extension'?

(A) Charles McCarthy (B) William Sewell

(C) Jensen (D) Nelso

287. Which one of the following is not a component of effective organization?

(A) Balanced organizational structure

(B) Adequate delegation of authority

(C) Clear line of authority

(D) An individual reporting to many superiors

288. The term 'Extension' is equated with extra-moral lectures of which University?

(A) Cambridge University (B) Nalanda University

(C) Lisbon University (D) Harvard University

289. In a constructive approach teachers should see themselves as ____ and colearners.

(A) Facilitators (B) Motivators

(C) Promoters (D) Developers

290. Kothari Commission (1964-66) emphasized on

(A) Expansion of Universal schooling

(B) Non-formal and continuing education

(C) Vocational education

(D) Reading materials

291. The programme aimed at enabling illiterate women to acquire functional skills, better awareness of health, hygiene and child care is

(A) National Female Literacy Mission

(B) Functional Literacy for Adult Women

(C) Female Farmers Functional Literacy and Training

(D) Total Literary Programme

292. The institutions established by the Ministry of Human Resource Development, Government of India in 1989 to provide education inexpensively to remote areas is

(A) JSS (B) NIOS

(C) SSA (D) DIET

293. In 1952 an important institution was created in India for furthering the curve of high education

(A) NCERT (B) AICTE

(C) NCTE (D) UGC

294. Which of the following leader has a natural ability to attract and inspire people ?

(A) Visionary leader (B) Spot leader

(C) Transformational leader (D) Charismatic leader

295. Who is identified as the champion of 'Radical Adult Education' ?

(A) Maslow (B) Peter Jarvis

(C) Paulo Friere (D) John Dewey

296. Arrange the following in order they appeared

(i) Non-formal education (ii) Social education

(iii) Extension education (iv) Continuing education

Codes:

(A) (iii) (ii) (i) (iv) (B) (ii) (i) (iv) (iii)

(C) (iv) (iii) (i) (ii) (D) (i) (iv) (iii) (ii)

297. Arrange the stages of communication in order of best sequence

(i) Encoding (ii) Decoding

(iii) Source (iv) Receiver

Codes:

(A) (iii) (ii) (i) (iv) (B) (iii) (iv) (i) (ii)

(C) (iii) (i) (ii) (iv) (D) (i) (ii) (iv) (iii)

298. Arrange the following tasks of the Department of Adult Continuing education in order in which these were implemented in Indian Universities

(i) Erradication of illiterary (ii) Field out reach

(iii) Population education (iv) Continuing education

Codes:

(A) (i) (ii) (iii) (iv) (B) (ii) (iii) (iv) (i)

(C) (i) (iii) (ii) (iv) (D) (i) (iv) (iii) (ii)

299. Arrange the following in correct order of their implementation

(i) IRDP (ii) MNP

(iii) Community Development (iv) Total Literacy Campaign

Codes:

(A) (i) (iii) (ii) (iv) (B) (iii) (i) (ii) (iv)

(C) (ii) (iii) (i) (iv) (D) (i) (ii) (iii) (iv)

300. Pick the correct sequence of implementation of the following programme :

(i) Mahila Samakhya (ii) Kasturba Balika Vidyalaya

(iii) Chipko movement (iv) Green Revolution

Codes:

(A) (iv) (i) (iii) (ii) (B) (iv) (i) (ii) (iii)

(C) (iv) (iii) (i) (ii) (D) (iv) (iii) (ii) (i)

301. Choose the correct sequence of Hierarchial theory of needs :

(i) Self actualization
(ii) Basic need
(iii) Physiological needs
(iv) Social needs

Codes:

(A) (iii) (ii) (i) (iv)
(B) (iv) (iii) (ii) (i)
(C) (ii) (iii) (iv) (i)
(D) (iii) (ii) (iv) (i)

302. Arrange the specific objectives of concurrent evaluation in order

(i) To identify the strengths and weaknesses of the project
(ii) To suggest corrective and remedial measures
(iii) To examine the operational strategies and implementation
(iv) To identify the factors responsible for improving the programme

Codes:

(A) (iii) (i) (iv) (ii)
(B) (i) (ii) (iii) (iv)
(C) (iv) (iii) (ii) (i)
(D) (iii) (i) (ii) (iv)

303. Pick the correct sequence of growth of educational and communication technologies.

(i) Interactive
(ii) Visual
(iii) Audio
(iv) Audio-visual

Codes:

(A) (iii) (iv) (ii) (i)
(B) (iii) (iv) (i) (ii)
(C) (iii) (ii) (i) (iv)
(D) (iii) (ii) (iv) (i)

304. Arrange the following list of media in order in which they are popularly used in Adult education. Use the codes given below :

(i) Television
(ii) Print media
(iii) Radio
(iv) Folk arts, kalajatha

Codes:

(A) (iv) (iii) (ii) (i)
(B) (iv) (ii) (iii) (i)
(C) (iv) (i) (iii) (ii)
(D) (iv) (ii) (i) (iii)

305. The full form of ICT is

(A) Information and Communication Technology
(B) International Commission Technology
(C) Information Consortium Technology
(D) Information for common techniques

306. Praxis term was used by

(A) Evan Illich (B) Gramsci

(C) Maslow (D) Paulo Friere

307. Arrange the following documents in chronological order :

(i) Kothari Commission Report (ii) Woods Dispatch

(iii) Radha Krishnan Education Report (iv) Secondary Education Report

Codes:

(A) (ii), (i), (iv), (iii) (B) (i), (ii), (iii), (iv)

(C) (ii), (iv), (i), (iii) (D) (iii), (ii), (i), (iv)

308. National Open School was renamed as National Institute of Open Schooling in

(A) 1989 (B) 2000

(C) 2001 (D) 2001

309. Which is not true about University Grants Commission?

(A) Provides fund to the Colleges and Universities

(B) Provides academic guidelines

(C) Provides guidelines to the qualification of teachers in Universities and Colleges

(D) Provides fund for the Elementary Education

310. Who coined the term 'extension'?

(A) Paulo Friere (B) Evan Illich

(C) Charles Mc carthy (D) John Dewy

311. Which of the following is more closer to adult education?

(A) Formal (B) Informal

(C) Open education (D) Non - Formal education

312. Which of the following is the best criteria for choosing a teaching aid ?

(A) Attractive and costly

(B) Easy to use

(C) Made by teachers themselves

(D) Learner specific and the level of content

313. Arrange the following in the order of their appearance

(i) Gram Shikshan Mohim

(ii) Community Development Programme

(iii) National Literacy Mission

(iv) Sarva Shiksha Abhiyan

Code:

(A) (ii), (i), (iii) and (iv) are correct

(B) (i), (iii), (ii) and (iv) are correct

(C) (iv), (iii), (ii) and (i) are correct

(D) (iii), (ii), (iv) and (i) are correct

314. National Literacy Mission was started in

(A) 1978 (B) 1980

(C) 1986 (D) 1988

315. First Folk High School was established in Denmark in

(A) 1947 (B) 1944

(C) 1844 (D) 1888

316. Ernakulum is known for

(A) Jail Reform (B) Water Harvesting

(C) Total Literacy (D) Wasteland Development

317. Lever Act promoted the concept of

(A) Extension (B) Rural Development

(C) Vocational education (D) None of the above

318. Learning: The Trearure within is an outstanding publication in education by

(A) UNO (B) UNICEF

(C) UNESCO (D) World Bank

319. Satyen Maitra Award is given by

(A) NLMA (B) SLMA

(C) SRC (D UGC

320. Which could be the best sequence in communication process

(A) Coding- sending- receiving- decoding

(B) Sending- coding-receiving-decoding

(C) Coding-sendin- decoding-receiving

(D) sending- coding-decoding-receiving

321. Arrange Teaching Aids in terms of effectiveness from highest to lowest :

Use the following code:

(i) Educational movie (ii) Lecture

(iii) Educational excursion (iv) Using charts

Code :

(A) (iv), (i), (iii), (ii)
(B) (i), (ii), (iv), (iii)
(C) (iii), (i), (iv), (ii)
(D) (iii), (iv), (ii), (i)

322.

	List I		List II
i.	Rreading, writing and arithmetic	1.	CE
ii.	Extension eduication	2.	3R
iii.	Continuing education	3.	3H
iv.	Head, Hand, Heart	4.	EE

Code:

(A)	2	4	1	3
(B)	1	3	2	4
(C)	4	2	1	3
(D)	3	1	4	2

323. Arrange the following programme in order in which these were introduced by the Government of India:

(i) Social Education
(ii) Non-Formal Education
(iii) Distance Education
(iv) Sarva Siksha Abhiyan

Codes:

(A) (ii), (i), (iv), (iii)
(B) (i), (ii), (iii), (iv)
(C) (iii), (iv), (i), (ii)
(D) (iv), (i), (ii), (iii)

324. Arrange the following UGC' Extension Programmes in order in which these wer introduced in the Departments of Adult and Continuing Education. Use the code given below:

(i) 16th Point in 20 Point Programme
(ii) Area Development Approach
(iii) Mass Programme for Functional Literacy
(iv) Each one teach one

Codes:

(A) (i), (iii), (iv), (ii)
(B) (ii), (iii), (iv), (i)
(C) (i), (ii), (iii), (iv)
(D) (iii), (ii), (iv), (i)

325. Arrange the following institutions in order they were instituted:

(i) University Grants Commission, New Delhi
(ii) Indian University Association for Continuing Education, New Delhi
(iii) Indian Adult Education Association, New Delhi
(iv) National Institute of Open Schooling, New Delhi

Codes:

(A) (ii), (iii), (i), (iv)
(B) (iii), (i), (ii), (iv)
(C) (iv), (ii), (i), (iii)
(D) (ii), (iii), (ii), (i)

326. Arrange the following tasks of the Department of Adult Continuing Education in the order in which they are being executed. Use code given below:

(i) Field out reach
(ii) Extension
(iii) Teaching/Training
(iv) Research

Codes:

(A) (ii), (iv), (i), (iii)
(B) (iii), (iv), (ii), (i)
(C) (iv), (iii), (i), (ii)
(D) (i), (ii), (iii), (iv)

327. Arrange the following in the order in which they appeared :

(i) Prof. Ram Lal Parikh Review Committee Report.
(ii) Radhakrishnan Commission Report.
(iii) Kothari Commission Report.
(iv) University Grants Commission 6th Pay Commission for Teachers

Codes:

(A) (ii), (iii), (i), (iv)
(B) (i), (ii), (iii), (iv)
(C) (ii), (i), (iv), (iii)
(D) (iv), (iii), (ii), (i)

328. Arrange the following in the order in which they appeared. Use the code given below :

(i) Continuing Education
(ii) Adult Education
(iii) Life Long Education
(iv) Extension Education

Codes:

(A) (ii), (i), (iv), (iii)
(B) (i), (ii), (iii), (iv)
(C) (iii), (i), (ii), (iv)
(D) (iv), (iii), (i), (ii)

329. Arrange the following in order in which the following programmes were launched in India. Use the code given below :

(i) Farmers Functional Literacy Programme
(ii) Total Literacy Campaign
(iii) Post Literacy
(iv) Continuing Education

Codes:

(A) (ii), (i), (iii), (iv)
(B) (iv), (ii), (iii), (i)
(C) (i), (ii), (iii), (iv)
(D) (ii), (iii), (i), (iv)

330. Who used the term information and communication technology first?

(A) Stevenson
(B) Watson
(C) Simpson
(D) Sorenson

331. Jan Shikshana Sansthan is associated with

(A) National Population Programme
(B) National Literacy Mission
(C) National Adult Education Program
(D) All of the above

332. Measurement of Human Development is focussed on

(i) Education
(ii) Longevity
(iii) Standard of Living

Codes:

(A) (i), (ii), (iii) are correct
(B) (i), (ii) are correct
(C) (i), (iii) are correct
(D) (ii), (iii) are correct

333. Gram Shikshan Mohim was launched in the State

(A) Gujarat - Maharashtra
(B) Rajasthan - Maharashtra
(C) Gujarat - Maharashtra -Rajasthan
(D) Maharashtra

334. Population Education Project was funded by UNFPA in the year

(A) 1985
(B) 1987
(C) 1989
(D) 1988

335. Jan Shikshan Sansthan does not provide the service

(A) Voter's Education
(B) Vocational Training
(C) Skill Training
(D) Basic Education

336. Which order of the following States/Union Territory is correct in order of high literary States ?

(A) Kerala, Mizoram, Lakshdweep, Goa
(B) Kerala, Goa, Mizoram, Lakshdweep
(C) Kerala, Lakshweep, Goa, Mizoram
(D) Kerala, Mizoram, Goa, Lakshdweep

337. In the context of Right to Education which of the following statement is true ?

(A) You can file a suit if education is not provided
(B) In all schools there should be trained teachers
(C) It is the responsibility of the State to bring the child to school
(D) All of the above

338. Legal age of girls' marriage is

(A) 18 years
(B) 19 years
(C) 20 years
(D) 21 years

339. National Literacy Mission was launched on

(A) March 1988
(B) April 1988
(C) May 1988
(D) June 1988

340. Functions of State Resource Centre includes

(A) Training
(B) Development Learning Materials
(C) Development of Area Educational Profile
(D) All of the above

341. Who used the term 'social education' for adult literacy programme?

(A) Maulana Azad
(B) Aruna Asaf Ali
(C) Zakir Hussain
(D) Krishnama Chari

342. The Concept of Extension found its initial support from

(A) Land Grant Colleges
(B) Diffusion of Innovation
(C) Extra-mural lectures
(D) All of the above

343. Village Education Committee is responsible for

(A) Monitoring TLC at the village level
(B) Supervising the work of volunteers
(C) Reviewing the progress of TLC
(D) All of the above

344. National Literacy Mission gives

(A) Satyen Maitra Award
(B) Hari Om Ashram Award
(C) Shram Shree Award
(D) None of the above

345. Find the correct sequence in the step in adult learning in which they happen.

(A) Attention, interest, desire, conviction, action, satisfaction
(B) Satisfaction, interest, conviction, attention, action, desire
(C) Attention, interest, conviction, desire, action, satisfaction
(D) Interest, attention, action, satisfaction, desire, conviction

346. Arrange the elements of communication process in which they occur.

(A) Feedback - Message - Source - Receiver – Channel

(B) Source - Message - Channel -Receiver – Feedback

(C) Channel - Feedback -Receiver - Message - Source

(D) Message - Source - Channel -Receiver – Feedback

347. Using the code given below arrange the andragogical process in which they occur.

(i) Setting a climate for learning

(ii) Establishing a mechanism for mutual planning

(iii) Addressing interests, needs and values

(iv) Formulating objectives

(v) Designing learning activities

(vi) Implementing learning programme

(vii) Evaluating results

Codes:

(A) (ii), (i), (iii), (v), (iv) (vi), (vii)

(B) (iii), (ii), (i), (iv), (v), (vi), (vii)

(C) (i), (ii), (iii), (iv), (v), (vi), (vii)

(D) (vii), (i), (v), (iv), (vi), (iii), (ii)

348. With the use of code given below arrange the elements of experiential learning.

(i) Experience

(ii) Process

(iii) Generalization

(iv) Application

Codes:

(A) (i) (iii) (ii) (iv)

(B) (iv) (i) (iii) (ii)

(C) (ii) (i) (iii) (iv)

(D) (i) (ii) (iii) (iv)

349. Arrange the following methods in a sequence which creates an effective learning situation. Use the code given below:

(i) Educational movie

(ii) Lectures

(iii) Educational excursions

(iv) Using charts

Codes:

(A) (iv) (i) (iii) (ii)

(B) (i) (ii) (iii) (iv)

(C) (ii) (iv) (i) (iii)

(D) (iii) (ii) (i) (iv)

350. Arrange the following in order in which these programmes were launched. Use the code given below :

(i) FFLP (ii) TLC

(iii) PLC (iv) CEP

Codes:

(A) (ii) (i) (iii) (iv) (B) (iv) (ii) (iii) (i)

(C) (i) (ii) (iii) (iv) (D) (ii) (iii) (i) (iv)

351. Arrange the following in order of their introduction by the Government of India.

(i) Social Education (ii) Non-formal Education

(iii) District Primary Education (iv) Sarv Shiksha Abhiyan

Codes:

(A) (ii) (i) (iv) (iii) (B) (i) (ii) (iii) (iv)

(C) (iii) (iv) (i) (ii) (D) (iv) (i) (ii) (iii)

352. Arrange the following in sequence of methods of research in social science:

(i) Problem Identification (ii) Formulation of objectives

(iii) Data collection and Analysis (iv) Conclusion and Result

Codes:

(A) (i) (ii) (iii) (iv) (B) (iv) (ii) (iii) (i)

(C) (iv) (iii) (ii) (i) (D) (ii) (i) (iv) (iii)

353. Arrange the proper sequence of steps in writing a report. Use the code given below :

(i) Implementation (ii) Objective

(iii) Rationale (iv) Target

Codes:

(A) (iii) (ii) (iv) (i) (B) (ii) (i) (iii) (iv)

(C) (iv) (i) (ii) (iii) (D) (i) (ii) (iii) (iv)

354. Arrange the following programmes in order in which they were implemented in India:

(i) DAE (ii) SRC

(iii) SVP (iv) JSS

Codes:

(A) (ii) (i) (iii) (iv) (B) (i) (ii) (iii) (iv)

(C) (iii) (ii) (i) (iv) (D) (iv) (i) (iii) (ii)

355. Arrange the following functions of Management in the order in which they should be used. Use the code given below :

(i) Planning | (ii) Motivation

(iii) Organizing and Implementing | (iv) Controlling

Codes:

(A) (ii) (iii) (i) (iv) | (B) (i) (ii) (iv) (iii)

(C) (iii) (i) (iv) (ii) | (D) (i) (iii) (ii) (iv)

356. Arrange the programmes of extension in order there were introduced in the University Departments of Adult, Continuing Education and Extension. Use the code given below:

(i) 16 point programme

(ii) Area Development Approach

(iii) Mass Programme for Functional Literacy

(iv) Total Literacy Programme

Codes:

(A) (i) (iii) (iv) (ii) | (B) (ii) (iii) (iv) (i)

(C) (i) (ii) (iii) (iv) | (D) (iii) (ii) (iv) (i)

357. Arrange the following National Level Programmes on Adult and Continuing Education launched by Government of India in chronological order. Use the code given below :

(i) NAEP | (ii) NLM

(iii) TLC | (iv) CEP

Codes:

(A) (ii) (i) (iv) (iii) | (B) (iii) (iv) (ii) (i)

(C) (i) (ii) (iii) (iv) | (D) (iv) (ii) (i) (iii)

358. Education for all aimed to achieve

(A) Schooling to the age group of 6-14 years

(B) Promoting education for the girl child

(C) Both (A) and (B) are correct

(D) Both (A) and (B) are incorrect

359. Distance mode is used to provide an alternative system of school education through

(A) Zila Saksharata Samiti

(B) Indira Gandhi National Open University

(C) National Institute of Open Schooling

(D) Distance Education Council

360. Androgogy is known as

(A) Arts and Science of helping adults to learn

(B) Science of teaching children

(C) Science of behavioural study of adult

(D) None of the above

361. Inability to read, write and enumerate is a condition of illiteracy associated with persons in

(A) India (B) Sweden

(C) United Kingdom (D) United States of America

362. Teaching, Research and Extension is a popular concept in higher education taken from

(A) Radhakrishnan Education Commission

(B) Kothari Commission

(C) National Policy on Education 1986

(D) None of the above

363. University-community interaction is a

(A) Two way process (B) One way process

(C) Technology driven process (D) None of the above

364. Prior learning refers to

(A) Skills acquired formally through training.

(B) Skills acquired through informal learning and work experience.

(C) Skills acquired before going to school.

(D) Skills acquired in primary school.

365. Lifelong education is an expansion of the scope of

(A) adult education (B) population education

(C) legal education (D) continuing education

366. Village Education Committee is responsible for

(A) Reviewing the adult literacy programme of National Literacy Mission.

(B) Overseeing the structural and functional components of adult literacy programme in the village.

(C) Overseeing the structural and functional components of the 'education for all' programme in the village.

(D) All of the above.

367. Female foeticide is

(A) Sex determination and termination of pregnancy.

(B) Indiscriminate termination of pregnancy.

(C) Medical advised termination of pregnancy.

(D) None of the above.

368. National Literacy Mission was launched in

(A) 1978 (B) 1988

(C) 1998 (D) 1968

369. The opportunity of furthering knowledge and skills at any stage of life is commonly known as

(A) ABL (B) IPL

(C) CE (D) None of the above

370. Existence of gender bias is reflected in

(A) Sex-ratio

(B) Rate of sectoral growth of population

(C) G.D.P.

(D) Regional variation in population growth

371. Environment pollution is linked to

(A) Global warming (B) Ozone depletion

(C) Green house gases (D) All of the above

372. Right to Free and Compulsory Education for age group of 6-14 year Act was notified on

(A) 1st April, 2007 (B) 1st April, 2008

(C) 1st April, 2009 (D) 1st April, 2010

373. For conducting evaluation of learner competencies of literacy outcomes arrange the steps in order they should be.

(I) Sampling Frame

(II) Collection of background Information

(III) Selection of Test Administrators and Test Administration

(IV) Reporting the Result

Codes:

(A)	I	II	III	IV
(B)	IV	III	II	I
(C)	II	I	III	IV
(D)	III	II	I	IV

374. Arrange in order in which the following appeared :

(I) TLC (II) M.P.F.L.

(III) NAEP (IV) LLL

Codes:

(A)	IV	III	II	I
(B)	III	II	I	IV
(C)	II	III	IV	I
(D)	I	IV	III	II

375. Arrange in order of sequence the methodology used for designing an effective training programme :

(I) Determining and sequencing training contents.

(II) Operationalizing training process.

(III) Setting training objectives.

(IV) Programme effectiveness

Codes:

(A)	II	I	III	IV
(B)	III	II	I	IV
(C)	I	II	IV	III
(D)	III	I	II	IV

376. As per stated objectives of 'Sakshar Bharat' arrange these as has been listed in the Government of India document :

(I) Female Literacy (II) Skill Training

(III) Learning Environment (IV) Beyond Literacy

Codes:

(A)	III	II	I	IV
(B)	IV	III	II	I
(C)	I	IV	II	III
(D)	II	III	I	IV

377. Arrange the following in order of the University Departments of Adult, Continuing Education and Extension :

(I) Field outreach (II) Continuing Education

(III) Extension (IV) Teaching of degree programmes

Codes:

(A)	II	III	I	IV
(B)	III	II	I	IV
(C)	I	III	II	IV
(D)	IV	III	II	I

378. Arrange the communication process in order of best sequence :

(I) Sending message
(II) Coding
(III) Receiving
(IV) Decoding

Codes:

(A)	II	I	III	IV
(B)	I	III	II	IV
(C)	I	II	III	IV
(D)	IV	III	II	I

379. The schemes for the universalization of elementary education have been introduced by Government of India. Arrange them in order in which they appeared :

(I) District Primary Education Programme
(II) Social Education
(III) Non-Formal Education
(IV) Sarva Shiksha Abhiyan

Codes:

(A)	I	III	II	IV
(B)	II	III	I	IV
(C)	IV	III	II	I
(D)	II	I	III	IV

380. Developing a Training Programme should be viewed as a curriculum development process. Arrange the phases of process in order.

(I) Pre-Planning
(II) Recycling
(III) Planning
(IV) Implementation

Codes:

(A)	III	I	II	IV
(B)	IV	III	I	II
(C)	II	I	IV	III
(D)	I	III	IV	II

381. Arrange the roles and Tasks of grassroot level functionaries engaged in literacy work in order to

(I) Carry out evaluation

(II) Mobilise community support

(III) Impart functional literacy skills

(IV) Create favourable environment

Codes:

(A)	IV	II	III	I
(B)	II	IV	III	I
(C)	III	II	I	IV
(D)	II	III	I	IV

382. Arrange in order of steps, the method of conducting 'Social Survey' :

(I) Data gathering

(II) Data analysis and Tabulation

(III) Data Processing

(IV) Report Writing

Codes:

(A)	IV	III	II	I
(B)	II	III	I	IV
(C)	I	III	II	IV
(D)	III	II	IV	I

383. The main objective of "Education for All" is to

(A) Promote literacy among deprived sections of society

(B) Promote sectoral literacy among all sections of society

(C) Both (A) and (B) are correct

(D) Both (A) and (B) are incorrect

384. Alternate system of school education through distance mode is provided by

(A) Directorate of Adult Education

(B) State Resource Centre

(C) Jan Shikshan Sansthan

(D) National Institute of Open Schooling

385. The art and science of helping adults to learn is known as

(A) Pedagogy

(B) Pedology

(C) Andragogy

(D) None of the above

386. Illiteracy in India is associated with person's

(A) Inability to read, write and comprehend

(B) Inability to understand legal and technological processes

(C) Inability to use computers

(D) None of the above

387. Kothari Commission emphasized on the trinity of

(A) Information, Education and Communication

(B) Teaching, Research and Extension

(C) Teaching, Research and Development

(D) None of the above questions, each question carrying two (2)

388. University Extension Services leads to

(A) University-Community interaction

(B) Transfer of research to industry

(C) Formal teaching programme

(D) None of the above

389. Skills acquired through 'Prior learning' can be certified by

(A) National Institute of Open Schooling

(B) National Council of Vocational Training

(C) National Council of Education, Research and Training

(D) None of the above

390. LEAP stands for

(A) Life Expectancy Awareness Programme

(B) Life Enrichment Awareness Programme

(C) Lifelong Education and Awareness Programme

(D) Lifelong Education and Awareness Plan

391. Non-formal education of the Government is monitored at the village level by

(A) VEC (B) ZSS

(C) JSS (D) None of the above

392. Sex determination led termination of pregnancy is known as

(A) Infant mortality (B) Female foeticide

(C) Genocide (D) Homicide

393. International Literacy Day is celebrated on

(A) 5th September (B) 6th September

(C) 7th September (D) 8th September

394. Continuing education programme is a sequel to

(A) Need based requirement and provisions for further enrichment of knowledge of the people

(B) Post-literacy

(C) Adult basic literacy and further education

(D) All of the above

395. An adverse sex ratio is an indicator of

(A) Existence of gender bias (B) Rate of growth of population

(C) Rate of morbidity (D) Rate of mortality

396. Green House gases are linked to

(A) Water sanitation (B) Global Warming

(C) H1N1 Viruses (D) None of the above

397. Right to Free and Compulsory Education for 6-14 years of age group Act was notified on

(A) 1st April 2008 (B) 1st April 2009

(C) 1st April 2010 (D) 1st April 2007

398. Arrange in order in which the following schemes appeared ?

I. LLL II. NAEP

III. TLC IV. MPFL

Codes:

(A) II, IV, III, I (B) IV, II, III, I

(C) I, II, III, IV (D) III, II, IV, I

399. As per stated objectives of 'Sakshar Bharat' arrange these as has been listed in the Government of India Document.

I. Learning Environment II. Skills Training

III. Beyond Literacy IV. Female Literacy

Codes:

(A) III, II, I, IV (B) IV, III, II, I

(C) III, IV, I, IV (D) II, III, IV, I

400. Arrange the following in order of introduction in the University Departments of Adult, Continuing Education and Extension.

I. Extension

II. Continuing Education

III. Field outreach

IV. Teaching of Degree Programmes

Codes:

(A) III, II, I, IV
(B) II, III, IV, I
(C) I, II, III, IV
(D) IV, III, II, I

401. Arrange the schemes for the universalization of elementary education as they appeared in order of sequence.

I. Non Formal Education
II. Social Education
III. Sarva Shiksha Abhiyan
IV. District Primary Education Programme

Codes:

(A) I, III, IV, II
(B) II, III, I, IV
(C) II, I, IV, III
(D) III, II, I, IV

402. Arrange the roles and tasks of grass root functionaries engaged in literacy in an order of sequence.

I. To create favourable environment

II. To mobilise community participation

III. To carry out evaluation

IV. To impart literacy skills

Codes:

(A) IV, I, II, III
(B) III, II, I, IV
(C) II, I, IV, III
(D) I, II, III, IV

403. For conducting evaluation of learner competencies of literacy arrange, the steps involved in the order they should be.

I. Selection of test Administrators and Test Administration

II. Sampling frame

III. Collection of background information

IV. Reporting the result

Codes:

(A) II, III, IV, I
(B) III, II, IV, I
(C) IV, III, II, I
(D) III, II, I, IV

404. Arrange in order of sequence the methodology used for designing an effective training programme.

I. Setting Training Objectives

II. Programme Effectiveness

III. Determining and sequencing Training Content

IV. Operationalizing Training Process

Codes:

(A) I, II, III, IV (B) IV, II, III, I

(C) I, III, IV, II (D) II, IV, III, I

405. Arrange the Communication Process in order of sequence.

I. Coding II. Receiving

III. Sending message IV. Decoding

Codes:

(A) III, II, I, IV (B) I, III, II, IV

(C) IV, II, III, I (D) I, III, IV, II

406. Developing a programme should be viewed as curriculum development process. Arrange the phases of process in order.

I. Planning II. Recycling

III. Pre-planning IV. Implementation

Codes:

(A) III, I, IV, II (B) IV, III, II, I

(C) II, III, I, IV (D) IV, II, III, I

407. Arrange in order of steps the survey techniques.

I. Data Processing II. Data Analysis and Tabulation

III. Data Gathering IV. Report Writing

Codes:

(A) III, I, II, IV (B) I, III, IV, II

(C) II, IV, I, III (D) III, II, I, IV

408. Rabindranath Tagore had set up at Shantiniketan

(A) Viswabharathi (B) Rabindrabharathi

(C) Sangeetbharathi (D) Gyanabharathi

409. Mahatma Gandhi's idea of education for illiterates was through

(A) Adult Education (B) Functional Literacy

(C) Basic Education (D) Population Education

410. Characteristics of "Total Literacy Campaigns"

(A) Improved andragogy with emphasis on learning outcome.

(B) To cover all the districts of India.

(C) To introduce child vaccination.

(D) To generate awareness about ICDS.

411. One of the factors responsible for poor female literacy rate in India

(A) Class based inequality (B) Religion based inequality

(C) Caste based inequality (D) Gender based inequality

412. Integrated approach to attain the higher level of literacy means

(A) To use audio-visual system (B) To remove illiteracy

(C) To cover backward areas (D) To cover drop out children

413. "Jana Shikshana Sansthan" was earlier known as

(A) Bharatheeya Vidyapeetha (B) Gujarat Vidyapeetha

(C) Kishan Sansthan (D) Shramik Vidyapeeth

414. "SRC" stands for?

(A) Space research centre (B) Space Requirement centre

(C) State Resource Centre (D) State Random Census

415. Partnership with Universities for adult education means

(A) To undertake action for neo-literates

(B) To involve Higher educational institutions in literacy

(C) To generate awareness among women

(D) To support NGOs

416. "Social Education" was integrated with

(A) Community Development Programme

(B) Population Education Programme

(C) Environmental Education Programme

(D) Malaria Eradication Programme

417. Which step is correct after the Data Collection for Social Research ?

(A) Analysis of the data (B) Report writing

(C) Formulation of hypothesis (D) None of the above

418. The Central Advisory Board of Education (CABE) recommended in 1974 the following:

(A) Introduction of Non-Formal education in Formal System.

(B) To start separate department of Non-Formal education.

(C) To start Adult Education programme.

(D) To concentrate on Population education.

419. NCERT specially plays an important role for framing Education policy of

(A) Primary education

(B) Secondary and Higher secondary

(C) Higher education

(D) Preprimary education

420. Experimental Research Design must address to

(A) Random sample

(B) Lottery system of sample

(C) Stratified random sample

(D) Control group and experimental group

421. Audio-visual Aids includes

(A) Buzz session (B) Group discussion

(C) Charts (D) T.V.

422. Slow progress of literacy in India is due to

(A) Poor monitoring (B) Population Explosion

(C) Environmental degradation (D) Lack of Peaople participation

423. Source of secondary data is

(A) Gazzetted documents of Government

(B) Information collected through questionnaire

(C) Door to door data collection

(D) None of the above

424. Impact of effective communication is

(A) Positive (B) Cheerful

(C) Negative (D) Resistance

425. 'Animator' in Adult Education programme is

(A) Motivator (B) Promoter

(C) Prerak (D) Facilitator

426. "Folk Schools" are located in

(A) Africa (B) Denmark

(C) England (D) West Indies

427. Dr. Zakir Hussain Memorial lecture is organized by

(A) Indian Universities Association of Continuing Education

(B) Rajeev Gandhi Foundation

(C) University Grants Commission

(D) Indian Adult Education Association

428. Arrange the following in the order in which they appeared by using the following code :

(i) Gram Shikshan Mohim

(ii) Farmer's Functional Literacy Programme

(iii) Community Development Programme

(iv) Social Education

Codes:

(A) (ii) (iii) (iv) (i)

(B) (ii) (iv) (iii) (i)

(C) (iv) (iii) (i) (ii)

(D) (iii) (i) (iv) (ii)

429. Arrange the following in the order in which they appeared by using the codes as below :

(i) Population

(ii) Food, Cloth and Shelter

(iii) Environment Education

(iv) Pollution

Codes:

(A) (iv) (ii) (i) (iii)

(B) (i) (ii) (iv) (iii)

(C) (ii) (iii) (i) (iv)

(D) (ii) (iv) (iii) (i)

430. Arrange the following in the order in which they appeared by using the codes as below

(i) Internet

(ii) Radio

(iii) TV

(iv) Book

Codes:

(A) (iv) (ii) (iii) (i)

(B) (ii) (iii) (iv) (i)

(C) (ii) (iv) (iii) (i)

(D) (iii) (ii) (iv) (i)

431. Arrange the following in the order in which they appear. Use the code as given below :

(i) Agricultural

(ii) Industrial

(iii) Post-industrial

(iv) Pastoral

Codes:

(A) (iv) (i) (ii) (iii) (B) (i) (ii) (iii) (iv)

(C) (i) (iv) (iii) (ii) (D) (iv) (iii) (ii) (i)

432. Arrange the following in the order in which they appear. Use the codes as given below:

(i) Infant (ii) Old

(iii) Young (iv) Child

Codes:

(A) (iv) (i) (ii) (iii) (B) (i) (ii) (iii) (iv)

(C) (i) (iv) (iii) (ii) (D) (iv) (iii) (ii) (i)

433. Arrange the following in the order in which they appear. Use the codes as given below:

(i) Political (ii) Biological

(iii) Environmental (iv) Social

Codes:

(A) (iv) (i) (ii) (iii) (B) (iii) (ii) (iv) (i)

(C) (ii) (i) (iii) (iv) (D) (i) (iv) (ii) (iii)

434. "Illiteracy is a National shame" who said it ?

(A) Pt. Jawaharlal Nehru (B) Mahatma Gandhiji

(C) Rabindranath Tagore (D) Sardar Vallabhbhai Patel

435. Field outreach programme has been initiated by :

(A) U.G.C (B) NLM

(C) SRC (D) SLM

436. Three "R" in Education includes :

(A) Skill of running fast, skill of reading fast, skill of working fast.

(B) Training of Hand, Heart and Head

(C) Training of reading, writing and counting

(D) None of the above

437. "Bharat Gyan Vigyan Jatha" promotes :

(A) Vocational skill training (B) Teaching of science in school

(C) Bharatiya Gyan Vidyapeeth (D) Popularisation of science

438. Adult Educator should be a :

(A) Democratic leader (B) Autocratic leader

(C) Natural leader (D) Combination of above all

439. MPFL stands for :
(A) Man Planning for Literacy
(B) Management Programme for Functional Literacy
(C) Man power for Literacy
(D) Mass Programme for Functional Literacy

440. Formal education is :
(A) More rigid (B) More open
(C) More flexible (D) None of the above

441. The slogan "Education for All" by 2000 is given by :
(A) NLM (B) UNO
(C) UNESCO (D) UNICEF

442. "Jan Shikshan Nilayam" is not different from :
(A) Jan Shikshan Sansthan (B) JSN
(C) Janata College (D) BSSL

443. Who plays a very crucial role for the welfare of the population ?
(A) WHO (B) UNICEF
(C) UNFPA (D) UNO

444. "International Literacy Day" is celebrated every year on :
(A) 8th September (B) 2nd October
(C) 3rd March (D) IIth September

445. The first total Literate district in India was :
(A) Tamil Nadu (C) Mumbai
(B) Banaskantha (D) Ernakulam

446. Point No. 16 of the 20 - Point Programme of 1982 emplasises on :
(A) Adult Education (B) Population Education
(C) Child Education (D) Environment Education

447. Where was "Gram Shikshana Mohim" Started ?
(A) Bihar (B) Rajasthan
(C) Gujarat (D) Maharashtra

448. "Development is of the Man, by the Man and for the Man" who has said ?
(A) Julius K. Nyerere (B) Malcohm Knowles
(C) Malcohm S. Adiseshiah (D) Dr. Madhuri Shah

449. ASPBAE, is related to :

(A) Farmer's Education
(B) Adult Education
(C) Worker's Education
(D) Population Education

450. Frank LauBach contribution to adult-education is :

(A) Each one Teach one Method
(B) Non-Formal Education Approach
(C) Formal Education Approach
(D) Incidental Education Approach

451. NAEP was launched in the year:

(A) 1947
(B) 1985
(C) 1978
(D) 1998

452. "Tagore Literacy Award" is being given for an outstanding work in :

(A) Promotion of Literacy work among men
(B) Promotion of Literacy work among women
(C) Promotion of Literacy work among youth
(D) None

453. "Human Rights Day" is celebrated on :

(A) 10th November
(B) 10th December
(C) 10th July
(D) 10th September

454. Anti-Arrack agitation of Nellore District of Andhra Pradesh was organised mainly by :

(A) Neo-literate women of the district
(B) Self-Help Groups of the district
(C) Panchayat members of the district
(D) Neo-literate men of the district

455. NLM was launched by the then Prime Minister :

(A) Lal Bahadur Shastri
(B) Mrs. Indira Gandhi
(C) Rajiv Gandhi
(D) Narasimha Rao

456. Population density is a measurement of :

(A) Number of houses where people live in
(B) Number of people in per square k.m.
(C) Types of Houses where people live
(D) Distribution of population in the area

457. The sex ratio in India as per 2001 census is :

(A) 927 : 1000 (B) 933 : 1000

(C) 945 : 1000 (D) 929 : 1000

458. "World Population Day" is celebrated on :

(A) 6th July (B) 15th July

(C) 8th July (D) 11th July

459. Arrange the following in the order in which they appeared. Use the code given below.

(i) Sarva Shiksha Abhiyan (ii) Total Literacy campaign

(iii) NAEP (iv) AEP

Codes:

(A) (iii) (iv) (ii) (i) (B) (iv) (ii) (iii) (i)

(C) (i) (ii) (iii) (iv) (D) (iv) (i) (iii) (ii)

460. Arrange the following in the order in which they appeared. Use the code given below.

(i) Literate (ii) Illiterate

(iii) Semiliterate (iv) Neo-literate

Codes:

(A) (ii) (i) (iii) (iv) (B) (iv) (iii) (ii) (i)

(C) (i) (ii) (iii) (iv) (D) (ii) (iv) (i) (iii)

461. Arrange the following in the order in which they appeared. Use the code given below.

(i) MPFL (ii) FFLP

(iii) RPFL (iv) NAEP

Codes:

(A) (i) (ii) (iii) (iv) (B) (ii) (i) (iii) (iv)

(C) (ii) (iii) (iv) (i) (D) (ii) (iv) (iii) (i)

462. Arrange the following days in the correct order of occurence month wise as they are being celebrated throughout the year :

(i) National Literacy Day (ii) International Literacy Day

(iii) International Human Rights Day (iv) International Women Day

Codes:

(A) (iv) (i) (ii) (iii) (B) (iv) (iii) (ii) (i)

(C) (iv) (ii) (iii) (i) (D) (iv) (ii) (i) (iii)

463. Arrange the following in the order in which they appeared. Use the code given below.

(i) New Education Policy
(ii) NAEP
(iii) FFLP
(iv) World Declaration on Education for All

Codes:

(A) (iii) (iv) (ii) (i)
(B) (iii) (ii) (i) (iv)
(C) (iii) (i) (ii) (iv)
(D) (iii) (iv) (i) (ii)

464. Arrange the following activities in the correct order of occurence in the management of adult education programme :

(i) Planning
(ii) Staffing
(iii) Training
(iv) Organizing

Codes:

(A) (i) (iii) (iv) (ii)
(B) (i) (iv) (iii) (ii)
(C) (i) (iv) (ii) (iii)
(D) (i) (ii) (iii) (iv)

465. Arrange the following in the order in which they appeared. Use the code given below.

(i) Child
(ii) Infant
(iii) Youth
(iv) Old man

Codes:

(A) (ii) (i) (iii) (iv)
(B) (ii) (iii) (iv) (i)
(C) (ii) (i) (iv) (iii)
(D) (ii) (iv) (iii) (i)

466. National Literacy Mission was launched in :

(A) 1986
(B) 1987
(C) 1988
(D) 1990

467. The Task of Adult Education programme is :

(A) To develop interest in education
(B) To identify reasons for resistance to programme
(C) To import functional literacy for quality of life improvement
(D) None of the above

468. Satyen Mitra Award is given by :

(A) YMCA
(B) IAEA
(C) BGVS
(D) NLM

469. Sex Ratio is an Index describing the :
(A) Existence of Gender Discrimination
(B) Rate of Morbidity
(C) Rate of Population Growth
(D) Rate of Mortality

470. Indian Adult Education Association was started in the year :
(A) 1940 (B) 1932
(C) 1936 (D) 1939

471. The concept of Social Education was introduced during :
(A) First Five year plan (B) Second five year plan
(C) Third Five year plan (D) Fourth five year plan

472. Which World Organisation addresses Special Mandate for Literacy ?
(A) UNICEF (B) UNPF
(C) UNDP (D) UNESCO

473. Population studies are specifically concerned with :
(A) Prevention of Infant Mortality Rate (B) Democracy
(C) Demography (D) Quality of life

474. "Gram Shiksha Mohim" was started in :
(A) Bihar (B) Gujarat
(C) Tamil Nadu (D) Maharashtra

475. "Window Period" is associated with :
(A) TB (B) Malaria
(C) HIV/AIDS (D) High Fever

476. Who has Advocated "Rural Universities will support the Basic Education"?
(A) Sarojini Naidu (B) Sardar Patel
(C) Jawaharlal Nehru (D) Mahatma Gandhi

477. In which year the "NLM - UNESCO Award" was instituted?
(A) 1995 (B) 1996
(C) 1997 (D) 1998

478. ASPBAE is related to
(A) Childrens education (B) formal education
(C) Adult education (D) Workers education

479. Edusat is associated with :

(A) Alternative Satellite Learning
(B) Distance Education Learning
(C) Satellite Education
(D) Virtual Education

480. Frank Laubach's contribution to Adult Education is:

(A) Women's Functional Literacy Programme
(B) Functional Literacy Programme
(C) Folk Education Programme
(D) "Each One Teach One" Method

481. World declaration on "Education For All " was made in :

(A) Germany
(B) Malaysia
(C) India
(D) Thailand

482. "Cultural Action For Freedom" is a book written by :

(A) Roby Kidd
(B) James Draper
(C) Malcohm Knowles
(D) Paulo Freire

483. Fifth UNESCO International Adult Education Conference (CONFINTEA) was c onvened in Hamburg in :

(A) 1997
(B) 1990
(C) 1991
(D) 1993

484. "Nehru Literacy Award" and "Tagore Literacy Award" is given by :

(A) NLM
(B) Planning Commission
(C) IAEA
(D) JNU

485. "Anti - Arrack Agitation" was organised in :

(A) Tamil Nadu
(B) Karnataka
(C) Gujarat
(D) Andhra Pradesh

486. Which one of the following is not correctly matched ?

(A) NLM : 1988
(B) NAEP : 1978
(C) TLC : 1991 - 1992
(D) PLC : 1994 - 1995

487. (i) "Pedagogy is the Art and Science of Teaching Children to Learn",

(ii) "Andragogy is not the Art and Science of Helping Adults to Learn".

(A) (i) and (ii) are true
(B) (i) is true and (ii) is false
(C) (i) is false and (ii) is true
(D) (i) and (ii) are false

488. (i) "Sarva Shiksha Abhiyan" is being implemented by Government of India for Universalisation of Elementary Education.

(ii) DPEP is equal to SSA.

(A) (i) is false and (ii) is true (B) (i) and (ii) are true

(C) (i) is true and (ii) is false (D) (i) and (ii) are false

489. (i) JSS deals with Vocational Education.

(ii) JSN deals with Continuing Education.

(A) (i) and (ii) are false (B) (i) is true and (ii) is false

(C) (i) and (ii) are true (D) (i) is false and (ii) is true

490. (i) National Institute of Open Schooling conducts Continuing Education.

(ii) Open Basic Education Programme is a Past Function of NIOS.

(A) (i) and (ii) are true (B) (ii) is true and (i) is false

(C) (i) is true and (ii) is false (D) (i) and (ii) are false

491. (i) Population Education is Quality of Life.

(ii) Population Studies includes Demography.

(A) (i) is true and (ii) is false (B) (i) and (ii) are false

(C) (i) is false and (ii) is true (D) (i) and (ii) are true

492. (i) HIV leads to Full Blown AIDS.

(ii) AIDS leads to Full Blown HIV.

(A) (i) and (ii) are true (B) (i) and (ii) are false

(C) (i) is true and (ii) is false (D) (i) is false and (ii) is true

493. (i) Self - Help Groups make Economic Empowerment of Women.

(ii) Self - Help Groups deny Empowerment of Women.

(A) (i) is false and (ii) is true (B) (i) is true and (ii) is false

(C) (i) and (ii) are true (D) (i) and (ii) are false

494. (i) "Medium is the Message" is pronounced by Marshal Mc Luhan.

(ii) "Motivation is an Energy change within the person" Pronounced by Mc Donald.

(A) (i) is false and (ii) is true (B) (i) and (ii) are true

(C) (i) is true and (ii) is false (D) (i) and (ii) are false

495. (i) ICT Includes Audio-visual, Folk Story Telling

(ii) NICT includes Computers, e-learning, Internet and Web-casting.

(A) (i) is false and (ii) is true (B) (i) is true and (ii) is false

(C) (i) and (ii) are true (D) (i) and (ii) are false

496. We have now Four types of Terminologies Identify the correct order.

(A) Illiterate, Literate, Neo-Literate, Semiliterate

(B) Illiterate, Semi-literate, Neo-Literate, Literate

(C) Neo-Literate, Literate, Illiterate, Semiliterate

(D) Semiliterate, Illiterate, Literate, Neo-Literate

497. We have now Four types of Media Identify the correct order - in which they appeared in India.

(A) Print, Film, TV and Virtual

(B) TV, Print, Virtual and Film

(C) Film, TV, Virtual and Print

(D) Virtual, TV, Print and Film

498. Arrange the following concepts in order in which it appeared in India. Use the code given below :

(i) 3 R's

(ii) Eradication of Illiteracy

(iii) Area Development

(iv) Cent percent Literacy

Codes:

(A) (iv) (iii) (ii) (i)

(B) (ii) (iii) (i) (iv)

(C) (i) (ii) (iii) (iv)

(D) (iii) (i) (iv) (ii)

499. Arrange the following Books in order in which they appear and use the code given below and select the correct answer :

(i) Pedagogy of the oppressed

(ii) History of Adult Education

(iii) An Encyclopaedia of Adult Education

(iv) Modern practice of Adult Education from Andragogy to Pedagogy

Codes:

(A) (i) (iv) (ii) (iii)

(B) (iii) (ii) (i) (iv)

(C) (ii) (iii) (iv) (i)

(D) (iv) (ii) (iii) (i)

500. Arrange the following in order in which they appeared and use the code given below: and Select the correct answer.

(i) Social Education

(ii) NAEP

(iii) TLC

(iv) CEP

Codes:

(A) (ii) (i) (iii) (iv)

(B) (i) (ii) (iii) (iv)

(C) (iii) (i) (iv) (ii)

(D) (iv) (ii) (iii) (i)

501. Arrange the following in order to obtain Master's Degree in the Non-Formal mode. Use the code for Selecting the correct.

(i) Adult Education Centre
(ii) Continuing Education Centre
(iii) Open School
(iv) Open University

Codes:

(A) (iv) (iii) (ii) (i)
(B) (ii) (iii) (i) (iv)
(C) (i) (ii) (iii) (iv)
(D) (iii) (i) (iv) (ii)

502. Choose the following in correct order. Use the code given below and select the correct answer.

(i) Message
(ii) Sender
(iii) Channel
(iv) Receiver

Codes:

(A) (ii) (iii) (i) (iv)
(B) (i) (ii) (iii) (iv)
(C) (iv) (i) (ii) (iii)
(D) (iii) (i) (iv) (ii)

503. Arrange the following process of Research Design by using the code :

(i) Identification of the problem
(ii) Review of Literature
(iii) Objectives
(iv) Formulating Hypothesis

Codes:

(A) (iv) (ii) (i) (iii)
(B) (i) (iii) (iv) (ii)
(C) (iii) (ii) (i) (iv)
(D) (i) (ii) (iii) (iv)

504. Indian Adult Education Association was launched in the year :

(A) 1979
(B) 1978
(C) 1976
(D) 1977

505. The DAE was established by the Government of India during the year :

(A) 1993
(B) 1992
(C) 1994
(D) 1991

506. Non-formal education is concerned with the age group of :

(A) 6 - 14 years
(B) 7 - 15 years
(C) 7 - 14 years
(D) 6 - 15 years

507. Andragogy is :

(A) Teaching Adults to Learn
(B) Teaching Children to Learn
(C) Making Adults Literate
(D) Study of Adult Behaviour

508. Total Literacy Campaign was related only to :

(A) Teaching Adults (B) 3 R's

(C) Basic Literacy (D) Skill Development

509. The first fully literate District under Total Literacy Campaign was :

(A) Pondicherry (B) Ernakulam

(C) Nellore (D) Bijapur

510. NLM aims at imparting :

(A) Functional Literacy to Non-Literate Persons

(B) Literacy to Neo-Literates

(C) Adult Literacy Programmes

(D) Mass Education

511. According to India's 2001 Census, the literacy rate among the population aged seven years is :

(A) 65.38 per cent (B) 68.3 per cent

(C) 64.5 per cent (D) 67.2 per cent

512. The sex ratio in India according to 2001 census is :

(A) 927 : 1000 (B) 933 : 1000

(C) 945 : 1000 (D) 929 : 1000

513. NLM was launched to achieve the objective of :

(A) Making 100 million literates in the age group of 15 - 35 years

(B) Teaching children in the age group 5 - 15 years

(C) Making all the adults functionally literate

(D) Making India a fully literate country

514. "By education I mean an all round drawing out of the best in Child and Man, body, mind and spirit", is quoted by :

(A) Sri Aurobindo (B) Swami Vivekananda

(C) M. K. Gandhi (D) Adult Education

515 "Any organised, systematic, educational activity carried on outside the framework of the formal system to provide selected types of learning to particular sub-groups in the population, adults as well as children" is known as :

(A) Non-Formal Education (B) Informal Education

(C) Formal Education (D) Adult Education

516. The main objectives of Gram Shikshan Mohim was :

(A) To Eradicate illiteracy among the adults in the age group of 14 - 50 years

(B) To experiment the mass literacy programmes

(C) To provide functional literacy programmes to adults

(D) None of the above

517. What is the other name of Polyvalent Education Centre ?

(A) Shramik Vidyapeeth

(B) Gram Shikshan Mohim

(C) Jan Shikshan Sansthan

(D) Community Education Centre

518. The World Conference on Education for All is held in :

(A) Thailand

(B) Singapore

(C) India

(D) China

519. Identify the correct order of the process in which we receive communication:

(A) Sender, Message, Carrier, Receiver

(B) Message, Carrier, Sender, Receiver

(C) Carrier, Message, Receiver, Sender

(D) Receiver, Carrier, Message, Sender

520. Identify the correct order of their appearance:

(A) Correspondence Education, Open University System, Distance Education, EDUSAT

(B) Correspondence Education, Distance Education, EDUSAT, Open University System

(C) Distance Education, Correspondence Education, EDUSAT, Open University System

(D) EDUSAT, Distance Education, Correspondence Education, Open University System

521. Identify the correct order of their appearance :

(A) State Resource Centre, Gram Shikshan Mohim, Jan Shikshan Nilayam, Jan Shikshan Sansthan

(B) Gram Shikshan Mohim, State Resource Centre, Jan Shikshan Sansthan, Jan Shikshan Nilayam

(C) Jan Shikshan Sansthan, Jan Shikshan Nilayam, State Resource Centre, Gram Shikshan Mohim

(D) Jan Shikshan Nilayam, Jan Shikshan Sansthan, Gram Shikshan Mohim, State Resource Centre

522. Identify the correct order according to their increasing order of highest literacy rates

(A) Kerala, Mizoram, Lakshadweep, Goa and Delhi

(B) Mizoram, Kerala, Delhi, Goa and Lakshadweep

(C) Lakshadweep, Mizoram, Kerala, Delhi and Goa

(D) Goa, Mizoram, Kerala, Lakshadweep and Delhi

523. Identify the correct order according to their decreasing order of lowest literacy rates

(A) Bihar, Jharkhand, Jammu and Kashmir, Arunachal Pradesh and Uttar Pradesh

(B) Jharkhand, Bihar, Arunachal Pradesh, Uttar Pradesh and Jammu and Kashmir

(C) Uttar Pradesh, Jharkhand, Jammu and Kashmir, Arunachal Pradesh and Bihar

(D) Jharkhand, Uttar Pradesh, Bihar, Jammu and Kashmir and Arunachal Pradesh

524. Arrange the following programmes in the order in which they appeared. Use the code given below:

(i) National Adult Education Programme

(ii) Total Literacy Campaign

(iii) Post Literacy Campaign

(iv) Continuing Education Programme

Codes:

(A) (i) (ii) (iii) (iv)

(B) (ii) (i) (iii) (iv)

(C) (iii) (i) (iv) (ii)

(D) (i) (iii) (ii) (iv)

525. Arrange the following Commissions/Committees in the order in which they appeared. Use the code given below :

(i) Kothari Commission

(ii) Ram Lal Parikh Committee

(iii) Radha Krishna Committee

(iv) University Grants Commission

Codes:

(A) (i) (ii) (iii) (iv)

(B) (ii) (iii) (iv) (i)

(C) (iii) (i) (iv) (ii)

(D) (i) (iii) (ii) (iv)

526. Arrange the following Institutions in the order in which they appeared. Use the code given below :

(i) National Council for Educational Research and Training

(ii) National Institute of Educational Planning and Administration

(iii) District Institute of Education and Training

(iv) District Resource Centre

Codes:

(A) (i) (ii) (iii) (iv)
(B) (ii) (i) (iii) (iv)
(C) (iii) (i) (iv) (ii)
(D) (i) (iii) (ii) (iv)

527. Arrange the following Institutional Organizations in the order in which they appeared.

(A) UNESCO, UNICEF, UNFPA and WHO
(B) UNICEF, UNESCO, WHO and UNFPA
(C) WHO, UNFPA, UNICEF and UNESCO
(D) UNFPA, WHO, UNESCO and UNICEF

528. Arrange the following programmes in the order in which they appeared.

(A) Social Education, Adult Education, Community Development and Distance Education
(B) Distance Education, Community Development, Adult Education and Social Education
(C) Adult Education, Distance Education, Social Education and Community Development
(D) Community Development, Social Education, Distance Education and Adult Education

529. The main objective of "Education For All" is to be :

(A) Promote a learning society
(B) Promote literacy among men and women
(C) Promote literacy among deprived sections of society
(D) None of the above

530. In NAEP the initial focus was:

(A) 15 - 25 age group
(B) 15 - 30 age group
(C) 10 - 25 age group
(D) 15 - 35 age group

531. Farmers Training and Functional Literacy Programme aimed at popularization of :

(A) High yielding variety of seeds through adult education
(B) Completing farmers literacy from village to village

(C) To literate poor and marginalized farmers

(D) To literate farmer women

532. International Conference on Population and Development in Cairo, adopted a programme of Action for :

(A) 5 years (B) 10 years

(C) 20 years (D) 25 years

533. 'Paradigm Shift' in POPED includes:

(A) Reproductive Health (B) Small Family Norms

(C) Favourable Sex-Ratio (D) Crude Birth Rate

534. Fifth Five Year plan emphasized the need of :

(A) Non-formal Education

(B) Community Development Programme

(C) Adult Education

(D) Correspondence Education

535. A book that Roby Kidd wrote was :

(A) Padagogy of the Oppressed (B) Culture Action for Freedom

(C) How Adult Learn (D) Small is Beautiful

536. Literacy Award given by NLM for outstanding work in this area is known/ called :

(A) Nehru Award (B) Tagore Award

(C) Satyen Maitra Award (D) None of the above

537. The Indian Adult Education Association instituted the 'Nehru Literacy Award' in :

(A) 1962 (B) 1965

(C) 1968 (D) 1969

538. Rashtriya Mahila Kosh was established in :

(A) 30 March 1992 (B) 30 March 1993

(C) 30 March 1994 (D) 30 March 1995

539. Main objective of the National Policy on Women Empowerment 2001 was:

(A) Women's progress, Development and Empowerment

(B) Education for Women and Girls

(C) Gender Equality

(D) Economic Independence

540. The National Institute of open learning conducts:

(A) Only Primary School Courses

(B) Courses from Primary to Higher Secondary

(C) Vocational Courses

(D) All the above

541. Kothari Commission emphasized on :

(A) Non Formal Adult and Continuing Education

(B) Expansion of Universal Schooling

(C) Preparation of Literature and Reading Material

(D) Arrangement for Continuing Education Programmes

542. SRC's functions do not include :

(A) Supervision of ZSS
(B) Material Development

(C) Training
(D) Research and Evaluation

543. Life Long Education is an organizing principle providing a total system for all education pertaining to :

(A) Non-Formal Education
(B) Learning to Learn

(C) Post Literacy
(D) Neo-Literate

544. New Education Policy was the part of plan of Government of India :

(A) Seventh Five Year Plan
(B) Tenth Five Year Plan

(C) First Five Year Plan
(D) Fourth Five Year Plan

545. National Literacy Mission includes:

(A) Each One Teach One

(B) Farmer's Functional Literacy

(C) New Area Development Approach

(D) Total Literacy campaign

546. Bharat Gyan Vigyan Jatha aims at :

(A) Inculcating religious temperament

(B) Inculcating scientific temperament

(C) Inculcating non alliance temperament

(D) Inculcating non violence temperament

547. VEC is responsible for :

(A) Reviewing TLC at the village level

(B) Supervising the work of VT's

(C) Observing the progress of neo-literates

(D) All the above

548. Integrated Pace and Content Learning is :

(A) A method of teaching

(B) A method of creating proper environment

(C) A essential approach for launching successful literacy campaign

(D) An assured provision for reentry and future learning

549. Which of the following is the most important in case of good communication between Teacher and Learner ?

(A) The subject matter is well organized

(B) Learning objectives are well understood by learner

(C) Learner is made to realize the learning material

(D) Use of good text books

550. Arrange the following in the order of Low Literacy Rate States in India, according to census of India 2001

(A) Jammu and Kashmir, Arunachal Pradesh, Uttar Pradesh and Bihar

(B) Uttar Pradesh, Rajasthan, Orissa, Bihar

(C) Bihar, Uttar Pradesh, Rajasthan, Orissa

(D) Orissa, Rajasthan, Uttar Pradesh and Bihar

551. Arrange the following programmes in order in which they were classified in India. Use the code given below:

I. DAE

II. SRC

III. SVP

IV. JSS

Codes:

(A) II, I, IV and III

(B) III, IV, I and II

(C) I, II, III and IV

(D) III, II, IVand I

552. Arrange the following tasks of the department of Adult Continuing Education in the order in which they are being implemented. Use code given below :

I. Field out reach

II. Extension

III. Research

IV. Teaching/Training

Codes:

(A) IV, III, II and I

(B) III, II, I and IV

(C) II, III, IV and I

(D) I, II, III and IV

553. Arrange the following in the order of universalisation of Primary Education introduced by the Government of India after Independence:

I. Social Education

I. Non-Formal Education

III. District Primary Education

IV. Sarva Shiksha Abhiyan

Codes:

(A) I, II, III and IV
(B) III, IV, II, and I
(C) I, III, IV and II
(D) II, IV, III and I

554. Arrange the principles of Planning and Management followed in implementing any Adult Education Programmes :

(A) Planning, Organising, Implementing, Monitoring and Evaluation, Supervision
(B) Planning, Implementing, Monitoring, Supervision and Evaluation
(C) Planning, Organising, Implementing, Monitoring and Supervision
(D) Preplanning, Implementing, Monitoring, Supervision and Evaluation

555. We have now four types of mass media which are also available for Adult Education. Identify correct order in which they are being used.

(A) Print, Radio, T.V., Folk Arts and Kalajatha
(B) Folk Arts and Kalajatha, Radio, T.V., Print
(C) Folk Arts and Kalajatha, Print, Radio, T.V
(D) T.V., Radio, Folk Arts and Kalajatha, Print

556. Arrange the following National Level Programmes on Adult and Continuing Education launched by Government of India in chronological order. Use the following code :

I. NAEP
II. NLM
III. TLC
IV. CEP

Codes:

(A) I, III, IV and II
(B) I, II, III and IV
(C) IV, III, II and I
(D) II, IV, I and III

557. Which could be the best sequence in any communication process ?

(A) Coding - sending - receiving - decoding
(B) Sending - coding - receiving - decoding
(C) Coding - sending - decoding - receiving
(D) Sending - coding - decoding – receiving

558. World Declaration on "Education For All" was made in :

(A) 1990
(B) 1996
(C) 1980
(D)1992

559. NAEP was launched in :

(A) 1997
(B) 1972
(C) 1976
(D) 1978

560. Farmers Training and Functional Literacy programme was launched in :

(A) 1968 (B) 1962

(C) 1965 (D) 1967

561. International Population Day is celebrated on :

(A) 18 July (B) 11 July

(C) 20 July (D) 10 July

562. UGC initiated POPED activities in the year :

(A) 1978 (B) 1983

(C) 1988 (D) 1992

563. International Literacy Day is celebrated on :

(A) 18 July (B) 8 Sep

(C) 2 Oct (D) 19th NOV

564. "Padagogy of the oppressed" was written by :

(A) Ivan Ilich (B) Paulo Freire

(C) Bertson (D) None of the above

565. NLM was launched in :

(A) April 1996 (B) December 1990

(C) May 1988 (D) Jan 1989

566. Dr. Zakir Husain Memorial Lecture is organized by:

(A) Jamia Millia

(B) International Council for Adult Education

(C) Asian South Pacific Bureau of Adult Education

(D) Indian Adult Education Association

567. National Commission For Women was established in :

(A) 1990 (B) 1987

(C) 1994 (D) 1962

568. National Policy on Women Empowerment was launched in :

(A) 1999 (B) 2001

(C) 2000 (D) 2002

569. The changed name of National Open School is :

(A) National Flexible School

(B) National Distance Education Centre

(C) National Institute of Open Schooling

(D) National Institute of Open learning

570. National Adult Education Programme defined adult education as :

(A) Literacy, Functionality and Conscientization

(B) Functional Literacy, Productivity and Awareness

(C) Productivity, Mass Education and Literacy

(D) Conscientization, Functionality and Literacy

571. The major role of SRC in CEP is to provide help in :

(A) Developing package for vocational Education

(B) Provide professional support in CEP's

(C) Preparation of curriculum framework for neo-literates

(D) To monitor and evaluate Literacy programme

572. Life Long Education is regarded as :

(A) Education that does not end with schooling but it is a life long process

(B) Shifting from formal to non-formal

(C) Life Skill Education for better health

(D) Education for parent hood

573. New Education Policy was launched in :

(A) 1986 (B) 1980

(C) 1987 (D) 1989

574. The first Total Literate District was :

(A) Chittoor (B) Ernakulam

(C) Ajmer (D) Bankura

575. Mopping up programme means :

(A) Linking up the illiterates to developmental programmes

(B) Making literate the left out

(C) To be sensitive towards illiterates

(D) Empowering the illiterates

576. Continuing Education means :

(A) Weekend and evening programme for professional.

(B) Organising instructional programmes in specialized area

(C) Organising extension activities for grass-root level

(D) It is a educational process which organised learning for updating and overcoming the barriers of knowledge and skill

577. A nodal Prerak of CEC :

(A) Designs Curriculum and Learning Material

(B) Facilitates the functioning of CEC's under his/her control

(C) Integrates National issues and concerns with the learning activities

(D) Design and Implements Training for different functionaries

578. Education Technology is best defined as :

(A) Use of gadgets

(B) Developing Learning Material

(C) Systematic Applications of Learning theories in Teaching

(D) Systematic Applications of Technology in Education

579. Arrange the following in decreasing order of "High Literacy" rate states in India according to the census of India 2001 :

(A) Mizoram, Kerala, Goa and Delhi

(B) Kerala, Mizoram, Goa and Delhi

(C) Delhi, Goa, Mizoram and Kerala

(D) Goa, Kerala, Delhi and Mizoram

580. Arrange the following in the order in which the following programmes were launched in India, use the code given below :

(i) FFLP

(ii) TLC

(iii) PLC

(iv) CEP

Codes:

(A) (ii), (iii), (iv) and (i)

(B) (i), (ii), (iii) and (iv)

(C) (iii), (ii), (i) and (iv)

(D) (iv), (iii), (i) and (ii)

581. Arrange the following UGC's Extension programme on Adult Education introduced in the Dept. of Adult and continuing Education. Use the code given below : Adult Education under

(i) 16 point in 20 point programme

(ii) Area Developm. Approach

(iii) Mass Programme for Functional Literacy

(iv) Total Literacy Campaign

Codes:

(A) (i), (ii), (iii) and (iv)

(B) (iv), (iii), (ii) and (i)

(C) (iii), (ii), (i) and (iv)

(D) (i), (iv), (iii) and (ii)

582. Arrange the following in the order of promoting continuing Education among neo-literates in India launched by the Govt. of India after Independence :

(i) Jan Shikshan Nilayam
(ii) Open Basic Education
(iii) Jan Shikshan Sansthan
(iv) Continuing Education Prog.

Codes:

(A) (iii), (ii), (iv) and (i)
(B) (i), (iii), (ii) and (iv)
(C) (iv), (i), (iii) and (ii)
(D) (i), (ii), (iii) and (iv)

583. Arrange the following principles of planning and management in the order in which they should be use the code given below:

(i) Planning
(ii) Organising and Implementing
(iii) Management
(iv) Monitoring and Evaluation

Codes:

(A) (iv), (i), (ii) and (iii)
(B) (i), (ii), (iii) and (iv)
(C) (ii), (iii), (iv) and (i)
(D) (iii), (ii), (i) and (iv)

584. Arrange the following list of media in order in which they are popularly used in Adult Education. Use the code given below :

(i) Folk Arts
(ii) Kalajatha
(iii) Print Media
(iv) Radio

Codes:

(A) (ii), (iii), (iv) and (i)
(B) (i), (ii), (iv) and (iii)
(C) (iii), (i), (ii) and (iv)
(D) (ii), (iii), (i) and (iv)

585. Arrange the functional hierarchy of functionaries serving in continuing Education programme at District level :

(A) District programme Co-ordinator, Block-Co-ordinator, Prerak and Assistant Prerak
(B) Assistant Prerak, Prerak, Block-Co-ordinator and District Programme Coordinator
(C) Block-Co-ordinator, District Programme Co-ordinator, Assistant Prerak, and Prerak
(D) District Programme Co-ordinator, Block-Co-ordinator, Prerak and Assistant Prerak

586. What is the sequence for preparing a research report in Adult Education ?

(A) Research problem, Objectives, Methodology, Data Analysis and Findings, Discussions, Conclusion

(B) Objectives, Research problem, Methodology, Data Analysis and Findings, Discussions

(C) Objectives, Methodology, Data Analysis, Research problem and Findings, Discussions, Conclusion

(D) Research problem, Methodology, Data Analysis, Objectives and Findings, Discussions, Conclusion

587. International Literacy day is celebrated on :

(A) 18th July (B) 8th September

(C) 2nd October (D) 19th November

588. NLM was launched by then Prime Minister Rajiv Gandhi on :

(A) 5th May 1988 (B) 7th May 1989

(C) 5th May 1989 (D) 7th May 1988

589. Non formal programme was launched in :

(A) 1972-73 (B) 1975-76

(C) 1978-79 (D) 1981-82

590. Gram Shikshan Muhim was launched in :

(A) Gujarat (B) Kerala

(C) Rajasthan (D) Maharashtra

591. Paradigm Shift in 'POPED' includes :

(A) Reproductive Health (B) Small Family Norms

(C) Favourable Sea Ratio (D) Crude Birth Rate

592. World conference on population and development (1994) was held at :

(A) New Delhi (B) Mexico

(C) Cairo (D) New York

593. Integrated pace and content learning is :

(A) A method of teaching

(B) A method of creating proper environment

(C) A essential approach for launching successful literacy campaign

(D) An assured provision for re-entry and further learning

594. V.E.C. is responsible for :

(A) Reviewing TLC at the village level

(B) Supervising the work of VT's

(C) Observing the progress of Neo-literates

(D) All the above

595. Post literacy programmes have to be developed in the context of life long education. These have to fulfil four major goals namely :

(A) Functional, Instructional, Life Skill, Literacy

(B) Remediation, Continuation, Application, Communitisation

(C) Vocational, Nonformal, Population Education, Life Skill Education

(D) All above

596. National Adult Education Programme defined adult education as :

(A) Literacy, Functionality 8 Conscientization

(B) Functional Literacy, Productivity and Awareness

(C) Productivity, Mass Education 8 Literacy

(D) Conscientization, Functionality 8 Literacy

597. The new name of national open school is :

(A) National Flexible School

(B) National distance education centers

(C) National School of open schooling

(D) National School of Open Learning

598. Anti Arrack agitation of Nellore district of Andhra Pradesh was organised mainly by

(A) The NGO's of the district

(B) Neo-literate women of the district

(C) Women Panchayat member of the district

(D) None of the above

599. Main objective of the National Policy on woman empowerment 2001 :

(A) Women's progress, Development 8 Empowerment

(B) Education for Women 8 Girls

(C) Gender equality

(D) Economic Independence

600. The world conference on human rights was held in 1993 at :

(A) Vienna (B) Hamburg

(C) Mexico City (D) Cairo

601. The main objective of education for all is to be :

(A) Promote a learning society

(B) Promote literacy among men and women

(C) Promote literacy among deprived sections of society

(D) None of the above

602. The first total literate district in the country was :

(A) Chittor

(B) Ernakulam

(C) Ajmer

(D) Bankura

603. J. S. S. was previously known as :

(A) Shramik Vidyapeeth

(B) Jan Shikshan Nilayam

(C) Gram Shikshan Muhim

(D) Janata College

604. World population day is celebrated on :

(A) 11th July

(B) 12th July

(C) 11th September

(D) 12th September

605. Population density is measurement of :

(A) Types of Houses where people live

(B) Number of people in per square k.m.

(C) Distribution of population in the area

(D) None of the above

606. The sex ratio in India as per 2001 census is :

(A) 927 : 1000

(B) 933 : 1000

(C) 945 : 1000

(D) 929 : 1000

607. Arrange the following in the order in which they appeared. Use the code given below:

(i) Gram Shikshan Mohim

(ii) Farmers Functional Literacy Programme

(iii) Community Development Programme

(iv) Social Education

Codes:

(A) (ii) (iii) (iv) (i)

(B) (ii) (iv) (iii) (i)

(C) (iv) (iii) (i) (ii)

(D) (iii) (i) (iv) (ii)

608. According to the census of India 2001, arrange the following states in the order of High Literacy Rate :

(A) Kerala, Mizoram, Lakshadweep Goa and Delhi

(B) Mizoram, Lakshadweep, Goa Kerala and Delhi

(C) Mizoram, Lakshadweep, Goa, Delhi and Kerala

(D) Lakshadweep, Goa, Delhi, Kerala and Mizoram

609. According to the census of India 2001, arrange the following in the order of low literacy rate:

(A) Arunachal Pradesh, Uttar Pradesh, Bihar, Jharkhand and Jammu and Kashmir

(B) Bihar, Jharkhand, Jammu & Kashmir, Arunachal Pradesh and Uttar Pradesh

(C) Jharkhand, Jammu & Kashmir, Arunachal Pradesh, Uttar Pradesh and Bihar

(D) Jammu & Kashmir, Arunachal Pradesh, Uttar Pradesh, Bihar and Jharkhand

610. Indicators for quality of life improvement programme under APEEAL are designed in the following areas :

(A) Biological, Social, Economic and Environmental

(B) Biological, Social, Environmental and Humanistic

(C) Food, Housing, Sanitation and Pollution Free Environment

(D) Health, Economic and Environmental

611. The three key components of development as indicated by UNDP reports are :

(A) Adult Literacy, Education, Income

(B) Longevity, Knowledge and Income

(C) Health Care, Home, Intelligence

(D) Hygiene, Nutrition, Income

612. Arrange the following in the order in which they appeared. Use the code given below :

(i) Population Growth (ii) Food, shelter, housing

(iii) Environmental Education (iv) Pollution

Codes:

(A)	(i)	(ii)	(iii)	(iv)
(B)	(ii)	(iii)	(iv)	(i)
(C)	(iv)	(ii)	(iii)	(i)
(D)	(i)	(iv)	(ii)	(iii)

613. Arrange the following in the order in which they appeared. Use the code given below:

(i) Infant (ii) Old

(iii) Young (iv) Child

Codes:

(A)	(i)	(iv)	(iii)	(ii)
(B)	(ii)	(iii)	(iv)	(i)
(C)	(iv)	(ii)	(iii)	(i)
(D)	(i)	(ii)	(iii)	(iv)

614. Arrange the following in order in which they appeared. Use of the code given below :

(i) Computer (ii) Radio

(iii) TV (iv) Books

Codes:

(A)	(iv)	(ii)	(iii)	(i)
(B)	(ii)	(iii)	(iv)	(i)
(C)	(ii)	(i)	(iv)	(iii)
(D)	(i)	(ii)	(iii)	(iv)

615. Indian Adult-Education Association was started i n the year :

(A) 1932 (B) 1936

(C) 1939 (D) 1940

616. 'Nehru Literacy Award' was consitituted by :

(A) IAEA (B) IUACE

(C) Directorate of Adult Education (D) Ministry of HRD

617. The concept of Social Education was initiated during :

(A) First Five Year Plan (B) Second Five Year Plan

(C) Third Five Year Plan (D) Fourth Five Year Plan

618. NLM was started in the year :

(A) 1982 (B) 1989

(C) 1988 (D) 1990

619. The lowest literacy rate is in the state of:

(A) UP (B) MP

(C) AP (D) Bihar

620. International Literacy Day is celebrated every year on:

(A) 15th August (B) 14th November

(C) 8th September (D) 2nd October

621. The first total literate district in India was :
(A) Chittoor (B) Ernakulam
(C) Ajmer (D) Bankura

622. The National Adult Education Programme was started in the year :
(A) 1975 (B) 1976
(C) 1977 (D) 1978

623. Which age group is specially targetted by Adult Education Programme
(A) 6-14 Years (B) 15-35 Years
(C) 35-60 Years (D) Above 60 Years

624. The Adult Education movement in Denmark was known as :
(A) Folk High Schools (B) Grammer Schools
(C) Public Schools (D) Residential Schools

625. Continuing Education is essentially an instructional programme for :
(A) School Dropouts (B) Married Women
(C) Non-Resident Indians (D) All the age Groups

626. Adult Learning ultimately should lead to
(A) Modifiaction of Habits (B) Modification of Attitudes
(C) Modification of Behariour (D) Modification of Aptitude

627. The New Education Policy was approved in the parliament in
(A) 1985 (B) 1986
(C) 1984 (D) 1981

628. What was the literacy rate in India as per 2001 census ?
(A) 65.38 per cent (B) 72.96 per cent
(C) 61.14 per cent (D) 64.84 per cent

629. Andragogy means:
(A) Teaching Adults (B) Guiding Adults
(C) Helping Adults Learn (D) Lifelong Learning

630. When is the International Women's Day observed?
(A) 2nd October (B) 19th November
(C) 25th December (D) 8th March

631. Area Development Approach depends on :
(A) Major Planning (B) Minor Planning
(C) Micro Planning (D) Macro Planning

632. Who has said 'illiteracy is a Sin and Shame'?

(A) Zakir Hussain
(B) Jawaharlal Nehru
(C) Mahatma Gandhi
(D) Sarojini Naidu

633. The objectives of Nehru Yuvak Kendra is to involve young people in

(A) Literacy activities
(B) Adult Education activities
(C) National Development activities
(D) NLM activities

634. Which of the following programmes would focus on developing leadership?

(A) Area Based Approach
(B) Workers Education
(C) Nehru Yuvak Kendra
(D) Shramik Vidyapeeth

635. Who has said 'Medium is the message'?

(A) David Mc Lleland
(B) Thorndike
(C) Abraham Maslow
(D) Piaget

636. The Post - Literacy centre in the previous pattern of Adult Education is callled

(A) Grama Siksha Mohim
(B) Jankalyan Nilayam
(C) Jan Siksha Nilayam
(D) Jan Siksha Sansthan

637. Which world organisation addresses special mandate for Literacy Programmes?

(A) UNDP
(B) UNESCO
(C) UNFPA
(D) UNICEF

638. State was supposed to provide free and compulsory elementary education to all the

children of 6-14 years age group by:-

(A) 1960
(B) 1965
(C) 1970
(D) 1975

639. Population Studies are Specifically concerned with :

(A) Quality of Life
(B) Demography
(C) Prevention of Infant Mortality Rate
(D) Democracy

640. An illiterate person is one who is :

(A) Uneducated
(B) No interest in liberal ideas
(C) Lacks Skill in Reading Writing and Numeracy
(D) Lacks appreciation for literature

641. Which one is the main cause of growth of illiterates in India?

(A) Stagnation in Education

(B) Lack of Schooling

(C) High Dropout Ratio

(D) Low Enrollment in Primary Education

642. Where was 'Gram Shikshana Mohim' started?

(A) Andra Pardesh (B) Bihar

(C) Tamil Nadu (D) Maharashtra

643. Who has advocated 'Rural Universities will support the Basic Education'?

(A) Mahatma Gandhi (B) Jawaharlal Nehru

(C) Sardar Patel (D) Sarojni Naidu

644. The 'Window Period' the period in which the person gets infected with virus of HIV AIDS but dose not show any sign in Medical Investigation :

(A) 0-1 Month (B) 1-3 Months

(C) 3-5 Month (D) 5-7 Months

645. The three R's include

(A) Reading Writing and Arithmetic

(B) Reading Drawing and Painting

(C) Reading Recitation and Listening

(D) Reading Comprehending and Writing

646. Where was the UN conference on Environment and Development held in 1992?

(A) Paris (B) London

(C) Rio-De-Janeiro (D) Jakartha

647. UNICEF, Primarily deals with :

(A) Children (B) Adults

(C) Old age (D) Women

648. State Resource Centre for Adult and Continuing Education is known as :

(A) NGO (B) Quasi - Government Body

(C) Government Organisation (D) Statutory Body

649. What are the three main functions of University system?

(A) Teaching, Research and Extension

(B) Teaching, Lecture and Tutorial

(C) Reasearch, Demonstration and Practice

(D) Teaching, Research and Consultation

650. In which year the 'Total Literacy Campaign' was launched in India?

(A) 1990 (B) 1991

(C) 1992 (D) 1993

651. What is the changed name of open school?

(A) National Flexible School

(B) National Assistance Education Centre

(C) National Insititute of Open Schooling

(D) National Institute of Open Learning

652. Point No:16 of the 20-point programme of 1982 emphasise on :

(A) Formal Education (B) Adult Education

(C) Children Education (D) Workers Education

653. Adult Education Programme is:

(A) Teacher Need Based (B) Centre Oriented

(C) Learner Need Based (D) skill based

654. "Development is of the Man, By the Man and for the Man" who has said?

(A) Malcom. S. Adiseshiah (B) Julius K.Nyerere

(C) Molcom Knowles (D) J.R. Kidd

655. 'Edusat' means

(A) Satellite Education (B) Distance Education

(C) Virtual Education (D) Alternative Education

656. In which year the 'NLM-UNESCO Award' was instituted?

(A) 1995 (B) 1996

(C) 1997 (D) 1998

657. What is Sex Ratio (Female per thousand Male) in India as per 2001 census report?

(A) 963 (B) 953

(C) 933 (D) 943

658. ASPBAE is related to

(A) workers education (B) Adult education

(C) Formal education (D) children education

659. Which of the following is the right age of marriage for Boys and Girls in India?

(A) 18 years for Girls and 20 years for Boys

(B) 18 years for Girls and and 21 years for Boys

(C) 19 years for Girls and 22 years for Boys

(D) 20 years for Girls and 21 years for Boys

660. Frank LaucBach contribution to adult-education is :

(A) Each one Teach one Method

(B) Functional Literacy Programme

(C) Farmers' Functional Literacy Programme

(D) Women's Functional Literacy Programme

661. Connectionism or the S - R Theory of Learning was advocated by

(A) Thorundike (B) Watson

(C) Piaget (D) Gessalt

662. In which year was the First nigh school started?

(A) 1923 (B) 1924

(C) 1925 (D) 1926

663. German Adult - Education is known as :

(A) GAEA (B) GEA

(C) DVV (D) GUAE

664. 'Animator' in Adult Educational Programme are :

(A) Facilitators (B) Communicators

(C) Teachers (D) Researchers

665. World declaration on education made in

(A) 1990 (B) 1996

(C) 1980 (D) 1988

666. The main objective of 'Education For All' is to :

(A) Promote a learning society

(B) Promote literacy among men and women

(C) Promote literacy among deprived section of society

(D) None of above

667. International Population Day is celebrated on :

(A) 10th july (B) 11th July

(C) 18th July (D) 20th july

668. International Literacy Day is celebrated on :

(A) 18th July (B) 8th September

(C) 2nd October (D) 19th November

669. Human Rights Day is celebrated on :

(A) 15th July (B) 20th September

(C) 10th November (D) 10th December

670. NAEP was launched in the year :

(A) 1977 (B) 1972

(C) 1976 (D) 1978

671. National Adult Education Programme defined adult education as :

(A) Literacy, Functionality and Conscientization

(B) Functional Literacy, Productivity and Awareness

(C) Mass Education, Fundamental Education, Basic Education

(D) Liberal Education, Literacy and Education For Women

672. The World conference on Human Rights was held in the year 1993 at :

(A) Vienna (B) Hamburg

(C) Mexico City (D) Cairo

673. Farmer's Training and Functional literacy programme was launched in the year :

(A) 1968 (B) 1962

(C) 1965 (D) 1967

674. Rastriya Mahila Kosh was established in :

(A) 30 March 1992 (B) 30 March 1993

(C) 30 March 1994 (D) 30 March 1995

675. National Policy on Women Empowerment was launched in the year :

(A) 1999 (B) 2000

(C) 2001 (D) 2002

676. Fifth Five Year Plan emphasised the need of :

(A) Non-Formal Education

(B) Community Development Programme

(C) Adult Education

(D) Correspondence Education

677. Bangkok Conference on adult educators and experts (1965) envisaged the concept of :

(A) Non-Formal Education
(B) Distance Education
(C) Functional Literacy
(D) Community Education

678. 'Cultural Action For Freedom' is a book written by :

(A) Malcom Knowle
(B) Paulo Freire
(C) James Draper
(D) Roby Kidd

679. 'Learning to be' is an outstanding publication of the :

(A) UNICEF
(B) UNESCO
(C) IAEA
(D) ASPBAE

680. A book written by Roby Kidd is :

(A) Padagogy of the Oppressed
(B) Cultural Action For Freedom
(C) How Adult Learn
(D) Small is Beautiful

681. The 'Concept of Hierarchy of Needs' is advocated by :

(A) David Mac'lleland
(B) Glen Eyford
(C) Abraham Maslow
(D) J.R. Kidd

682. 'Insight Learning' is associated with :

(A) Kohler
(B) Maslow
(C) Thorndike
(D) Skinner

683. NLM aims at imparting literacy to

(A) 100 million illiterates
(B) 150millionilliterates
(C) 200 million illiterates
(D) 300 million illiterates

684. Literacy Award being given by NLM for outstanding work is known as :

(A) Nehru Award
(B) Tagore Award
(C) Satyen Maitra Award
(D) None of the above

685. Tagore Literacy Award is being given for an outstanding work is :

(A) in the promotion of literacy work among women
(B) in the promotion of literacy work among youths
(C) in the promotion of literacy work among farmers
(D) in the promotion of literacy work among labourers

686. New Education Policy was launched in the year :

(A) 1986
(B) 1980
(C) 1987
(D) 1989

687. TLC Project have been launched in the country in :

(A) more than 500 districts
(B) 400 districts
(C) more than 400 districts
(D) 500 districts

688. The first total literate district in India was :

(A) Chittoor
(B) Ernakulam
(C) Ajmer
(D) Bankura

689. Dr. Zakir Husain Memorial Lecture is organised by :

(A) Jamia Millia Islamia
(B) International Council For Adult Education
(C) Asian South Pacific Bureau of Adult Education
(D) Indian Adult Education Association

690. Nehru Literacy and Tagore Literacy award is given by :

(A) Jamia Millia Islamia
(B) Indian Adult Education Association
(C) National Literacy Mission
(D) Planning Commission

691. The incidence of bonded labour is high among:

(A) Factory Workers
(B) Agricultural workers
(C) Garment Industrial Workers
(D) mass media

692. Anti Arrack agitation of Nellore District of Andhra Pradesh was organised mainly by:

(A) The NGO's of the district
(B) Neo-literate women of the district
(C) Women panchayat members of district
(D) Self-Help Groups of the district

693. Life-long Education is regarded as :

(A) education that does not end with schooling but it is a life long process
(B) shifting from formal to non-formal
(C) life skill education for better health
(D) education for parent hood

694. Environmental conservation is a part of :

(A) Non-Formal Education Programme
(B) Population Education Programme

(C) Adult Education Programme

(D) None of the above

695. Who was the author of 'Buniyadi Talim' in Pre-Independent India ?

(A) Mahatma Gandhi (B) Jawaharlal Nehru

(C) Netaji Subhash Chandra Bose (D) Bal Gangadhar Tilak

696. Which of the following system of education is concerned with adult education?

(A) Formal (B) Informal

(C) Open Leaving System (D) Non-formal education

697. The National Open School conducts :

(i) Only primary school education

(ii) Courses from primary to higher secondary school level

(iii) Vocational courses

(iv) Quality of life improvement courses

Codes:

(A) (i) only (B) (i) and (iii)

(C) (i), (iii) and (iv) (D) All the above

698. Match the order of the concepts/terms in List-I with the that is List-II.

List - I		**List - I**
(A) Andragogy	i.	Maslow
(B) Conscientization	ii.	Malcome Knowles
(C) How Adult Learn	iii.	Roby kidd
(D) Motivational Theory	iv.	Paulo Freire

Codes:	(A)	(B)	(C)	(D)
(A)	i	iii	ii	iv
(B)	ii	iv	iii	i
(C)	iv	iii	ii	I
(D)	ii	iii	iv	i

699. Non-Formal Education :

(A) Refers to education incidentally picked up in life situations

(B) Refers to an organised, systematic educational activities carried on outside the frame work of the formal system

(C) Refers to education organised in a systematic manner extending from primary level to the university

(D) None of the above

700. You are conducting an awareness programme on HIV/AIDS for truck drivers at a local dhabha/cafe eating place which combination of communication technologies would you use :

(A) Storytelling, OHP and film projector

(B) Video film, LCD projector and charts

(C) Charts, banners, distribution of leaflets, storytelling with OHP and video-film

(D) Lecturing with charts and distribution of leaflets

701. Population Education mean :

(A) Education about the different types of people in different countries

(B) Education about the impact of a large population on development

(C) Education about family planning and contraceptives

(D) Education about the reasons for the population growth in India

702. Which one of the follwing is known as father of adult education ?

(A) Nalcolm Knowles (B) Philip Coombs

(C) Roby Kidd (D) James Draper

703. The main objectives of the National Policy on Women Empowerment 2001, is :

(A) Women's progress development and empowerment

(B) Education for Women and Girls

(C) Gender Equality

(D) Economic Independence

704. Continuing Education means :

(A) Weekend and evening programmes for professionals

(B) Organising instructional programmes in a specialized area

(C) Organising extension activities for grass-root level

(D) It is an educational process which organised learning for updating and overcoming the barriers of knowledge and skill.

705. 'Paradigm Shift' in POPED includes :

(A) Reproductive Health (B) Small Family Norm

(C) Favourable Sex Ratio (D) Crude Birth Rate

706. UGC initiated POPED activities in the year :

(A) 1978 (B) 1983

(C) 1988 (D) 1992

707. World population reached the six billion mark on :

(A) 12 October 1999
(B) 12 September 1999
(C) 12 November 1999
(D) 12 December 1999

708. HIV/AIDS is more a

(A) Socio-Medical Problem
(B) Ecological problem
(C) Human problem
(D) paleontological problem

709. Participatory Research aims at :

(A) Mobilizing and empowering community members to develop and conduct research and use research outputs
(B) Developing the discipline of adult education
(C) Solving problems of people
(D) Posing question of ethics of research

710. Integrated Pace and content learning is :

(A) A method of teaching
(B) A method of creating proper environment
(C) An essential approach for launching a successful literacy campaign
(D) An assured provision for re-entry and further learning

711. A nodal prerak of CEC :

(A) Design curriculum and learning material
(B) Facilitates the functioning of CECs under his/her control
(C) Integrates national issues and concerns with the learning activities
(D) Design and implements training for different functionaries

712. **SRCs function do not include :**

(A) Supervision of ZSS
(B) Material Development
(C) Training
(D) Research and Evaluation

713. **The following programmes were launched in India, indicate the chronological order of launching of the programmes :**

(A) DPEP, NLM, NFE, Sarva Shikshan Abhiyan
(B) NFE, NLM, DPEP, Sarva Shikshan Abhiyan
(C) Sarva Shikshan Abhiyan, DPEP, NLM, NFE
(D) NFE, DPEP, NLM, Sarva Shikshan Abhiyan

714. Indicate the correct order of activities in the management of adult education programme :

(A) Organizing, training, staffing, planning evaluation
(B) Staffing, training, planning, organizing, evaluation

(C) Planning, organizing, staffing, training, evaluation

(D) Planning, staffing, training, organizing, evaluation

715. The Mumbai statement on adult education resolved in favour of opening

(A) Community halls to adult learners

(B) School, colleges and universities to adult learners

(C) Buildings of chambers of commerce to adult learners

(D) Marriage halls to adult learners

716. As per census 2011, the state\union having higest sex ration in india is

(A) Punjab

(B) West Bengal

(C) Kerala

(D) Rajasthan

717. The concept of distance education is

(A) New and non-traditional

(B) Traditional

(C) New and traditional

(D) None of the above

718. The active means of communication is

(A) Play

(B) Workshop

(C) Street play

(D) All of the above

719. Sarva Shiksha Abhiyan (SSA) is Government of India's flagship programme for achievement of

(A) Universalization of Elementary Education (UEE) in a time bound manner.

(B) Universalization of Secondary Education in a time bound manner.

(C) Universalization of Higher Education in a time bound manner.

(D) Universalization of Skill Development in a time bound manner.

720. According to 2011 Census, the sex ratio in India (upto the age group of 6 years) is

(A) 914

(B) 927

(C) 930

(D) 943

721. The scheme of Jan Shikshan Sansthan (JSS) aim to impart education

(A) For all, including the poor and the rich.

(B) For the poor, the illiterate and the neo-literate.

(C) Only for the poor women who are illiterates and neo-literates.

(D) Only for the poor male adults who are illiterates and neo-literates.

722. The beneficiaries of continuing Education Programmes are

(A) Neo-literates (B) School dropouts
(C) Common villagers (D) All of the above

723. Village is an example of
(A) Institution (B) Community
(C) Organisation (D) None of the above

724. The population education clubs in Universities and Colleges primarily
(A) Integrate population and development education messages in the teaching/learning materials (both print and non-print)
(B) Produce films on population
(C) Stage street plays on alcoholism
(D) Organize poetry competitions on population themes.

725. Legal literacy program in India
(A) Encourages citizens to use litigation as a strategy for grievance redressal.
(B) Generates awareness of rights and duties as knowledge so that people live in consonance with the rule of law.
(C) Encourages citizens to enrol in law colleges as law students.
(D) Encourages citizens to become lawyers.

726. Which educational concept was developed by Grundwig ?
(A) Community schools (B) Community colleges
(C) Folk colleges (D) Folk high schools

727. The medium of communication that has the widest reach in India is
(A) Print (B) Radio
(C) Television (D) Internet

728. Which of the following is the characteristic of an adult learner ?
(A) Maturity (B) Slow learning
(C) Experience (D) All of the above

729. Factors responsible for effective learning are
(A) Motivation (B) Presentation skills
(C) Expertise of teachers (D) All of the above

730. Essential condition for women empowerment is (Use the code given below)
(A) Educational development
(B) Health and nutritional facilities
(C) Reservation in family headship
(D) Proper training and orientation

Codes:

(A) (A), (B) and (C)
(B) (A), (B) and (D)
(C) (B), (C) and (D)
(D) (A), (C) and (D)

731. Identify the potential non-formal learning centres that are available in the country. (Use the code given below) :

(A) Primary health centres
(B) Community centres
(C) Cooperative societies
(D) Religious organizations

Codes:

(A) (A), (B), (C), (d)
(2) (A) and (B)
(3) (B) and (D)
(D) (B), (C), (D)

732. The importance of motivation in adult learning :

(A) Creates interest in learning
(B) Facilitates cooperation in learning
(C) Establishes individual democracy
(D) Ensure proper use of human resources

733. The main approaches to post literacy and continuing education are : (Use the codes given below :)

(A) Institutional approach
(B) Open/distance learning approach
(C) Computer-assisted approach
(D) Web-based approach

Codes:

(A) (A), (B), (D)
(B) (A), (B), (C), (D)
(C) (B), (C), (D)
(D) (B), (A), (C)

734. Select the types of lifelong learners by their roles. (Use the codes given below) :

(A) Learners as reflective agents for ideas
(B) Learners as creators of painting
(C) Learners as self actualizing agents for skills
(D) Learners as mediators for disputes

Codes:

(1) (A) and (C)
(2) (A) and (D)
(3) (B) only
(D) (C) and (D)

735. National Institute of open schooling also offers vocational education programmes for a variety of target groups such as : (Use the codes given below)

(A) Farmers (B) Weavers

(C) Doctors (D) Carpenters

Codes:

(A) (A), (B) and (D) (2) (B) and (D)

(C) (A), (B), (C) and (D) (4) (B) and (C)

736. Vocational education facilitates : (Use the code given below)

(A) Removal of unemployment

(B) Economic development

(C) Meeting the needs of organized and unorganized sectors.

(D) Preparation of students for self-employment.

Codes:

(A) (A), (B) and (C) (B) (A), (B), (C) and (D)

(C) (C) and (D) (D) (A), (C) and (D)

737. Methods of teaching usually preferred for adult learners are : (more than one option is possible) (use the code given below) :

(A) Brain storming method (B) Lecture method

(C) Group discussion method (D) Seminar method

Codes:

(1) (B) and (C) (B) (C) and (D)

(3) (A) and (D) (4) (A) and (C)

738. Arrange the following procedure for offering information dissemination service. (Use the codes given below)

(A) Judge (B) Weigh the options

(C) Analyse (D) Search

Codes:

(A) (A), (B), (C), (D) (B) (D), (C), (B), (A)

(C) (D), (A), (B), (C) (D) (A), (D), (B), (C)

739. Arrange the steps from beginning to end involve in organizing Adult/ continuing education, extension and field outreach activities. Use the code given below :

(A) Planning the extension work

(B) Identification of community needs

(C) Rapport building

(D) Selection of Projects

Codes:

(A) (A), (B), (C), (D) (B) (B), (A), (C), (D)

(C) (B), (A), (D), (C) (D) (A), (C), (D), (A)

740. Arrange the following processes of searching information on a given social issue. (Use the codes given below)

(A) Finalize Query formulation options on the issue.

(B) Identify database on the issue.

(C) Finalize strategy for search on the issue.

(D) Conducting the search on the issue.

Codes:

(A) (B), (C), (A), (D) (B) (B), (C), (D), (A)

(C) (A), (C), (B), (D) (D) (A), (B), (C), (D)

741. Arrange the following public policies in the chronological order on which they were implemented. (Use the codes given below)

(A) National policy on Women Empowerment

(B) National population Policy

(C) National policy on Education

(D) National policy on Health

Codes:

(A) (A), (B), (D), (C) (B) (C), (A), (B), (D)

(C) (B), (C), (D), (A) (D) (C), (B), (A), (D)

742. Arrange the skills of a good communicator in order to perform professional tasks. Use the codes given below :

(A) Observation (B) Empathy

(C) Encouragement (D) Summarising

Codes:

(A) (B), (C), (A), (D) (B) (C), (A), (B), (D)

(C) (A), (B), (C), (D) (D) (B), (A), (C), (D)

743. Arrange the process of communications from beginning to end using the code given below :

(A) Encode (B) Conceive

(C) Decode (D) Interpret

Codes:

(A) (A), (B), (C), (D) (B) (B), (A), (C), (D)

(C) (B), (C), (A), (D) (D) (C), (B), (A), (D)

744. Arrange the following programmes in order in which they were launched. Use the codes given below :

(A) Non-formal Education

(B) National literacy mission

(C) District Primary Education Programme

(D) Sarva Shiksha Abhiyan

Codes:

(A) (A), (B), (C), (D) (B) (B), (C), (A), (D)

(C) (A), (C), (D), (B) (D) (C), (D), (A), (B)

745. Arrange the following tasks of the department of adult and continuing education in the order in which they are being implemented. (Use the codes given below)

(A) Field outreach or outreach in the community

(B) Extension activities on the campus

(C) Research

(D) Teaching

Codes:

(A) (A), (B), (C), (D) (B) (D), (C), (B), (A)

(C) (C), (B), (A), (D) (D) (B), (C), (A), (D)

746. Arrange the principles of planning and management followed in implementing any adult education programmes. (Use the codes given below)

(A) Planning (B) Organising

(C) Implementing (D) Monitoring and Evaluation

Codes:

(A) (A), (C), (B), (D) (B) (B), (A), (C), (D)

(C) (A), (B), (C), (D) (D) (B), (A), (D), (C)

747. Arrange the following States according density of population. (Use the code given below)

(A) West Bengal (B) Tamil Nadu

(C) Maharashtra (D) Uttar Pradesh

Codes:

(A) (C), (D), (B), (A)
(B) (D), (B), (C), (A)
(C) (D), (C), (A), (B)
(D) (A), (C), (B), (D)

748. Arrange the following according to learning steps from beginning to end. (Use the code given below)

(A) Reinforcement
(B) Motivation
(C) Perception
(D) Reward

Codes:

(A) (C), (B), (A), (D)
(B) (B), (C), (A), (D)
(C) (A), (C), (B), (D)
(D) (D), (A), (B), (C)

749. Arrange the following programmes in the order in which they were launched. (Use the code as given below)

(A) National policy on Education
(B) Nai Talim
(C) Social Education Programme
(D) Saakshar Bharat Abhiyan

Codes:

(A) (A), (C), (B), (D)
(B) (B), (C), (A), (D)
(C) (C), (B), (D), (A)
(D) (C), (A), (B), (D)

750. National Youth Programe, which began in 1974, promoted in the commonwealth countries came into existence for :

(A) Child development
(B) Youth development
(C) Only female youth development
(D) Senior citizen development

751. Socialist Pedagogy reflects _____ at a given time thinks about Education Upbringing, about the relationship between the individual and society, and about social welfare for its marginalized members.

(A) How a given society
(B) How the teacher
(C) How the school owner launched the open basic Education Programme
(D) How the parents

752. The National Institute of open schooling, offer a basic Education Programme, as an alternative educational programme, equivalent to ____ of the formal education system.

(A) The College Education Programme
(B) The Senior Secondary Education Programme

(C) The Secondary Education Programme

(D) The Elementary Education Programme

753. Teaching aids are meant to :

(A) Engage the teachers' sense and increase interaction with the content, leading to increased memory relention.

(B) Engage the students' sense and increase interaction with the content, leading to increased memory relention.

(C) Engage the education inspectors' sense and increase interaction with the content, leading to increased memory relention.

(D) engage the school owners' sense and increase interaction with the content, leading to increase memory relention.

754. The "cascade" approach to training adult educators involves providing initial training.

(A) Of all adult education instructors in an area.

(B) For selected resource persons who then become responsible for training others.

(C) For selected supervisors of adult education in an area.

(D) For selected senior citizens participating in the adult education programme in an area

755. The post-literacy materials which are being supplied to adult education centres for neoliterates via in the form of _____.

(A) Short story, drama and poetry

(B) Legal case summaries

(C) Press reports published in newspapers

(D) Essays written in prose form

756. The National Rural Health Mission was launched in 2005 in India _____.

(A) To provide health services for all citizens

(B) To provide health services in rural areas

(C) To provide health services for women

(D) To provide health services for childrens

757. Change in one variable leading and change in another variable is called as:

(A) Average (B) Standard deviation

(C) Correlation (D) ANOVA

758. An Interview based on a identified list of questions is called as _____.

(A) Structured interview (B) Open discussion

(C) Personal interview (D) Psychological interview

759. Which district was declared as totally literate in 1989 ?

(A) Kolhapur
(B) Nellore
(C) Ernaculam
(D) Gorakhpur

760. Which of the following factors have not weakened the caste system ?

(A) Industrialization and urbanisation
(B) The quick means of transportation
(C) The Constitution of India
(D) The policy of reservations

761. Mahatma Gandhi and Dr. Zakir Hussain supported education that emphasized

(A) The concerns of only heart
(B) The concerns of only head and heart
(C) The concerns of head, heart and hand
(D) The concerns of commerce

762. Which of the following is a probability sampling design ?

(A) Quata sampling
(B) Snowball sampling
(C) Cluster sampling
(D) Purposive sampling

763. The main difference between a child learner and an adult learner is that the adult learner

(A) Learns by imitation
(B) Relies on experience, teacher and the text book
(C) Relies on technology
(D) Relies on the text book

764. The problem solving method of teaching usually involves

(A) The teacher mentioning the problem and the learner finding the solutions
(B) The learners mentioning the problem and the teacher finding the solution
(C) The teachers mentioning both the problem and finding the solution
(D) The examiners mentioning the problem and the learners finding the solution

765. Which international organisation coordinates the Education for all programme at the global level ?

(A) UNDP
(B) UNESCO
(C) IMF
(D) UNFP

766. Which of the following stages are found in a learning cycle in it ?

(A) Active experimentation (B) Reflective observation

(C) Ignoring (D) Disseminating

Codes:

(A) (A) and (B) (B) (A) and (C)

(C) (B) and (C) (D) (C) and (D)

767. Which of the following is not a national values ?

(A) Patriotism (B) Literacy for all

(C) Nepotism (D) National Integration

768. Which one of the following is not the methods of teaching adult education?

(A) Story telling technique (B) Alphabetical technique

(C) Poetry-recitation technique (D) Interview technique

769. Which of the following is not a correct statement?

(A) A test can be reliable without being valid

(B) A test cannot be valid without being reliable

(C) A test can be reliable and valid both

(D) A test can be valid without being reliable

770. Which one of the following does not form part of the Continuing Education Programme ?

(A) Health and hygiene Education (B) Women's Education

(C) School Education (D) Civic Education

771. The Ministry of youth Affairs and sports organises each year in January.

(A) National Youth Festival

(B) National Child Festival

(C) National Women's festival

(D) National senior citizen's festival

772. The book "India's changing villages" is written by

(A) Dr. S.C. Dubey (B) Dr. M.N. Srinivas

(C) Dr. T.B. Bottomore (D) Shri. Jaiprakash Narayan

773. Select among the following the role of preraks (Stimulators) in the adult education programme ?

(A) Establishing a library and reading room

(B) Serving food

(C) Serving the disabled

(D) Organising games and sports

Codes:

(A) (A), (B), (C), (D)
(B) (B) and (C)
(C) (C) and (D)
(D) (A) and (D)

774. The main objective of a questionnaire in social research is

(A) To collect authentic data
(B) To find out authentic result
(C) To find out authentic source
(D) To find out authentic process

775. Which of the following practices would not lead to 'malnutrition' ?

(A) Breast feeding
(B) Imbalanced nutrition
(C) Balanced nutrition
(D) Under Nutrition

Codes:

(A) (A) and (C)
(B) (A) and (B)
(C) (B) and (C)
(D) (C) and (D)

776. Which of the following were given the status of National Technology Mission ?

(A) Immunization
(B) Employment
(C) Prohibition
(D) Literacy

Codes:

(A) (A) and (B)
(B) (A) and (D)
(C) (C) and (D)
(D) (B),(C) and (D)

777. The nature and characteristics of adult education are

(A) It is community specific
(B) It is participatory
(C) It is problem solving
(D) It is exponential

Codes:

(A) (A), (B), (D)
(B) (A) and (C)
(C) (A), (B) and (C)
(4) (A) and (B)

778. The Programme Continuing Education in Universities during seventies led to several conferences held at several places. Which of the following are the correct places where conferences were held to start the programme of Adult and Continuing Education.

(A) Simla
(B) Hyderabad
(C) Srinagar
(D) Udaipur

Codes:

(A) (A) and (B) (B) (B) and (C)

(C) (A), (B) and (C) (D) (A), (B) and (D)

779. Mention the names of two great philosophers who were also great educationists.

(A) Sri Aurobindo (B) Plato

(C) Prof. Satish Dhawan (D) Rakesh JhunJhunwala

Codes:

(A) (A) and (D) (B) (B) and (C)

(C) (B) and (D) (D) (A) and (B)

780. Which of the following are the characteristics of extension education ?

(A) Need based (B) Formal

(C) Flexible (D) Learner centered

Codes:

(A) (A) and (B) (B) (B) and (C)

(C) (A), (C) and (D) (D) (B), (C) and (D)

781. Point out the names of Behavioural Scientists from among the names given below :

(A) A.H. Maslow (B) French and Bell

(C) Keith Davis (D) Kurt Lewin

Codes:

(A) (A) and (B) (B) (B) and (C)

(C) (A) and (D) (D) (C) and (D)

782. An extension worker should be a _____.

(A) Teacher and trainer (B) Leader and guide

(C) Researcher in a laboratory (D) Motivator

Codes:

(A) (A), (B) and (D) (B) (A), (C) and (D)

(C) (A), (B) and (C) (D) (B), (C) and (D)

783. The UGC acknowledged in 1977 that the universities have largely been concerned with teaching and researches, they advised other functions _____.

(A) Annual Lectures

(B) Lecture by every new professor

(C) Practice teaching for all teachers

(D) Extension

784. The National Institute of open schooling conducts

(A) Only primary school classes courses

(B) Courses from primary school classes to higher secondary school classes

(C) Vocational courses

(D) Only secondary school classes courses

Codes:

(A) (A) only
(B) (B) and (C)
(C) (C) only
(D) (C) and (D)

785. Select the following agencies, which are closely associated in its organisation of skill development :

(A) State Resource Centres
(B) Jan Shikshan Sansthan
(C) National and State open schools
(D) Directorate of health services

Codes:

(A) (A) and (B)
(B) (A), (C) and (D)
(C) (A) only
(D) (A), (B) and (C)

786. Which of the following are closer to adult education as compared to other features mentioned below ?

(A) Formal
(B) Non-formal
(C) Teacher centered
(D) Learner centered

Codes:

(A) (A) and (B)
(B) (B) and (C)
(C) (A) and (D)
(D) (B) and (D)

787. Which of the following are the human channels of communication ?

(A) Family and friends

(B) Community fair and festivals

(C) News papers

(D) Mobile phones

Codes:

(A) (A) and (C)
(B) (A) and (B)
(C) (B) and (C)
(D) (C) and (D)

788. Which of the following strategic areas is emphasized in the Common Wealth Youth Programme ?

(A) National Youth policy

(B) Scientific and Technological development

(C) Youth empowerment

(D) Marketing and Brand promotion

Codes:

(A) (A) and (B)
(B) (B) and (C)
(C) (B) and (D)
(D) (A) and (C)

789. The principal function of continuing education will be to provide :

(A) Learning activities
(B) Tailoring training
(C) Cultural activities
(D) Sports activities

Codes:

(A) (A), (B) and (C)
(B) (B), (C) and (D)
(C) (A), (C) and (D)
(D) (A) and (B)

790. Arrange the steps involved in conducting total literacy campaign in an adopted area :

(A) Organisation of literacy centre
(B) Environment building
(C) Survey
(D) Evaluation

Codes:

(A) (C), (A), (B), (D)
(B) (A), (C), (B), (D)
(C) (C), (B), (A), (D)
(D) (B), (A), (C), (D)

791. Arrange the following important days in order in which they are celebrated (from January to December)

(A) International Literacy Day
(B) Girl Child Day
(C) Earth Day
(D) World Population Day
(E) NSS Day

Codes:

(A) (B), (D), (A), (C), (E)
(B) (D), (A), (B), (E), (C)
(C) (B), (C), (A), (D), (E)
(D) (B), (C), (D), (A), (E)

792. Arrange the following programme of education according to their implementation :

(A) DPEP
(B) POA
(C) NPE
(D) Mahila Samakhya

Codes:

(A) (A), (B), (C), (D)
(B) (D), (C), (A), (B)
(C) (C), (D), (B), (A)
(D) (B), (C), (D), (A)

793. Arrange the following acts/policies in order of their implementation:

(A) Right to Education
(B) National Policy for Women Empowerment
(C) New Panchayat Raj Act
(D) National Policy on Education

Codes:

(A) (D), (C), (B), (A)
(B) (C), (D), (B), (A)
(C) (D), (C), (A), (B)
(D) (A), (B), (D), (C)

794. Arrange the plan according to their establishment :

(A) Vishveshvarayya's plan
(B) Bombay plan
(C) The People's plan
(D) Gandhian plan

Codes:

(A) (A), (B), (C), (D)
(B) (B), (C), (A), (D)
(C) (B), (C), (D), (A)
(D) (C), (B), (D), (A)

795. Arrange the principles of planning and management followed in implimenting the adult education programmes:

(A) Planning
(B) Organising
(C) Implementing
(D) Monitoring and Evaluation

Codes:

(A) (A), (C), (B), (D)
(B) (B), (A), (C), (D)
(C) (A), (B), (C), (D)
(D) (B), (A), (D), (C)

796. Arrange the steps in conducting "Sequential exploratory mixed methods" research.

(A) Collecting quantitative data
(B) Collecting qualitative data
(C) Analysing qualitative data
(D) Analysing quantitative data

Codes:

(A) (A), (B), (C), (D)
(B) (B), (C), (A), (D)
(C) (A), (D), (B), (C)
(D) (D), (C), (B), (A)

797. Arrange the following steps in the process of extension. Use the codes given below :

(A) Teaching
(B) Deciding goals

(C) Reconsideration | (D) Evaluation

Codes:

(A) (A), (B), (C), (D)
(B) (B), (A), (D), (C)
(C) (A), (B), (D), (C)
(D) (B), (C), (D), (A)

798. Arrange the states by population in descending order. Use the codes given below :

(A) Maharashtra
(B) Uttar Pradesh
(C) West Bengal
(D) Bihar

Codes:

(A) (A), (C), (D), (B)
(B) (B), (A), (D), (C)
(C) (C), (A), (B), (D)
(D) (D), (A), (C), (B)

799. Arrange the steps in orgainising the research data. Use the code given below :

(A) Analysing
(B) Classifying
(C) Tabulating
(D) Editing

Codes:

(A) (A), (C), (D), (B)
(B) (B), (C), (A), (D)
(C) (C), (D), (A), (B)
(D) (B), (C), (D), (A)

800. Evaluation is :

(A) A subjective opinion
(B) A continuous process
(C) An integral part of the total system of education
(D) Wastage of money and time

Codes:

(A) (A) and (B)
(B) (B) and (C)
(C) (C) and (D)
(D) (B) and (D)

801. The main objectives of National water mission are _____.

(A) Conservation of Water and minimizing wastage.
(B) Examine all related aspects of development.
(C) Ensuring its more equitable distribution at National and state levels.
(D) Sale and Purchase of water.

Codes:

(A) (A) and (D)
(B) (B) and (C)
(C) (A) and (C)
(D) (C) and (D)

Answers

1	(D)	20	(C)	39	(A)	58	(D)
2	(C)	21	(B)	40	(B)	59	(C)
3	(C)	22	(C)	41	(B)	60	(A)
4	(B)	23	(C)	42	(D)	61	(D)
5	(A)	24	(A)	43	(C)	62	(B)
6	(D)	25	(C)	44	(B)	63	(C)
7	(C)	26	(D)	45	(A)	64	(C)
8	(A)	27	(C)	46	(B)	65	(D)
9	(A)	28	(A)	47	(A)	66	(C)
10	(D)	29	(A)	48	(C)	67	(C)
11	(C)	30	(B)	49	(A)	68	(A)
12	(C)	31	(A)	50	(C)	69	(B)
13	(A)	32	(A)	51	(B)	70	(B)
14	(B)	33	(D)	52	(A)	71	(A)
15	(C)	34	(D)	53	(D)	72	(B)
16	(B)	35	(B)	54	(D)	73	(A)
17	(D)	36	(B)	55	(B)	74	(D)
18	(D)	37	(A)	56	(D)	75	(C)
19	(C)	38	(D)	57	(A)	76	(A)

77	(D)	111	(A)	145	(A)	179	(C)
78	(D)	112	(C)	146	(D)	180	(C)
79	(C)	113	(C)	147	(B)	181	(A)
80	(B)	114	(C)	148	(C)	182	(B)
81	(B)	115	(A)	149	(C)	183	(D)
82	(C)	116	(B)	150	(A)	184	(C)
83	(C)	117	(A)	151	(B)	185	(B)
84	(D)	118	(B)	152	(D)	186	(A)
85	(A)	119	(A)	153	(C)	187	(B)
86	(B)	120	(B)	154	(B)	188	(C)
87	(C)	121	(B)	155	(D)	189	(D)
88	(D)	122	(D)	156	(D)	190	(A)
89	(C)	123	(C)	157	(B)	191	(C)
90	(C)	124	(B)	158	(C)	192	(C)
91	(B)	125	(B)	159	(A)	193	(C)
92	(D)	126	(A)	160	(A)	194	(B)
93	(B)	127	(C)	161	(A)	195	(C)
94	(C)	128	(C)	162	(B)	196	(C)
95	(A)	129	(B)	163	(B)	197	(D)
96	(D)	130	(A)	164	(B)	198	(B)
97	(A)	131	(B)	165	(B)	199	(C)
98	(D)	132	(A)	166	(A)	200	(B)
99	(D)	133	(A)	167	(D)	201	(A)
100	(B)	134	(D)	168	(D)	202	(B)
101	(B)	135	(D)	169	(B)	203	(D)
102	(C)	136	(B)	170	(B)	204	(C)
103	(D)	137	(C)	171	(D)	205	(D)
104	(A)	138	(D)	172	(A)	206	(C)
105	(A)	139	(A)	173	(A)	207	(A)
106	(A)	140	(D)	174	(D)	208	(A)
107	(A)	141	(A)	175	(D)	209	(B)
108	(A)	142	(B)	176	(A)	210	(D)
109	(D)	143	(B)	177	(C)	211	(C)

110	(C)	144	(A)	178	(B)	212	(B)
213	(C)	247	(D)	281	(B)	315	(C)
214	(C)	248	(A)	282	(A)	316	(C)
215	(D)	249	(C)	283	(A)	317	(A)
216	(A)	250	(D)	284	(B)	318	(C)
217	(D)	251	(D)	285	(B)	319	(A)
218	(B)	252	(A)	286	(A)	320	(D)
219	(A)	253	(C)	287	(D)	321	(C)
220	(C)	254	(D)	288	(A)	322	(A)
221	(B)	255	(B)	289	(A)	323	(A)
222	(C)	256	(A)	290	(A)	324	(D)
223	(D)	257	(C)	291	(B)	325	(B)
224	(A)	258	(D)	292	(B)	326	(B)
225	(A)	259	(B)	293	(D)	327	(C)
226	(D)	260	(A)	294	(D)	328	(A)
227	(B)	261	(C)	295	(C)	329	(C)
228	(B)	262	(D)	296	(B)	330	(A)
229	(B)	263	(B)	297	(C)	331	(C)
230	(B)	264	(A)	298	(D)	332	(A)
231	(D)	265	(C)	299	(B)	333	(D)
232	(B)	266	(D)	300	(D)	334	(B)
233	(C)	267	(C)	301	(C)	335	(D)
234	(A)	268	(B)	302	(A)	336	(D)
235	(D)	269	(A)	303	(D)	337	(D)
236	(C)	270	(C)	304	(B)	338	(A)
237	(A)	271	(D)	305	(A)	339	(C)
238	(B)	272	(D)	306	(D)	340	(D)
239	(C)	273	(B)	307	(D)	341	(A)
240	(A)	274	(A)	308	(A)	342	(D)
241	(C)	275	(C)	309	(D)	343	(D)
242	(B)	276	(C)	310	(C)	344	(A)
243	(A)	277	(B)	311	(D)	345	(A)
244	(C)	278	(B)	312	(D)	346	(B)

245	(B)	279	(A)	313	(A)	347	(B)
246	(B)	280	(A)	314	(D)	348	(D)
349	(C)	383	(C)	417	(A)	451	(C)
350	(C)	384	(C)	418	(C)	452	(B)
351	(B)	385	(D)	419	(A)	453	(A)
352	(A)	386	(C)	420	(D)	454	(A)
353	(A)	387	(A)	421	(D)	455	(C)
354	(C)	388	(B)	422	(D)	456	(B)
355	(D)	389	(A)	423	(A)	457	(B)
356	(A)	390	(B)	424	(B)	458	(D)
357	(C)	391	(C)	425	(D)	459	(A)
358	(A)	392	(A)	426	(B)	460	(D)
359	(C)	393	(B)	427	(D)	461	(B)
360	(A)	394	(D)	428	(C)	462	(D)
361	(A)	395	(A)	429	(B)	463	(B)
362	(B)	396	(B)	430	(A)	464	(C)
363	(A)	397	(C)	431	(A)	465	(A)
364	(C)	398	(B)	432	(C)	466	(C)
365	(D)	399	(B)	433	(B)	467	(C)
366	(C)	400	(C)	434	(B)	468	(D)
367	(A)	401	(C)	435	(A)	469	(A)
368	(B)	402	(C)	436	(C)	470	(D)
369	(C)	403	(D)	437	(D)	471	(A)
370	(A)	404	(C)	438	(A)	472	(D)
371	(D)	405	(B)	439	(D)	473	(C)
372	(D)	406	(A)	440	(A)	474	(D)
373	(C)	407	(A)	441	(D)	475	(C)
374	(B)	408	(A)	442	(B)	476	(D)
375	(D)	409	(C)	443	(C)	477	(D)
376	(A)	410	(A)	444	(A)	478	(C)
377	(A)	411	(D)	445	(D)	479	(B)
378	(A)	412	(C)	446	(A)	480	(D)
379	(D)	413	(D)	447	(D)	481	(D)

380	(D)	414	(C)	448	(A)	482	(D)
381	(B)	415	(A)	449	(B)	483	(A)
382	(C)	416	(A)	450	(A)	484	(C)
485	(D)	519	(A)	553	(A)	587	(B)
486	(D)	520	(B)	554	(A)	588	(A)
487	(B)	521	(B)	555	(C)	589	(C)
488	(C)	522	(C)	556	(B)	590	(D)
489	(C)	523	(A)	557	(D)	591	(B)
490	(C)	524	(A)	558	(A)	592	(C)
491	(D)	525	(B)	559	(D)	593	(A)
492	(C)	526	(D)	560	(D)	594	(D)
493	(B)	527	(B)	561	(B)	595	(D)
494	(C)	528	(D)	562	(B)	596	(B)
495	(A)	529	(C)	563	(B)	597	(C)
496	(B)	530	(D)	564	(B)	598	(B)
497	(A)	531	(A)	565	(C)	599	(A)
498	(C)	532	(C)	566	(D)	600	(A)
499	(A)	533	(B)	567	(A)	601	(C)
500	(B)	534	(C)	568	(B)	602	(B)
501	(C)	535	(C)	569	(C)	603	(A)
502	(B)	536	(C)	570	(B)	604	(A)
503	(B)	537	(C)	571	(C)	605	(B)
504	(B)	538	(B)	572	(A)	606	(B)
505	(C)	539	(A)	573	(A)	607	(C)
506	(A)	540	(D)	574	(B)	608	(A)
507	(A)	541	(B)	575	(B)	609	(B)
508	(C)	542	(D)	576	(D)	610	(A)
509	(B)	543	(A)	577	(B)	611	(B)
510	(C)	544	(A)	578	(D)	612	(B)
511	(C)	545	(A)	579	(B)	613	(A)
512	(B)	546	(B)	580	(B)	614	(A)
513	(A)	547	(D)	581	(A)	615	(C)
514	(C)	548	(A)	582	(D)	616	(A)

515	(A)	549	(B)	583	(B)	617	(A)
516	(B)	550	(C)	584	(C)	618	(C)
517	(A)	551	(D)	585	(A)	619	(D)
518	(A)	552	(A)	586	(A)	620	(C)
621	(B)	655	(B)	689	(D)	723	(B)
622	(D)	656	(D)	690	(B)	724	(A)
623	(B)	657	(C)	691	(B)	725	(B)
624	(A)	658	(B)	692	(B)	726	(D)
625	(D)	659	(B)	693	(A)	727	(B)
626	(C)	660	(A)	694	(B)	728	(D)
627	(B)	661	(A)	695	(A)	729	(D)
628	(D)	662	(A)	696	(D)	730	(B)
629	(C)	663	(C)	697	(D)	731	(A)
630	(D)	664	(A)	698	(B)	732	(C)
631	(C)	665	(A)	699	(B)	733	(B)
632	(C)	666	(C)	700	(D)	734	(A)
633	(C)	667	(B)	701	(B)	735	(A)
634	(C)	668	(B)	702	(A)	736	(B)
635	(A)	669	(D)	703	(A)	737	(D)
636	(C)	670	(D)	704	(D)	738	(B)
637	(B)	671	(B)	705	(B)	739	(B)
638	(A)	672	(A)	706	(B)	740	(B)
639	(B)	673	(D)	707	(A)	741	(D)
640	(C)	674	(B)	708	(A)	742	(C)
641	(D)	675	(C)	709	(C)	743	(B)
642	(D)	676	(C)	710	(A)	744	(A)
643	(A)	677	(A)	711	(B)	745	(B)
644	(A)	678	(B)	712	(D)	746	(C)
645	(A)	679	(B)	713	(B)	747	(C)
646	(C)	680	(C)	714	(C)	748	(B)
647	(A)	681	(C)	715	(B)	749	(B)
648	(B)	682	(A)	716	(C)	750	(B)
649	(A)	683	(A)	717	(A)	751	(A)

650	(A)	684	(C)	718	(D)	752	(D)
651	(C)	685	(A)	719	(A)	753	(B)
652	(B)	686	(B)	720	(A)	754	(B)
653	(C)	687	(C)	721	(B)	755	(A)
654	(B)	688	(B)	722	(D)	756	(B)
757	(C)	769	(A)	781	(C)	793	(A)
758	(A)	770	(C)	782	(A)	794	(B)
759	(C)	771	(A)	783	(D)	795	(C)
760	(D)	772	(B)	784	(B)	796	(B)
761	(C)	773	(D)	785	(D)	797	(B)
762	(C)	774	(A)	786	(D)	798	(B)
763	(B)	775	(A)	787	(B)	799	(B)
764	(A)	776	(B)	788	(D)	800	(B)
765	(B)	777	(C)	789	(C)	801	(C)
766	(A)	778	(D)	790	(C)		
767	(C)	779	(D)	791	(D)		
768	(D)	780	(C)	792	(C)		

www.ingramcontent.com/pod-product-compliance
Ingram Content Group UK Ltd.
Pitfield, Milton Keynes, MK11 3LW, UK
UKHW020249290926
15470UKWH00002B/822

9 789390 384020